L.F. BJORKLUND
1971

ROAD AGENTS AND TRAIN ROBBERS

ROAD AGENTS
AND
TRAIN ROBBERS

Half a Century of Western Banditry

HARRY SINCLAIR DRAGO

Illustrated with photographs

Endpaper drawing by Lorence F. Bjorklund

DODD, MEAD & COMPANY

NEW YORK

ISBN: 0-396-06785-9
Library of Congress Catalog Card Number: 72-12439
Printed in the United States of America
by The Cornwall Press, Inc., Cornwall, N. Y.

Foreword

WESTERN OUTLAWRY has claimed the attention of a far greater number of writers, magazine commentators, folklorists, and competent historians than any other activity connected with the settling of the West. It has produced an endless miscellany of articles, pamphlets, and books. No matter how minor the outlaw may have been, someone has put him into print.

Although most of such narratives can be dismissed as trash, they have aided the researcher in weeding out fact from fiction. As a consequence, readers interested in the history of banditry, beginning with the road agents of California and ending with the horseback outlaws of Missouri, Kansas, Oklahoma, and the other prairie states, have become as critical and discerning as those in any other field.

From year to year, reader interest in matters relating to the coming of age of the American West continues to grow. It is our greatest story and needs no embellishment; the truth is sufficient. For half a century and more I have been trying to tell that story, presenting what I found to be the truth, even though it has meant contradicting many of my peers. Of all the fan letters I have received I have always treasured most one from an old Kansas cowman, who wrote: "I like your books because you try to tell it as it was."

I have written this book about road agents, bank and train robbers without any thought of glamorizing them. Some were men of great courage, strangers to fear; others were savage brutes who killed when there was no need for killing. All, or nearly all, were ignorant men, devoid of any trace of education. But whatever else they were, they were criminals and deserved the fate that overtook so many of them. A little army of sheriffs, United States marshals, Wells, Fargo detectives and other special agents tracked them down and in shoot-outs either killed or captured them and hustled them off to long terms of imprisonment. The badge wearers were hard men, too; they had to be to survive.

Gentlemanly Black Bart, the king of California's road agents, may arouse your sympathy. In many ways he was an incredible little man. He had a sense of whimsy and humor that no other bandit ever exhibited. For seven years he outwitted Wells, Fargo's Chief of Detectives Hume and the best men the express company could put on his trail. Of course he was a thief. But he apparently enjoyed jousting with the law, and he might never have been apprehended save for a telltale laundry ticket that got into the wrong hands.

Immediately preceding the years in which Black Bart was compiling his remarkable record of twenty-seven successful stage robberies, the ubiquitous Tom Bell, Rattlesnake Dick, and other outlaws had terrorized the Mother Lode country of California with their killings and plundering. Trails and highroads were not safe for travelers or shipments of gold. The banks were vulnerable, but, strangely, they were seldom molested. The bandits seemingly preferred ambushing a gold shipment in transit to cracking a bank vault.

However it was, the savagery of the bands of *Californios* (Californians of Spanish-Mexican extraction), such as the one led by Tiburcio Vasquez, the so-called Wild Man, led to the successful state-wide campaign that eliminated them. Unquestionably the Spanish-speaking Californians were being oppressed, racial prejudice relegating them to the role of second-class citizens. It was as their champion that Vasquez first gained power. Soon, however, he was preying on his own people.

Racial prejudice in California could be traced back to 1854, when John Rollin Ridge published his paperback *The Life and Adventures of Joaquin Murrieta, Celebrated California Bandit*. It is a preposterous little book. It got to a slow start and then caught fire. People believed it, and the name of Joaquin Murrieta, the bloody avenger of the wrongs done him and his people by white men, became the most frightening sound in California history.

California outlawry spilled back across the Sierras in the great rush to Washoe and the Comstock Lode in 1859. Some found rich pickings in Nevada; others did not tarry there long. Tales of gold being found at the grass roots all over Boise Basin, Idaho, and in the Clearwater River Basin, sent them scurrying north. Henry Plummer, a handsome young desperado, wanted for robbery and murder in California and Nevada, left the Comstock and headed for Lewiston, at the mouth of the Clearwater, where he was in position to hear the reports filtering back across the Bitterroots of the fortunes being washed out of Grasshopper Creek at Bannack City and the new bonanza in Alder Gulch. Plummer lost no time getting there, and instead of depending on the uncertainty that he might find in a gold pan, he had himself elected sheriff as a much quicker way of getting rich.

Plummer has been called the most consummate villain. Certainly he put together the most efficient and murderous gang of road agents the West ever knew. He was the Law, and as such he easily arranged to be thirty or forty miles from the scene of the holdups and killings that were occurring every few days. But he overplayed his hand and ended up becoming the first man hanged on the gallows he himself had built at Bannack.

The Civil War was over and the eyes of the country were on the West, on the Colorado mines bonanza—first gold, then silver. Denver had become the Queen City of the Plains. In the mountains and in South Park the treasure coaches were being stopped and looted by the Reynolds Gang and by other bands of desperadoes. When newspaper headlines disclosed that mining production in Colorado had been falling off for the past month and a half, it caused some concern in Denver, especially among the birds of passage who were always ready to take off at the first sign of trouble. Several hundred miles to the north, Deadwood Gulch and the scattered camps in the Black Hills were booming, with new strikes being reported every few days. The news, coming when it did, touched off a minor exodus from Denver. Several thousand men and women entrained for Cheyenne and then proceeded the rest of the way by stagecoach.

Gold-mad Deadwood welcomed them. Farthest east of all important American mining camps, it hit the headlines with a bang. But when it began to fade and the noise and hoopla had subsided, the departing thousands headed back west, ears cocked for news of the next great discovery.

The rush to the Black Hills set the scene for the last, gaudy act of stagecoaching. The final curtain fell when the Fremont, Elkhorn, and Missouri Valley put its rails into Rapid City in 1880. But long before then, holding up stagecoaches had become a secondary consideration with the ex-road agents and prairie bandits, who had discovered that robbing the steam cars could be accomplished almost as easily and was far more lucrative.

It would be silly to say—as did Burton Rascoe, who established himself as an authority on outlawry by ridiculing the errors of other writers—that "Jesse James *invented* train robbery." By my count, no fewer than seven such robberies had occurred prior to the wrecking and robbery of a Chicago and Rock Island express at Adair, Iowa, by the James-Younger Gang on July 21, 1873. The first train robbery in the United States occurred at Seymour, in southern Indiana, in 1866, and was committed by the three Reno brothers and one of their brothers-in-law. They hit the dinky railroad, the Ohio and Mississippi, a second time a few weeks later, again at Seymour, and this time they killed the express messenger by tossing him through the open door of the baggage car while the train was in motion.

In Tennessee, Levi and Hilary Farrington robbed a Mobile and Ohio express at Moscow, Kentucky, in 1870. They struck a second time, looting a Nashville and Northwestern express car at Union City, Tennessee. Three weeks later, again near Union City, they climbed into the baggage car of another Nashville and Northwestern train and compelled the express messenger to open the safe, from which they took between $3,000 and $4,000. In the effete East, a Boston and Albany express was robbed and the messenger killed within sixty miles of Boston.

While accounts of these early robberies were reported in the newspapers, it was not until the double robbery of the Central Pacific's eastbound California Fast Express on November 6, 1870, at Verdi, Nevada, and six hours later at Independence, in the eastern part of the state, near old Fort Halleck, that robbing the steam cars became big business. The Verdi bandits alone made off with $40,000 in gold and currency. Undoubtedly young Jesse read the published accounts of the Verdi robbery and filed them away in his mind for future reference, for if he didn't "invent" train robbery, he unquestionably improved its technique.

Some writers have made much of the fact that Jesse Woodson James was faithful to his wife, loved his son and his mother, and that for a man who was on the dodge most of the time, his family life was admirable. With that I can agree, but when they proceed to label him the greatest of all outlaw leaders, I cannot go along. Jesse was often stubborn and gullible at the same time. He embarked on the Northfield adventure solely on Bill Chadwell's tales of the rich pickings to be found in faraway Minnesota, a country about which he (Jesse) knew nothing. Had Jesse been the peerless leader he is often reputed to have been, he never would have led his men out of the comparative safety of Missouri and set out for the north and disaster on the unsupported word of a small-time desperado and horse thief of Chadwell's caliber.

Next to the Coffeyville, Kansas, raid, which eliminated the Dalton Gang and took the lives of eight men, the shoot-out at Northfield between the James-Younger Gang and an aroused citizenry rates a close second. The Battle of Ingalls, in which the Doolin Gang dueled with a posse of deputy United States marshals, with the outlaws the victors, was the third and last of the great confrontations.

Contents

Illustrations

I

America on the Move—
Prelude to Gold and Violence

LESS THAN two years after word got out that gold had been discovered in quantity in the mountain streams of the Mother Lode, banditry began to flourish in California. It hardly could have been otherwise, for along with the thousands of honorable adventurers who risked everything—often their lives—in the mad rush to the new bonanza, came thieves, ex-convicts, and assorted other criminals. Eventually they were put down, imprisoned, hanged. However undesirable they were, they were part of the saga of the Overland Trail and the Forty-Niners.

No one can say how many men and women rode or trudged halfway across the continent to California in the years 1849–1852, in the greatest mass migration in American history. It was not the first time the young nation had witnessed such a streaming to the west. For almost a decade prior to the discovery of gold in California, other thousands of pioneers had been making their way across the plains and mountains to the so-called Oregon Country, which they envisioned as a golden land of opportunity, where a man could not do other than prosper.

Their optimistic confidence in what awaited them at the end of the trail was just a surfacing of the pioneering urge to be mov-

1

ing on, ever westward, that had been fermenting in America since post-colonial times. It had begun with the definite goal of getting beyond the Alleghenies and spreading out on the fertile lands of the new states—Ohio, Michigan, Indiana and Illinois—that had been carved out of the Old Northwest Territory.

In the mill towns along the Atlantic Seaboard, thousands of workers laid down their tools and organized themselves into colonization parties bound for the Middle West; in New England, scores of Yankees deserted their rocky hillside farms, put their families and goods into improvised covered wagons, and set out for the West; even staid Boston witnessed the departure of a company of three hundred colonists, bound for the fertile prairies of Ohio. Beyond the borders of New York State, roads were nonexistent or at best mere traces through the wilderness, quagmires in the rainy season and rocky traces at other seasons. But with completion of the Erie Canal in 1825, which connected the Hudson River with the Great Lakes, access to most of Ohio and its neighboring states became readily available. At the close of navigation, two years later, the number of persons passing through Buffalo had increased tenfold. From there, thousands had proceeded by schooner and lake steamer to their destinations.

Many of the newcomers discovered after a year or two that they had not bettered their lot by cutting themselves adrift from their native region and joining the movers. The land to which they had come was fertile and produced bountiful crops, but with flour selling for a dollar a barrel and shelled corn bringing as little as fifteen cents a bushel for want of a market, immediate prospects were discouraging. Instead of waiting for them to improve, many of the newcomers pulled up stakes for the second time and made their way farther west. There was so much movement in the several years that followed that the frontier was rapidly being pushed back. It crossed the Mississippi, and by 1831 was firmly established at Independence, Missouri, and the cluster of neighboring Missouri River ports. The Santa Fe Trade was booming, and Independence, strategically located at the head of the famous trail, was becoming the recognized jumping-off place for the Far West. There, and for the first time, fabulous tales were being told of the richness of distant Oregon and the equally remote Mexican state of California.

When Jim Marshall—James Wilson Marshall—left his native Hunterdon County, New Jersey, and headed west, he was far more interested in finding a place where he could put his roots down and prosper, than in adventure. By trade he was a wheelwright, a water mason, and a jack carpenter of sorts. After several years of indifferent success he was still pushing on westward. In 1843 he took passage by steamboat at St. Louis for Independence. He was thirty-three. Even with his various skills, the odds against his ever achieving a niche, however minor, in history, appeared beyond calculation.

Independence had never been busier. Its streets, dram shops, and mercantile establishments were thronged with colorful characters, plainsmen, trappers, and guides. Every other day caravans of arks (heavy freighters), loaded to capacity, were setting out for Santa Fe. Creating more commotion and attracting more attention were the long trains of covered wagons with their hundreds of pioneers bound for Oregon. The bustle and excitement of the takeoffs and the desperate optimism of the emigrants, which failed to waver despite the tales filtering back to Independence of trains being attacked and burned by the wild Plains Indians, must have tempted a man with itchy feet to join up.

Marshall, however, refused to take the plunge. Instead, he acquired a few acres of land near Fort Leavenworth, some thirty miles up the Missouri on the Kansas side of the river, and settled down to the hard work of turning under the prairie sod and establishing a farm. For a man of his temperament, it was an unlikely spot on which to settle down, for there he was exposed to the sight of an ever-increasing number of wagon trains setting out across the trackless plains for the Oregon Trail and the Columbia River Valley. To thousands of Americans, Oregon was becoming an almost holy word, a land of milk and honey.

When he calculated the returns from his first meager crop, Marshall's interest in farming, and in the agricultural possibilities of Oregon, waned. At Fort Leavenworth, our most important frontier military post, it was being freely predicted that the United States would soon be at war with Mexico, and that, when the unequal struggle ended, the American flag would be flying over the entire Spanish-speaking Southwest, including California. As the rumors spread they produced a quickened interest in that region, about which little was known other than what had been derived from the tales of hairy-headed scouts and mountain men, most of them consummate liars who, with one or two exceptions, had never set foot beyond the forbidding Sierra Nevada.

Although discounting much of what he had heard, early in May, 1845, Marshall joined a party of twenty fast-traveling horse-backers, unencumbered by women, children, or wagons, and set out for California by way of the Willamette River in Oregon—a long, roundabout course that relieved him of having to cross the high Sierras.

Soon after reaching the Oregon settlements, Marshall joined the large group of Argonauts—some sources say as many as two hundred—under the leadership of James Clyman, the favorably known frontiersman and Indian fighter, who were leaving for California. After being harassed by small parties of Klamath Indians as they coursed through the Siskiyou Mountains, the remainder of the long journey down the beautiful valley of the Sacramento River was an unmixed delight. In mid-July they reached Sutter's Fort (today's Sacramento), from where they spread out over the lower valley and the Delta country.

For Marshall, Sutter's Fort was the end of his journeying. With his various skills, he was a man made to order for John Sutter's needs. They got on so well together that Marshall soon was directing the building of the many improvements that the ambitious Swiss was installing on his little inland empire of New Helvetia.

At the time of Marshall's arrival the era of pastoral mission control of the land, as well as the comfortable, leisurely days of Spanish rule, had passed. Having won its independence from Spain, Mexico had supplanted the old order by sending in its own harsh and corrupt military and civil authorities to rule the country. They were hated and despised by the helpless *Californios* and scorned by the fewer than one thousand Americans who were largely concentrated in the Sacramento Valley.

The latter, though few in number, were bent on overthrowing the Mexican regime and raising the Stars and Stripes over California. The succession of events that followed—the short-lived Bear Flag Republic, the reappearance of Lieutenant Charles C. Fremont with his party of so-called Topographical Engineers (thirty-eight in number and unquestionably a unit of the American government), and the timely arrival of United States ships of war, under command of Commodores John Drake Sloat and Robert F. Stockton at Yerba Buena (San Francisco) and Monterey, suggest that the United States was acquainted with the situation and was not averse to its successful outcome. When Commodore Stockton ordered the Mexican flag lowered at Monterey, the capital, and the American colors run up, the upheaval, not without its comic-opera touches, was over, and California was American soil.

Sutter had been placed in a precarious position by the turnover; wanting the Americans to be victorious, he could not declare himself for them without putting in jeopardy the immense land grants he had received from the Mexican government. Although apparently having weathered the storm, he was filled with gloomy forebodings that the United States would refuse to honor the various titles to his domain. As history knows, his forebodings were to be realized beyond his reckoning. But the innocent catalyst, who was to destroy everything for John Sutter, was Jim Marshall.

In late autumn, 1847, the two of them rode up the South Fork of the American River and at Coloma selected the site for a new sawmill, construction of which was entrusted to Marshall. Having bossed Sutter's untutored laborers—Indian, Mexican and Chilenos—

on previous occasions, he knew how to get the maximum effort out of them. The work proceeded without a hitch, and by the first of the year the mill was completed.

When the water was let in, Marshall saw at once that the mill would have more power if the tailrace were deepened several feet. The additional work was completed in three weeks, and on January 24, 1848, the sluice gates were opened for the second time. The South Fork, released from its temporary imprisonment, came roaring in. Watching the turbulent action in the deepened tailrace with an engineer's understandable satisfaction over a job well done, Marshall was amazed to see flakes and nuggets of gold dancing in the rushing water.

It was a discovery that was destined to inflame the minds of men the world around. Gold in California! Gold in the sands of every mountain stream! California was never to be the same again. But Marshall's great discovery was to bring him no riches, and, ironically, it was to crush John Sutter and leave him broken and impoverished.

At first, fearful that his workers, on whom he depended to keep his little empire functioning, would drop their tools and rush off looking for gold, Sutter tried to keep the discovery secret. He might as well have tried to hold back Niagara. Sam Brannan, the erstwhile Mormon leader who, after his tiff with Brother Brigham, turned to promoting himself, had a store at Fort Sutter. The secret could not be kept from him. Arranging with the captain of a river launch to get him to San Francisco as quickly as possible, he sailed down the Sacramento. On his arrival, to the extent of his cash and credit, he purchased for the store, before prices skyrocketed, a stock of picks, shovels, boots, and such other articles as miners would need. Not till then did he break the startling news that had brought him hurrying downriver.

Its effect was cataclysmic; workmen threw down their tools, storekeepers closed their shops, and sailors by the score deserted their ships in a frantic rush to the gold fields, hoofing the intervening ninety miles if they could not find other means of transportation. Spring crops were left untended to wither in the fields, and the price of a three-dollar shovel soared to twenty-five dollars. Within three months, between two and three thousand gold seekers, braving the ice-cold waters of the American, Yuba, Feather, and other mountain streams, were burrowing in the sand and gravel bars in their frenzied quest for precious metal.

Save for the sailors who had left their ships to rot in San Francisco Bay, they were Californians of one kind or another, whites, Mexicans, Chilenos. With very few exceptions, they knew nothing about placer mining. But it was only the beginning, a making ready for the swarms of Forty-Niners who were heading for California from every corner of the globe.

Inevitably, chaos soon engulfed California, and although it received statehood in September of 1850, civil law could not be enforced. Mob rule—vigilante law—took its place. The days of what the late Joseph Henry Jackson, the able California historian, aptly labeled "the myth of the honest miner," were over. The days when a miner—after piling up a few rocks as a monument to show that he was working a certain stretch of gravel—could leave his claim for a week or more and return without finding that someone had jumped it, were gone. Half a hundred mining camps were spread out over the Mother Lode, and most of them were the scene of crime and violence, as such names as Hangtown and Murderer's Bar suggest.

In the diggings, racially prejudiced "miners' courts" dispensed a cruel brand of alleged justice, wasting no time in stringing up a suspected offender if he chanced to be a Mexican. In the absence of any legal authority to make a man secure in the possession of his life and property, only might made right.

No one was more vulnerable than John Sutter. Without hope of redress, he saw squatters taking possession of his choicest land at his embarcadero, occupying his fields and running off and slaughtering his cattle. This was climaxed by his being ejected from Fort Sutter for debt. In 1858, he received what was really the final blow, when the United States Land Commission declared his great

Sobrante and "general title" grants invalid, leaving him only the New Helvetia grant, which was already mortgaged to the hilt.[1] Lawyers' fees and other legal expenses consumed what little was left of his once considerable fortune. In 1864, reduced to dire need, he suffered his greatest humiliation when he was driven to accepting the paltry pension the State of California granted him.

Jim Marshall was already forgotten. But Sutter fought on, going to Washington to plead his case. There, for the last two years of his life, he made a nuisance of himself in the Halls of Congress, vainly petitioning the federal government to restore his land grants.

In his shabby room in a third-class hotel, he died on a hot July morning in 1880. That day, far away in California, on the Point Arenas run, Black Bart, the state's most accomplished road agent, stopped his twelfth Wells, Fargo stage and commanded the driver to "throw down the box."

Beneath its recently acquired gold-plated veneer, California was still California.

II

Joaquin Murrieta—
Fact and Fiction

By THE early 1850's it was becoming apparent that the gold-producing region of California had fairly well-defined bounds, beyond which precious metal was not to be found. It made mining an increasingly competitive business. The simplest solution was to rule out certain competitors, in this case the "foreigners"—a euphemism for all Mexican miners and the Chinese. This was accomplished by levying such crushing taxes on them that the Mexicans turned to other pursuits. The Chinese, still few in number, submitted, and continued to work the tail of once-productive mines and prospects that white men had abandoned; the Mexicans turned to the more lucrative field of outlawry—stealing cattle and running off horses.

In his hatred of the white man, spawned by the injustice that had been done him, the Mexican struck back. If a white miner was found with his throat split, it was assumed, without further evidence, that he had been slain by a Mexican. No doubt that was often true. But to the Mexican *gente*, such blows were struck only in retaliation for the wrongs that had been done them by the hated Yankees. Consider their position. California was their land; most of them had been born there, as had their fathers and many of their grandfathers.

9

Almost without exception Mexicans were expert horsemen, bold riders, inured to hardship. Living off the land in gangs of five to ten men, losing themselves in the foothills of the Sierra or wilderness fastnesses of the Coast Range, they led a wild, free life between forays. Whatever horses they stole in the north could be sold without much effort among the *rancheros* in the south. Shifting bases often, sheriffs and their deputies seldom knew where to look for the outlaws.

The incursions of the Mexican banditti began to come with such frequency and to exact such toll that throughout the great central valley of the state the cry was raised that something had to be done to suppress them. It could safely be assumed that the outlaws had a leader who was responsible for the crimes that were being reported almost daily. The press united in printing fiery editorials demanding that the state offer a reward for his capture, dead or alive.

According to what little information was available, his name was Joaquin. But that led to insolvable confusion, for it appeared that among the renegades there were at least five Joaquins of one surname or another. Since all five were presumed to be equally guilty, no effort was made to distinguish between them.

Reacting to the pressure put upon it to do something, the Legislature passed an act authorizing a Texan, Captain Harry Love, to raise a company of twenty mounted rangers. He was to muster them into the service of the state for three months, unless sooner discharged by the governor, and lead them in an attempt to capture or destroy the gang of robbers commanded by the "five Joaquins." Each of the five was named in the document. Murrieta headed the list, his name misspelled.

Captain Love and his band of rangers set out from Sacramento City on May 11, 1853, their enthusiasm for the job they had in hand having been whetted by Governor Bigler who, acting on his own responsibility, had posted a reward of a thousand dollars for the capture—or body—of any one of the five Joaquins named in the enabling act. But the big posse, not knowing where to find the quarry with which it was to come to grips and destroy, could be sure only of the daily wage the state was paying them. For weeks they were seen threading their way through the foothills to the east and west of the central valley. On July 25, with time running out on them, they were as far south as Panoche Pass, west of Tulare Lake, when they surprised and quickly surrounded a party of Mexican vaqueros who were lounging about a breakfast fire, their horses ground-tied a few yards away. In vain the Mexicans protested that they were mustangers, not outlaws. Suddenly there was shooting. One of the vaqueros was killed; another reached his horse but was shot down; two of the Mexicans escaped for the moment, only to be recaptured and headed for jail at Mariposa. On the way, one was drowned in crossing the San Joaquin River and the other was hanged by a Mariposa mob.

Captain Harry Love and his rangers not only got the thousand-dollar reward but shared between them an additional five thousand that an appreciative Legislature voted, in recognition of "the great service they had rendered the State." They brought back visual and gory evidence of this in the decapitated head, pickled in alcohol, of "Joaquin" (allegedly Joaquin Murrieta) and in the mutilated hand of Three-Fingered Jack (Manuel Garcia), a notorious outlaw.

It should be noted that, when Love exhibited the head in various parts of California, among the thousands who gaped at it were a few who had known Murrieta in life. None could find anything recognizable in what he had paid his money to see. A sister of Murrieta, living in Marysville, was induced to view the ghastly exhibit. A glance was enough. "That is not my brother," she said with finality.

The public prints found Captain Love and his "Joaquin" less and less newsworthy as the days passed, except for a brief flurry of interest when Bill Henderson, Love's lieutenant, who had performed the actual decapitation, had to be removed to a madhouse. According to the story, he had been dogged for nights by the ghostly visitations of "Joaquin," demanding that his head be returned. To escape from his tormentor, Henderson resorted to drink, but drunkenness only intensified his hallucinations and ended in madness.

In the succeeding months it became increasingly clear that banditry and other forms of outlawry had not been crushed. From the different camps on the Mother Lode, robberies and crimes of violence were being reported so frequently that no lone traveler or stage on the mountain trails and roads appeared safe from attack. What was even more disturbing was the fact that the marauders were not Mexicans. Organized in gangs of four or five men, they struck without warning and were seldom apprehended.

Many of the road agents were recognized by their victims, but no one ever claimed that he had seen Joaquin Murrieta, the real Murrieta. It convinced many doubting Thomases that he was one of the men killed at Panoche Pass by Captain Love and his rangers. For what it is worth, history does not reveal that he was ever seen in California again. However, among Mexicans—when they would talk—there were stories that he had made his way back to Sonora, whence he had come. But the facts are less than important in Murrieta's case; they are too few, too obscure to matter, for out of such unpromising clay was to be fashioned California's foremost legendary folk hero, four fifths myth and romantic twaddle. Today, more than a century after he was created, a perfect physical specimen of manhood, dashing, fiery Joaquin Murrieta rides the hills and vales of California, succoring the poor and helpless and crushing their oppressors, a veritable Robin Hood.

If his hands were red with other men's blood, it was only to avenge the wrongs and cruel injustice that had been done him. Any schoolboy could tell you how Joaquin and his younger brother had been falsely accused of stealing horses; how, while lashed to a tree trunk and being beaten into insensibility by his captors, he had been forced to witness the hanging of his brother and the ravishment of his Rosita, his beautiful wife.

It was a sizable score to settle. With a handful of followers, young men as disdainful of danger as he himself, he left a red trail behind him as he settled to his task. He laughed at the traps that were set to ensnare him; slipping through them, he struck swiftly and was gone.

Whether this is fact or fiction, the Murrieta legend, improved and expertly tailored over the years, to give it greater credibility, must be considered because of its association with California outlawry. It began when John Rollin Ridge, a young Cherokee Indian of mixed blood, published his little paper-covered book *The Life and Adventures of Joaquin Murrieta, Celebrated California Bandit* in San Francisco in 1854.[1] Regarding it, Joseph Henry Jackson, celebrated literary figure and Pulitzer Prize winner, commented some years after it was published: "It is not too much to say that Ridge, in his preposterous little book, actually created both the man, Murrieta, and the Murrieta legend as these stand today."[2]

When first published, Ridge's sensational book was only mildly successful, but five years later, when the *California Police Gazette* printed a pirated, better-written version, it caught on at once. Soon thereafter, Beadle's Dime Library published its own version of the Murrieta story and gave it nationwide circulation. The response was sensational. Spanish-language translations were published in Mexico and in most of the South American countries. At least half a dozen American publishers came out with pirated editions, all claiming to be the true and authentic "life" of Joaquin. The effect of such claims was snowballing and needed only the blessing of some recognized literary savant to give them validity. Incredibly, Hubert Howe Bancroft, California's most noted and most quoted historian, stepped into the breach. Reprinting Ridge's story in its entirety, with some additions of his own, he gave it the stamp of authenticity.

No longer was Joaquin to be confined to California's regional magazines, the paperbacks and the pulps. The sacrosanct *Saturday Evening Post* opened its pages to him. Poets and novelists of note began to find him worthy of their talents—steps leading to canonization (so to speak) by the motion-picture producers of Hollywood.

But despite the many attempts to alter it, the original Murrieta legend survived. We know, for instance, that by the end of 1853 he was dead or had disappeared; that John Rollin Ridge published his little book in 1854, a circumstance which very likely was not unrelated to the fact that a year later—time enough for certain interested parties to have read and drawn inspiration from it— bands of non-Mexican brigands were running wild on the Mother Lode and in the upper valley of the Sacramento.

Granted that being men of little or no education, they were not much addicted to reading. But there were exceptions. A notable one, time was to prove, was Dr. Thomas J. Hodges, who long after he had given up the practice of medicine and buckshot surgery for the more lucrative profession of banditry, was favorably known in the Rough and Ready diggings and other camps along the forks of the Yuba River.

Bold, more intelligent than the men with whom he soon surrounded himself, Hodges began his criminal career by concealing his identity, discarding his honest name and using the alias Tom Bell.

In less than two years from his first minor robberies, he was to make Tom Bell the most publicized and wanted outlaw in central California, pursued by sheriffs and numerous parties of "aroused citizens." The reliable Sacramento *Union* charged that he was "doubtless emulous of Joaquin. . . . It is incumbent upon our State authorities to take immediate steps in the premises."

In the late afternoon of October 4, 1856, on the banks of the Merced, the fate Tom Bell had so often tempted caught up with him. There was no flinching.

He was quite a fellow, this Tom Bell, as we shall see.

III

Your Money or Your Life

AMONG the many thousands of goldseekers who "rushed" to California, there were hundreds—many hundreds—who left no record whence they came or when they arrived. Especially is that true of the failures who drifted from mining to grand larceny and lie in unmarked graves. But for the letter to his mother, which he was permitted to write a few minutes before the noose was dropped over his head, alias Tom Bell would have been one of them.

The letter addressed to his mother led investigators to the little village of Rome, in north-central Tennessee, where, as Thomas Hodges, he had been favorably known. Old friends described him as a tall, handsome man, well over six feet, lean and muscular, with flaming red hair. At the outbreak of hostilities with Mexico he had joined a regiment of Tennessee volunteers as a medical orderly. When he returned from the Rio Grande, his face was disfigured by a blow he had received on the bridge of his nose, which appeared to have been inflicted by a saber. Of this he had nothing to say.

Some time later he removed to nearby Nashville, where he hung up his shingle, as the old saying had it, as Dr. Thomas Hodges. Nothing in the record suggests that he ever attended a medical college. But he knew something about medicine; as for a certified diploma, it was a time when one could be acquired by mail.

15

When he disappeared from Nashville is not known, but he definitely was trying his hand at placering on the Yuba River in the late months of 1853. It was at that time he first heard about the real Tom Bell, a likable, mild-mannered young man, who always had money to wager on the three-card monte games in Murphy's Diggings and Murderers' Bar, although he had no known occupation. The source of his income was disclosed when he was seen fleeing from the robbery of a Grass Valley store.

With panning gold rarely bringing in more than two or three dollars a day and his medical "practice" equally unrewarding, Hodges made some envious comparisons between his penury and the affluence of Tom Bell. When he had convinced himself that larceny was a more profitable profession than medicine—when conducted astutely—he made slits for eyeholes in a flour sack and, dropping it over his head to conceal his identity, took to the roads.

Apparently, things went his way for a time. But eventually sticking up a solitary passerby and relieving him of his poke became a bit too tame, and he attempted to hold up a freighting outfit that he had reason to believe was carrying treasure on the highway east of Auburn. It was a trap; sheriff's deputies were waiting, concealed in the roadside brush. Disarmed and put in irons, he was asked his name. "Tom Bell," he answered, which may or may not have been a decision of the moment.

In any event, it was as Tom Bell that he was tried and convicted. In May, 1855, he was sent up for ten years and placed in the state penitentiary on Angel Island, in San Francisco Bay. The Angel Island prison was a primitive, rat-infested institution, but it was almost escape-proof, due to the swirling riptides that constantly lashed the island. Tom Bell Hodges did not remain there long. He feigned a desperate illness so convincingly that the warden, not wanting him to die while in his custody, had him transferred to San Francisco County jail for examination and treatment. The prisoner showed some improvement, and to hasten his recovery he was given the freedom of the jail yard and other privileges.

It was while Tom Bell Hodges was incarcerated in the San

Francisco County jail that his career as one of California's master outlaws began. He became acquainted there with at least four of the desperate characters who were to form the nucleus of the bandit gang he was to put together. Among them, awaiting trial on a murder charge, was notorious Bill Gristy, alias White, whose known crimes included robbery, arson, and felonious assault.

Hodges appears to have recognized that in Gristy he had found the lieutenant he needed to guarantee the success of the plans he was contemplating. A breakout from the county jail occurred. A number of prisoners—some accounts say six and others as many as ten—escaped. Among them were Hodges and Gristy. By previous arrangement the gang rendezvoused in the hills east of Grass Valley. A rash of robberies and holdups followed, all attributed to Tom Bell and his gang. Sometimes two occurred almost simultaneously a hundred miles or more apart. What harassed lawmen could not understand was how "Tom Bell" could appear in two places at the same time. The testimony of his victims was equally confusing, some describing him as tall and snarling his commands; others insisting that he was of medium size, soft-spoken and almost apologetic. Of course it had not occurred to the man-hunters that there were two Tom Bells. Tom Bell Hodges must have enjoyed their bewilderment, even though murder had been added to the crimes for which he was wanted. It had happened on the road between Nevada City and Grass Valley. A teamster employed by a Sacramento brewery had delivered a load of beer in Nevada City and been paid for it. He was on his way home when the gang jumped him. Instead of complying with an order to hand over the money he had on him, he reached for a pistol. Hodges gave the word and guns blazed. Bill Gristy got the money, some three hundred dollars, so the story goes, which didn't amount to much when cut up six or seven ways.

Bell may have realized that he had made a mistake in permitting the gang to expand until there were so many mouths to feed that there was seldom enough in the pot to satisfy them. His dissatisfaction with the way things were going was whetted when two of his gang, both unimportant, busted into a saloon at Jackson, their purpose robbery, and found it crowded with Amador County deputies, who promptly unloaded on them, killing one and removing the other to the county jail.

The bandit leader's reaction was what might have been expected; he was through with the little stuff; he'd give California something to remember.

It does not seem so breathtaking today, but it was in 1856, principally because it had never happened before. For years, great amounts of treasure had been shipped from the different camps to branch banks and eventually to Sacramento and from there down the river to San Francisco. They had never been molested. It was unthinkable that they should be, for gold was the cement that held California together. But on the morning of August 11, when the triweekly Camptonville-Marysville stage rolled out of Camptonville, it was destined to win everlasting distinction in the annals of California outlawry.

As usual, veteran John Gear was handling the reins. Beside him sat Bill Dobson, the Langton Express Company's messenger, his rifle draped across his knees. They were two of a kind—hard-bitten, squint-eyed men. If they were a bit more alert than usual this morning it was because in the strongbox stowed away beneath the seat on which they sat was almost a hundred thousand dollars in gold dust, the property of Mr. Rideout, the Camptonville dealer in raw gold.

It was some thirty miles to Marysville, all of them mountain miles. Gear and Dobson could have negotiated the road with their eyes closed. It was well traveled, as mountain roads go, there being considerable going back and forth between Camptonville and Marysville—that day the stage was carrying a full load. Far enough ahead to escape the clouds of dust the team kicked up, Mr. Rideout, whose treasure was being transported, led the way astride a chestnut mare.

Rideout's purpose in personally escorting his gold to Marysville passes understanding. If he had any reason to suspect that the stage might run into trouble on this particular trip, he hardly would have failed to hire several trustworthy men to accompany him. He not only failed to do so but had not even bothered to arm himself.

For a good part of the way the road followed the winding course of Dry Creek. As usual at that time of the year, the creek bed was dry. But in late spring, when the annual runoff was at its height, the little mountain stream put a short section of its bed under water. To end that inconvenience, a piece of new road had been hacked through the manzanita and scrub timber for a short distance higher up the side of the ravine, the two forks coming together in half a mile. The lower road still got most of the traffic. John Gear took it as a matter of course; Mr. Rideout took the new fork. Asked later why he had, he said curtly, "It was cooler! There's never a breath of air stirring down below on a hot day."

He could hear the stage coming along, even catch glimpses of it. On rounding a bend, however, he realized that there was something decidedly wrong when three masked men stepped out of the roadside brush and ordered him down from the saddle, satisfied themselves that he was not armed, and ordered him to start walking. Having a lively interest in dealers in gold, it can be taken for granted that they recognized Rideout on sight.

Several days prior to the holdup, Tom Bell had selected the spot where the Camptonville stage was to be stopped. To assist him, he had chosen five reliable men, including Bill Gristy, his able lieutenant. As planned, all six were to remain concealed in the brush until the stage was about to pass, when, on signal from him, they were to leap out into the road, three on each side, and train their rifles on the driver and the express messenger. If John Gear failed to pull up his team and slap on the brakes, they were to shoot him.

The plan was a good one and undoubtedly would have succeeded had not Mr. Rideout made his untimely appearance on the upper road. The trio who had jumped him had lost some precious minutes. When a ruffle of gunfire shattered the afternoon quiet, they realized that they were not where they should have been.

Pushing Rideout out of the way, they went crashing down through the brush to the lower road.

Some accounts say that as many as thirty shots were fired in the attempted holdup of the Camptonville stage. It is a matter of record that Dobson, the express messenger, killed one of the bandits. There were other casualties. Those passengers who were armed had gotten into the fray. Three or four were wounded, and a Mrs. Tilghman, wife of a Marysville barber, was dead.

Bell and Gristy (if it was he) had picked up their mortally wounded companion and fled. When Rideout, who had recovered his horse, came riding up to the stage, Dobson commanded him to lose no time getting to Marysville with the news and alerting the town.

Due to their own ludicrous miscalculations, the holdup netted the bandits only several wounded men, one of them mortally. But they had stopped the Camptonville-Marysville stage, and their audacity shocked California. Not only had an innocent woman been killed but the very sanctity of safe travel by stagecoach was threatened.

Throughout the Northern Mines it was agreed that Tom Bell was the guilty party. For months, sheriffs of the different counties had been trailing him, but their individual efforts had not been successful. Now the cry was raised that the various counties unite in a campaign to run him to earth. Led by the Sacramento *Union* and the Marysville *Express,* newspapers throughout the region demanded that a massive man hunt should be organized and that the capture of Tom Bell should be the principal concern of all peace officers. Sacramento County hired a pair of professional detectives for the sole purpose of tracking down the outlaw. The sheriffs of Nevada, Placer, and Yuba counties swore in additional deputies and took up the hunt for Bell. They captured half a dozen members of the gang, but they failed to turn up the bandit leader.

But the hunt continued. It began to pay some fringe benefits. From Camptonville came word that a member of the Bell gang known as Monte Jack (Montague Lyon) had been wounded as he was escaping from the ranch of a Mexican named Ramirez. Monte Jack's name does not reappear in the Tom Bell chronicles, and it has been assumed that he died from his wound. A few days later the sheriff of Yuba County captured three of Bell's men in a shoot-out at the Oregon House, a suspected outlaw hangout. Before the week ended, Deputy Marshal Nightingale arrested five more of the outlaw's adherents. The net drew even closer when Sheriff Henson of Placer County and his posse surprised Bell, Ned Connor, a gang chieftain, and a third man known only as "Tex" as they were leaving the Franklin House near Auburn. There was a flurry of gunfire. Connor was killed. Bell and "Tex" made their getaway.

It was a narrow escape. The way things were going must have warned the gang leader that the law was closing in on him. He had further evidence of it within the week, when the Sacramento County detectives Harrison and Anderson took a man named Tom Brown into custody. They had evidence enough to convict the man of complicity in several of the crimes committed by the gang. How they induced him to talk is not known, but he agreed to lead them to a tent in the hills above the Mountaineer House, where Bill Gristy and four other Bell men were lying out.

The Mountaineer House was only one of a dozen similar roadside saloons where a traveler could get food, drink, and a night's lodging. Jack Phillips, the proprietor, a former "Sydney Duck" with a known criminal record, had long been suspected of being in Tom Bell's pay, supplying him with news of travelers who stopped at his place and supplying his men with food when they were occupying the tent in the hills above his establishment.

Harrison and Anderson, the detectives, enlisted two stout men to accompany them on the raid. Timing themselves so as to reach the vicinity of the tent after dark, they approached it undetected.

A light was burning inside. It cast grotesque shadows against the canvas. Harrison stopped to run over his plan again. It was simple enough. Brown, the informer, was to raise the flap and greet his fellow outlaws; Harrison and Anderson were to step in behind him and cover the five men; if there was any shooting, the detectives were to fling themselves to the ground and the two men outside were to riddle the tent with bullets.

There were five men inside. Four were seated; the fifth was on his feet at the far end of the tent fiddling with a mirror that hung from a tent pole. When the detectives rushed in, he snatched up a pistol and fired. Harrison killed him with a load of buckshot. Gristy snapped a shot over his shoulder and dived for the side wall, which he knew was not staked down. He was scrambling under it when a bullet from Anderson's rifle creased his scalp. It did not stop him. Though momentarily stunned, he reached his horse and escaped.

It had taken less than a minute. Gristy had got away; Walker, who had been at the mirror, was dead, and Pete Ansara was squirming on the ground with a load of buckshot in his thigh. The other two bandits spent the rest of the night behind bars in the Folsom jail.

Tom Bell had disappeared from his favorite haunts. So had Elizabeth Hood, the buxom proprietoress of the Western Exchange Hotel on the Sacramento–Nevada City road, and her three children, girls aged eight, nine and eleven. Putting together such pieces of evidence as became available some time later, it is reasonable to believe that Mrs. Hood was Tom Bell's woman or that she was his confederate in crime. Although travelers were never robbed in her establishment, they often were soon after leaving it, the assumption being that Mrs. Hood had tipped off her lover that a likely victim was, or soon would be, on the road traveling north or south, as the case might be.

With the dragnet the lawmen were drawing becoming uncomfortably close—he and Gristy having been within an inch of being captured within a week—Bell left the Northern Mines for the south, where he had never operated and could feel reasonably safe. Six miles above Firebaugh's Ferry on the San Joaquin he "acquired" a small ranch, got word to Gristy to join him, hired two old men to run the place, and brought Mrs. Hood and her children down from the north to keep house for him.

Gristy got the message and, accompanied by a Mexican, name unknown, rode south down the foothills toward the Stanislaus and the forks of the Tuolumne and the Merced. Having progressed as far south as Knight's Landing without being stopped or questioned, Gristy, with a false sense of security, suggested that they ride into town and enjoy a civilized meal. It was another of the miscalculations to which outlaws always seem to be prone. As they sat down to eat, Gristy was recognized by the proprietor of the hotel, who notified the undersheriff. A few minutes later, the outlaw and his Mexican companion were behind bars in the town's stone calaboose.

In the morning, after hours of questioning, Gristy broke down, admitted his identity, and made a full confession. When Judge Belt had put it in writing, Gristy signed it. Bell had trusted him, but Gristy was ready to betray him. He knew that any bargain he might strike with his captors could gain him only a few more weeks of life. To a man in his position, even a few days were precious. He had only one card to play and he laid it on the table, as the old saying had it: if the undersheriff and Judge Belt would agree to have him escorted safely back to Placer County, in which many of his crimes had been committed, he would tell them where to find Tom Bell.

The group gathered at the cell door conferred briefly. After all, Bell was the big fish they wanted. Judge Belt was of the opinion that the Mexican undoubtedly knew as well as Gristy did where the bandit leader was holed up, and that if they kept him in their custody, he could be made to lead them to Bell if Gristy's story proved to be a hoax. That settled the matter, and Gristy was taken north by three deputies. It was Saturday, September 27. The rest of the day was consumed in completing plans for the manhunt.

On Sunday morning the posse left Knight's Landing and headed up the river. The directions that had been elicited from Gristy proved to be accurate. Near the long slough that connected the Tulare Lakes with the San Joaquin, some six miles above Firebaugh's Ferry, they found the small ranch where Bell had holed up. As they approached the house warily, they were surprised to find

Sheriff Mulford of San Joaquin County and a number of his deputies in charge. It was Monday noon by now.

Mulford informed Judge Belt and the Knight's Landing men that he and his deputies, out looking for Tom Bell, had intercepted Gristy and his guards on their way north and that Gristy had repeated to him the directions he had given the judge.

The explanation was satisfactory. The leaders of the two parties agreed that they should join hands and wait for Bell to show up. In the meantime Mrs. Hood, her children, and the two aged caretakers were to be sent downriver to Stockton. This was done. With horses hidden, the united posses settled down to their vigil. It proved to be a long and unrewarding one.

For four days they waited without any sign of Bell or any member of his gang. On Friday evening, with the food in the house exhausted, Mulford reached the end of his patience and announced that, unless Bell put in an appearance by morning, he and his group would break camp and head for home. Morning came without bringing any sight of the bandit chieftain. The weary, bored posse broke up and began its retreat downriver. The Knight's Landing men hung on until noon before they pulled out. Judge Belt's party, with the exception of Bob Price of Sonora, intended to cross the San Joaquin at Firebaugh's Ferry. Price, to take a shortcut home, forded the river some distance above the ferry. Had he not done so, there is no telling how this narrative might have ended.

As he rode along, Price saw a rider turn abruptly into the willows some distance ahead of him. Alert as he passed the place where the man had left the road, he saw him trying to conceal himself in the trees. His suspicions thoroughly aroused, Price rode on a few yards before he signaled frantically for Judge Belt and his party to cross the river and join him at once.

The man in the willows was Bell. He had had the ranch under observation for days and knew how things had been going. Believing that the coast was now clear, he was making his way there. By chance, it was the greatest mistake he was ever to make, for as he regained the road he was confronted by the leveled guns of the judge and half a dozen men. Caught by surprise, all he could do was raise his hands and surrender.

According to the San Francisco *Alta*, reporting the confrontation a week later, the first words were spoken by Judge Belt. "I believe," said the judge, "that you are the man we have been looking for." Bell looked at him coolly for a moment and replied, "Very probably."

They led Bell down the road to a tall sycamore and dropped a rope over a convenient limb. Bell realized that this was the end. He met it bravely, asking only for permission to write a letter to Mrs. Hood, whom he addressed as "my dear and only friend," and to his mother.[1] Permission was granted. The noose was slipped over his head and he was yanked into the air to strangle to death.

It was five o'clock in the afternoon of October 4, 1856, an hour and a day that soon became meaningless. At the time, however, it was hailed as marking the end of outlawry in California. The Tom Bell gang had been broken up and many of its members hurried off to prison. But outlawry had not run its course. In fact, it was only beginning.

IV

Alias Rattlesnake Dick

In the end it has been almost invariably the excuse of men who followed the outlaw trade that they were pushed into a life of crime by circumstances beyond their control. Such protestations are usually found to be contrary to the facts.

Young Dick Barter, alias Rattlesnake Dick, appears to have been an exception to the rule. Although charged on at least three occasions of a crime he did not commit, he tried to go straight. But having been given a bad name, he could not buck the tide that had set in against him. In the spring of 1856, apparently concluding that he might as well have the game as well as the name, he committed his first robbery.

That was the year in which Tom Bell was running wild in the Northern Mines. That his path and Rattlesnake Dick's had sometimes crossed seems likely, for they had a mutual accomplice in the person of Jack Phillips, the proprietor of the notorious Mountaineer House on the Folsom road. But Bell was coming to the end of his career; the other's was just beginning, and it was in the years ahead that Rattlesnake Dick was to become a thorn in the side of lawmen.

Dick Barter and his older brother had reached early manhood in Quebec City, where their father, an English army officer, had been stationed and had married a French-Canadian woman, from whom the boys inherited their adventurous spirit and good looks.

After the death of their parents, they, as well as their sister and her husband moved to the United States. In 1850, joined by an elderly cousin, they made the long journey across the plains to Oregon and took up land in the vicinity of the growing village of Sweet Home, a few miles east of Corvallis. Confronted every few days by tales of rich new strikes being made on the rivers of the Mother Lode was more than the brothers could withstand. In the spring of the following year, accompanied by their cousin, they put Oregon behind them and headed south for California.

Everybody was talking about Rattlesnake Bar on the American, where the richest strikes yet recorded were being made. So the Barter brothers and their cousin joined the rush with high hopes. But they came to Rattlesnake only to discover that they were too late; the hundreds who had preceded them had put their mark on every foot of ground. Having no claim of their own, they had no choice but to go to work for men who had. Wages were high, but so was the price of grub. At the end of a month they had little to show for their labor. Like others in the same fix as themselves, they spent what time they could in prospecting the adjacent hills and streams, hoping to find a "color."

Luck was against them. After a year of unrewarding labor, Dick's brother and cousin informed him that they were returning to Oregon. They pleaded with Dick to leave with them, but he refused; he had come to the mines to make his fortune and he was still confident he would.

Although no one would admit it, it was apparent by early summer that the Rattlesnake Bar placers had been exhausted. Men began leaving the camp; claims that had been big producers could be had for a song. But there were few takers. Dick Barter's exuberance and spirited confidence that the Bar would make a comeback became the life of the diggings. One night when Dick walked into a saloon, a bearded old-timer greeted him with a cry of "Hooray for you, Rattlesnake Dick!" The group standing at the bar responded with a hearty "Right! Rattlesnake Dick!"

They were men twice or more his age, but the name they gave

him was not given in derision; they needed something more potent than whiskey to shore up their flagging spirits.

In the months that followed, Rattlesnake Bar suffered the usual traumatic experience common to all fading mining camps. New strikes were made but they proved to be of no consequence. In July, the proprietor of the general store discovered that someone was stealing cattle from the small herd he kept on hand for butchering. It afforded a man with a personal grievance against Dick an opportunity to even his score by accusing him of being the thief. Dick was arrested, tried, and found not guilty. But that did not erase the stigma that had been put on his name.

Later that same year he found himself in trouble again. A Mormon, working the gravel on the upper North Fork, reported that his mule had been stolen. On no better evidence than that he had been seen in the vicinity on the day the mule disappeared, young Dick was charged with the crime, arrested, tried, and convicted. Sentenced to two years in state prison, he was still languishing in the Folsom jail when the animal was found and the man who had stolen it confessed the crime.

With his name unjustly tarnished for the second time, Dick realized that there was no point in tarrying longer at Rattlesnake Bar. Still determined to lead an upright life, he struck out for Shasta County, nearly two hundred miles to the north, where he was unknown. As a further safeguard, he changed his name to Dick Woods.

For two years he moved about Shasta County, prospecting between jobs. Several thousand prospectors were on the move back and forth across the northern counties. He joined them, trying his luck on the South Fork of the Klamath, the Trinity and Lewiston rivers, doing just well enough to keep on trying. Doubtless among his widening circle of acquaintances were men against whom the law had a grudge. He was content to take them as he found them and asked no questions.

When the rush to French Gulch took place, he joined it. There he had the misfortune to be recognized by a man who had known him at Rattlesnake Bar. The expected happened; the man talked. Dick Woods was really Dick Barter, a two-bit thief who had been run out of Rattlesnake Bar. Untrue, of course, but devastating.

Dick could feel the chill that set in against him in many quarters. He gathered up his tools and disappeared. Weeks passed without his being seen. He had left the north and was camped out in the hills near Red Bluff. He had tried, as few young men have, to lead an honorable life. For the third time fate had cast him to the wolves. It might happen again, but whether it did or not, the tales that had been told about him would be remembered and repeated. His future held nothing.

After days of brooding, he shoved his pistol into the face of a passing traveler and relieved him of some four hundred dollars. He had made his decision. In what can only be put down as juvenile bravado, he said, "When they ask you who robbed you, tell them Rattlesnake Dick."

It was a name that the Mother Lode was to hear again and again in the years ahead.

During the summer of 1856 he pursued his new career of road agent with unqualified success. Of course he was small-fry in the eyes of the law, and after the attempted holdup of the Camptonville stage and the great hunt for Tom Bell got underway, the lawmen had no time to spend tracking him down.

With the hanging of Bell and the imprisonment of Bill Gristy and other Bell lieutenants, young Dick became obsessed with the idea that all he had to do to fill the vacuum their passing had left was to organize his own gang and take over. It was no longer possible to excuse what he was doing because of his youth and the tricks fate had played him; his latent criminal instincts had taken over, and he was as dangerous as any man who lived by the gun.

He had become acquainted with Jack Phillips, the unsavory proprietor of the Mountaineer House and a former Sydney Duck.[1] He was astute enough to realize that while the man ran errands and otherwise served men outside the law, he earned his living by preying upon them. And yet, though distrusting Phillips, Dick turned to him for advice when he began putting his gang together.

Phillips had a wide acquaintance among men whose profession was robbery. It so happened that just when he put out his "feelers," the second Vigilance Committee was giving San Francisco another housecleaning. As a consequence, known criminals were making a hasty exodus from the city. A number began dropping in at the Mountaineer House in response to the queries Phillips had sent out.

Dick had his choice of a score of the elite of California's robbers and renegades. He selected five. That was enough for what he had in mind. He didn't want a big, unmanageable gang such as Tom Bell had put together. He had a job in mind that would dwarf anything Bell had attempted. It was with that operation in mind that he selected his men. For his trusted lieutenant he chose George Skinner, a desperado of some distinction who had been in and out of prison for most of the years he had been in California. Hardly less noted was his brother, Cyrus Skinner. To that pair of worthies Dick added a big, husky horse thief and road agent who went by the name of Big Dolph Newton, a foreigner named Romero (said to have been an Italian) and Bill Carter, a drawling young Texan who was known to have a fast gun.

In Placer and Nevada counties the feeling of relief occasioned by the elimination of the Tom Bell gang and its leader faded when it became apparent that they were being scourged by a new band of marauders. Many of the robberies were minor ones. But they served their purpose; Rattlesnake Dick was testing his men, getting to know what he could expect from them when they found themselves in a tight corner. When ready to divulge the stroke that had been on his mind for months, he first discussed it with George Skinner. The latter liked the idea, and after they had ironed out some of the details, gave it his enthusiastic approval.

In his days in Shasta and Trinity County, Dick had learned how gold bullion from that wild, mountainous, heavily timbered country was shipped out by mule train, there being no roads over which a wagon could pass. Of course such a train, transporting as much as $100,000, moved under heavy guard, but he was convinced that at the right location it could be stopped and taken over.

It was at this point that they would be confronted with a problem on which the success or failure of the enterprise depended. Once in possession of the gold, how were they to move it? Surely it couldn't be done with the captured mules, for they were plainly branded W F, which everyone would identify on sight as the trademark of Wells, Fargo, by now the most important banking and express company on the Pacific Coast.

In putting his plans together, Dick had realized that it would not be safe to use the Wells, Fargo mules; instead, they would have to rustle a bunch of mules and substitute them for the animals that had brought the gold down from Yreka and the Klamath River mines. He knew where any number of mules were to be found, down near Auburn. It wouldn't take more than two men to steal as many as they needed. He would go, accompanied by the younger of the Skinner brothers. First, a spot for the holdup would have to be selected and a hideout located where the gang could hole up for a week undetected.

It was the custom for the gold train to leave Yreka on the first of the month. Allowing themselves plenty of time to get into position to intercept it, the gang set out for the north without attracting attention. In the foothills some miles below the tiny village of Redding, they jumped the Mexican muleteers. After cowing them with a flurry of shots, they tied them up and took possession of the gold. Using their horses as pack animals, they quickly disappeared into the mountains. As soon as they reached their hidden camp, Rattlesnake Dick and Cyrus Skinner took off to rustle the now sorely needed unbranded mules.

Everything had gone their way, but with a fortune in their hands their anxiety grew as days passed and Dick and young Skinner failed to return. They scouted the trails, thinking the two had lost their bearings. Nothing was seen of them, however.

George Skinner, who was giving the orders, refused to wait any longer, knowing that by now county officers and Wells, Fargo detectives were combing the country for them.

Skinner, still resourceful, secretly buried half of the loot and divided the other half between himself and his companions, which enabled them to make off with it. Luck was with them, and they reached their favorite hideout near Auburn. Anxious to learn what had become of his brother and Rattlesnake Dick, George Skinner decided to risk going into town to find out. The others went with him.

Being confident that the law was still looking for them far to the north, in the wilds of Trinity and Shasta counties, may have made them careless. If so, it was their mistake, for shortly after dark they ran head-on into a large posse under the leadership of Jack Barkeley, the Wells, Fargo detective. There was a brief battle. George Skinner was killed instantly. Romero, seriously wounded, made a run for the river, where Barkeley fished him out before he drowned. Big Dolph Newton and Carter threw down their guns and surrendered. Newton and Romero were sent to Angel Island for ten years. Bill Carter escaped a similar sentence by leading the officers to their hideout, where he and his companions had cached their share of the gold that had been brought down from the mountains with so much effort.

Strangely, the law did not connect Rattlesnake Dick with the robbery of the gold train, very likely because when it occurred he and Cyrus Skinner were languishing in the Placer County jail, charged with the attempted larceny of a number of mules from an American River rancher. Before they were brought to trial, they escaped. Cyrus Skinner was picked up a few days later and sent to state's prison for four years. Although he subsequently left California for Montana, he reappears in this narrative. Rattlesnake Dick, on the other hand, soon put together a new gang and continued to harass the foothill country.

For two years he appeared to bear a charmed life. He ranged over at least five counties, and although often cornered, managed to shoot his way to continued freedom. He sensed long before others did that the days of gang outlawry had passed. Operating as a lone bandit or with never more than one reliable man to side him, he found the rewards greater and escape much easier.[2]

The rewards posted for his capture appeared to amuse him, for he often stopped to scrawl a laconic message on them. Although he had stolen thousands of dollars, not including the mule-train fiasco, he had little to show for it. As for changing his course, it was too late for that now. The excitement and danger of the constant brushes with the law, the threat of capture and sudden death had became the spice of life. And then, in the early evening of July 11, 1859, it happened, and there is no explanation for it.

At half past eight, a neighbor hammered excitedly on the door of George Martin, deputy tax collector of Placer County, and told him that he had just seen Rattlesnake Dick ride past with a companion and turn into the road that led north. Why the man had not run around the corner to the sheriff's office with his news can very likely be attributed to the fact that Martin was a county official as well as the sheriff.

Martin hastily saddled his horse and hurried to the jail and courthouse in which the sheriff's office was located. Deputies Johnson and Crutcher were on duty. They agreed with Martin that there was no time to lose. Several minutes later the three men raced out of town in pursuit.

It was a clear, moonlit night, and they soon saw two riders loping along ahead of them. Where and why the two horsemen had tarried long enough to enable the deputies and Martin to overhaul them so quickly remains a mystery. Deputy Sheriff Johnson recognized Rattlesnake Dick and called on the two men to pull up and raise their hands. They did, but their hands did not come up empty. Dick's bullet severed Johnson's rein and mangled his left hand. His companion's slug struck Martin in the chest and tumbled him from the saddle. Crutcher, not knowing that Martin was dead, dropped down to see what he could do for him.

Not a shot had been fired at the bandits, and it seemed they would get away untouched, since Johnson, unable to control his horse with his shattered hand, was helpless for a minute, and Crutcher's attention was fixed on Martin. But Crutcher straightened up and fired a shot. Johnson, getting control of his mount, did likewise.

Later, both testified that they had seen the famous bandit sway in the saddle, then right himself and spur his horse down the road, his companion following.

A posse was out all night but discovered no trace of the bandits. But in the morning the driver and passengers of the Iowa Hill stage were startled to see a dead man lying at the side of the road as they neared the Junction House. The driver got down and examined the dead man. He had been shot twice through the chest and a third bullet had been fired into his head. Any one of the three shots would have been fatal.

With the assistance of several of the male passengers, the body was lifted to the roof of the stage and carried into town, where it was placed on the sidewalk in front of Masonic Hall. Word was sent around the corner to the sheriff's office. Deputy sheriff Crutcher came at once. A glance was enough for recognition. The dead man was Rattlesnake Dick.

Crutcher could account for two of the wounds but not the third. Johnson and he had fired but one shot each. Had Dick, to end his suffering, taken his own life—or had his companion fired a mercy shot?

That question might have been answered years later, when Aleck Wright, an associate of Dick and widely believed to have been the man with him on that fatal night, was tried for complicity in the killing of Deputy Tax Collector George Martin. Wright refused to talk, and the evidence brought against him was so flimsy that he was acquitted.

Rattlesnake Dick had no money on him and had to be buried at the county's expense, which presented another question that was never answered: Had Dick given his purse to Wright, or had the latter filched it?

Ironically, there is $40,000 in gold lying buried somewhere up in the Trinity foothills.

V

Tiburcio Vasquez: Tiger of the Dim Trails

ALTHOUGH in the decade and a half following the discovery of gold on the South Fork of the American the population of California had soared, the life-style of a great part of the state had not changed. In Spanish-speaking southern California the old manners and customs remained largely what they had been. That was true in lesser degree south from San Francisco Bay, down through San Mateo County and the Coast Range counties to Santa Barbara, where the scattered inhabitants were predominantly of Mexican origin. California, once their homeland, was no longer theirs. Not only had it been wrested away from them but they had been branded an inferior race.

In the main they were good people, humble, generous. Accustomed to making do with very little, they had neither the means nor the will to fight back. Among them were exceptions, of course —reckless young men who were determined to right the injustice that had been done their people. Setting out with that high resolve, they soon found there was only a thin, often indistinguishable line between their marauding and outright outlawry. As could have been predicted, they crossed it and became hunted men with a price on their heads.

35

The rugged fastnesses of the Coast Range, inhabited only by sheepherders and cowboys, offered them a safe and handy hideout. They struck without warning, robbing and killing and then disappearing into the mountains, where few sheriffs and their deputies dared to follow. When nothing else offered, they raided the little villages and *plazas* along the coast seemingly for the pure hell of it, plundering the *ricos* and sharing the spoils with the poor.

Half a dozen or more Mexican bandit leaders surfaced briefly during the 1860's and 1870's, only to be quickly eliminated by gunfire or hustled off to prison. It was a different story with durable Tiburcio Vasquez, the tiger of the dim trails. He was a rather small man, weighing not more than 140 pounds, with a cruel face and blazing dark eyes that held no mercy even in repose. He successfully jousted with the law-enforcement agencies of California for fifteen years before life was jerked out of him in the jail yard at San Jose on March 19, 1875.

Born of an Indian mother, Vasquez was a half-blood. Although there are conflicting accounts of where and when he was born, the consensus is that he was no more than fifteen when Joaquin Murrieta was believed to have been killed at Panoche Pass by Love and his rangers. Despite the disparity in their ages, some accounts have it that the two men were not only friends but that young Tiburcio Vasquez's campaign to end the oppression of his people had been inspired by Murrieta. That is utter nonsense; Vasquez was a loner; all that his bloody trail did for the Mexican *gente* was to cause it deeper humiliation.

With horses being the equivalent of legal tender in California, he began his lawlessness as a horse thief. He must have been fairly successful, for when he showed up periodically in Monterey, the Mecca for men engaged in the outlaw trade, he always had money to spend in the cantinas and brothels. He fancied himself as a lady killer and did not confine his quest to the women whose favors were for sale. Too many tales are told of his kidnapping the daughter of a Mexican rancher in the Livermore Valley for there not to be some truth in them. The most believable agree that the father of the girl pursued and overtook the couple. A bullet from the father's gun shattered the young bandit's right arm, and he fled.[1]

Having been put out of action for several months by his injury, Tiburcio slipped back into Monterey and spent his enforced idleness with a minimum of discomfort. It was at this time that he struck up a close acquaintance with one of the numerous Garcia brothers, either Miguel or Juan. He was associated with both at one time or another.

The Garcias were small-time cattle thieves. Still, they could talk to Tiburcio as equals. They were presently obsessed with one of those "great" ideas that afflict their kind from time to time, usually with disastrous results. The gist of it was that in Sonoma and Mendocino counties, north of the Bay, thousands of cattle were being fattened for the San Francisco market. A small herd could be rustled almost as easily as a dozen head. Vasquez bought the idea; there was nothing he wanted more than to make a big score that would establish him as a bandit leader.

When they were ready, they slipped out of Monterey. Several days later they crossed the Sacramento River at Vallejo without being questioned and lost themselves in the gentle valleys and hills of Sonoma and Mendocino counties. The country was not unfamiliar to Tiburcio Vasquez. Two years back, following the stabbing to death of a man in Monterey, of which he had been accused, he had hidden out in Mendocino County until the charges against him had been dropped. Cattle were now to be found in every direction, but the climate had changed in his absence; ranchers had largely supplanted their *vaqueros* with young Texans, who took a dim view of rustlers. Ignoring the changes that had taken place, Vasquez and his companions made their strike and were quickly apprehended.

San Quentin, California's new prison across the bay from San Francisco, was waiting to receive him. He had served less than two years of his five-year sentence when he escaped in a prison break. In the remarkably short period of two months he was back in San Quentin, this time on a larceny conviction in Amador

County. He served a year on the larceny conviction, plus the three years he already owed the state, and was discharged on August 13, 1863. He was back again a short time later on an armed-robbery conviction. It was not until June 4, 1870, that he walked out a free man. The prestige of being a three-time loser elevated him to a position of prominence among California's desperadoes.

An Italian butcher employed at the New Almaden Quicksilver Mines, near San Jose, was shot and stabbed to death in his bed. The four or five hundred dollars he was known to have had in his possession was missing, indicating that robbery was the motive. On whatever evidence was found, the authorities charged Vasquez with the crime. When they began looking for him, he was safe in his lair in the Arroyo Cantua, deep in the Coast Range mountains.

To relieve his boredom, he began putting a small gang together. Francisco Barcenas and Garcia Rodriguez, with whom he had become acquainted in San Quentin, were the only members who were known outside Monterey County. Led by Vasquez, they made a number of forays, robbing country stores and inns on the stage roads. Early in the summer, they held up their first stage a few miles north of the town of Hollister. The driver pulled up his horses when ordered to do so. After making sure that the stage was not transporting treasure of any kind, passengers were ordered out and lined up at the side of the road, hands raised. After they had been stripped of their money and other valuables, they were made to lie face down in the dust with their hands and ankles tied. This treatment of passengers became a Vasquez trademark when the victims submitted without resistance.

Congratulating themselves on the haul they had made, the bandits were jogging along a few minutes later when Thomas McMahon, the prosperous Hollister groceryman, came riding down the road. He was returning from a business trip to nearby Gilroy. This was an unexpected prize. McMahon had plenty of fight in him, and when the bandits began going through his pockets, he objected strenuously. He knew Vasquez. Unmindful of the danger he ran, he gave him a tongue-lashing in Spanish, a language far more expressive than English at such moments. Vasquez had killed men on less provocation. But he just laughed and galloped off with some seven hundred dollars of the storekeeper's money in his saddlebag.

But the day was not over yet. The sheriff of San Benito County was thirty-some miles away in Monterey. With him, by chance, was that formidable man-hunter, Sheriff Harry Morse of Alameda County. When word of the double holdup reached them, they picked up a Santa Cruz constable and the three set out to intercept Vasquez and his companions. The officers, believing that the bandits would be heading back to their sanctuary in the Arroyo Cantua, were successful in cutting their trail. There was a brief fight. The constable killed Francisco Barcenas; Vasquez and Rodriguez, both seriously wounded, made their escape. Rodriguez was captured two days later and was returned to San Quentin, where he died a short time later. Tiburcio Vasquez was safely back in the mountains and slowly recovering from the gunshot wound in his chest.

It was not until the spring of 1873 that he began scourging the country again. He had put together a new gang, with José Chavez, an experienced outlaw, as his lieutenant. One of his men, Moreno by name, had a wife living in the Mexican *barrio* at Hollister. The story goes that Vasquez risked capture by visiting her on occasion. When Moreno learned how matters stood, he went out to get Vasquez. That was his mistake. He was not seen again, and the supposition was that Tiburcio had killed him and tossed the body into a handy ravine.

The new Vasquez gang made its first strike far up the San Joaquin River, at Firebaugh's Ferry, early in July, looting a general store and making off with a sizable amount of goods and money. For the remainder of the summer they scourged the San Joaquin Valley, robbing stores, waylaying travelers, and stopping stage-coaches. On August 26, they staged what began as just one more of their routine store robberies, at Tres Pinos, a San Benito County settlement, a few miles south of Hollister. It proved to be the straw that broke the camel's back as far as the State of California was concerned. When the robbery of Andrew Snyder's Tres Pinos store appeared in newspaper headlines as "The Tres Pinos Tragedy —Three innocent people killed and several seriously injured," Governor Booth decided that the state had had enough of Tiburcio Vasquez.

The robbery of Snyder's store began as so many others had. Two of the bandits entered and engaged Snyder's clerk in conversation. A few moments later, five more of the gang arrived. After tying their horses at the hitch-rail, three of them, including Vasquez, stationed themselves outside the door; the other two went in. Leveling their pistols at the clerk and the several customers, (including a young boy), they ordered them to lie face down on the floor and then proceeded to empty the till, strip the victims of their cash and valuables, and finally to ransack the place, taking whatever they fancied.

The four bandits were ready to leave when there was a burst of gunfire outside. A sheepherder, William Redford, unaware of what was happening, had turned in off the road and was walking toward the store, when Vasquez ordered him to stop. The herder, confused or not understanding the command, did not obey. Guns blazed and he fell dead. Two teamsters, busy at their wagons a short distance away, had not been molested, but they ran up to the store now to learn the meaning of the shooting. Vasquez clubbed one of them unconscious with his pistol, and as the other, James Riley, turned to run, shot him through the heart as he was dodging around the corner of the building.

Between Snyder's store and the hotel, both on the same side of the road, there was an open space of some seventy-five yards. When a man stepped out on the wooden porch of the hotel, Vasquez snatched his rifle from its saddle scabbard and fired. The man on the porch leaped back untouched, but Vasquez's slug killed an elderly man named Davidson, who was standing with his wife just inside.

A young boy, the brother of the one who was lying on the

floor, shoved his head in at the back door of the store to see what was taking place. Chavez saw the lad. Chasing and overtaking him in the stable yard, he clubbed him unconscious with the barrel of his pistol.

When Vasquez and his gang jogged out of Tres Pinos, laden with plunder, they left behind them three dead men and a man and boy hovering on the brink of death. The tragedy horrified the public. For two months, hastily organized posses rode up and down the San Joaquin Valley and trailed through the Coast Range. They saw nothing of Vasquez. The rumor spread, hopefully, that he had left the country. Actually, he had, and was safe in the Cahuenga Hills, just north of Los Angeles, a region he had never molested in the past.

In December he surfaced again, after lying low for weeks. Riding into the little Fresno County town of Kingston at the head of his gang, he robbed both stores there. Ten days later, he and his lieutenant, José Chavez, held up the Los Angeles and Owens River stage. Other robberies followed.

In January the state acted, offering a reward of $3,000 for the capture of Tiburcio Vasquez, dead or alive. Newspapers denounced the sum as inadequate, and the Legislature upped the reward to $8,000.

Now, at last, it seemed that a united, organized effort was to be made to run Vasquez to earth. Harry Morse, the formidable sheriff of Alameda County, was put in charge. A better man could not have been found. He was shrewd, indomitable, and tireless. He had been watching Vasquez for a long time, filing away for future reference what he was able to learn about the man.

Among the Mexicans in Alameda and the adjoining counties Morse had what he termed "sources," who passed bits of information on to him. Before starting out on the big hunt for the bandit, he was convinced that Vasquez would eventually be found far to the south. But when he set out with his handpicked posse, he spent weeks combing the Coast Range before he turned southward, making sure that his man was still somewhere ahead of him and not behind. In a book he published later, Morse wrote that between March 11 and the first week in May, 1874, he and his men rode more than 2,700 miles.

It is safe to say that by the middle of December the posse had logged twice that many miles. In all that time, nearing ten months by now, Vasquez had been quiet, save for the minor robbery of a sheepman near San Gabriel Mission. That incident further convinced Morse that his man was hiding out somewhere south of Tehachapi Pass in the mountainous Kern County. He also realized that time was running out; that the state would not continue to finance the expensive and so far unproductive chase much longer.

Looking back from this distance, it is obvious that Vasquez knew Morse was closing in on him, for he dispersed his men and ordered them to make their way back north as best they could, hoping, of course, that the posse would pick up their trail and lead pursuit away from himself. It was a bold move and might have succeeded had not the break in the case come when it did.

Morse and his party were in the Cahuenga Hills, well inside the Los Angeles County line, when he bribed (or "induced," as he put it) a Mexican herder to supply him with the information he needed: Vasquez was in Alison Canyon in the adobe home of George Allen, better known as "Greek George," a fence for thieves. Morse should have closed in on the place at once. Instead, he posted his men to watch it while he rode into town to confer with Sheriff Rowland, of Los Angeles County.

It was not a question of overstepping his jurisdiction that took Morse into town; he was not only the sheriff of Alameda County but he had been authorized by the state to pursue his search for Vasquez wherever it might lead him. His purpose in conferring with Rowland was to extend to him the courtesy of taking part in the capture of the notorious outlaw. Rowland would have none of it. He declared that he had had Greek George's adobe under surveillance for some time, and there was no one living there but Greek George and his Mexican woman. In the angry confrontation that followed, Rowland advised Morse to gather up his men and get out of Los Angeles County at once; that he was capable of enforcing the law without any outside assistance.

Some accounts have it that he went so far as to threaten to place Morse under arrest if he didn't comply. That is unlikely. Morse was no man's fool. He realized that Rowland had his eyes on the reward California was offering for the capture of Vasquez, and that he (Morse) had foolishly put him in a position to collect it. "There was nothing for Morse to do but assent," says the usually reliable Joseph Henry Jackson. "He rode back to the Tejon, gathered his party, and turned north the way he had come."

Rowland swore in a group of deputies at once, among them George Beers, the Los Angeles correspondent of the San Francisco *Chronicle*, thus making sure that what he was doing would have the proper amount of publicity, and they set out for Greek George's adobe. Before coming in sight of the house, they stopped a wagon and arranged with the driver to take two of them, hidden under a piece of canvas, up to the building. Undersheriff Johnson and the other man, reporter Beers, leaped out and rushed the door. Greek George's woman tried to block the way. Johnson thrust her aside and ran into the house in time to see Vasquez leap through a rear window and make for his horse. Johnson fired and missed, but a blast from Beers' shotgun, loaded with buckshot, brought Tiburcio down. An hour later, he was behind bars in the Los Angeles County jail, waiting for a doctor to remove the slugs from his legs.

Being charged with the killing of Redford and Davidson at Tres Pinos, Vasquez should have been brought to trial in San Benito County, but since that county had no jail deemed strong enough to hold him, a change of venue was obtained to Santa Clara County, and he was remanded to the San Jose jail. On January 5, 1875, he was brought to trial. It did not take long. On January 9, the jury rendered its verdict. It was "guilty as charged," and death by hanging the penalty.

His lawyers took an appeal at once. He had been ably defended, a fund having been raised to provide him with adequate counsel.

Most of the subscribers were Mexicans, but not all, for, as usually happens when a known killer is on trial for his life, there was an outpouring of undeserved sympathy for him. When he was running wild, the cry had been to hunt him down and eliminate him; now sentimentalists, mostly women, were demanding mercy and keeping him supplied with delicacies.

On January 23, two weeks after the verdict had been rendered, Vasquez was brought before Judge Belden for sentencing. "Your life has been an unbroken record of lawlessness and outrage, a career of pillage and murder, a synonym for all that is wicked and infamous," Belden informed him. "I now sentence you to be hanged by the neck until dead on March the nineteenth."

On March 12, word was received from Sacramento that the High Court had denied the appeal. Sheriff Adams began preparing for the event. Since Santa Clara County did not have a gallows, Adams borrowed one from Sacramento County [2] and set it up in the San Jose jail yard. As required by California statute, invitations to witness the hanging of Tiburcio Vasquez were put in the mails.

During the weeks of his incarceration Vasquez had stubbornly refused the ministrations of a priest, but as the time of his execution neared, he permitted Father Serda, the chaplain, to spend several hours a day with him. He dictated several letters; one of them asking the forgiveness of those he had wronged and another addressed to his followers, pleading with them to change their ways and not to seek to avenge his death. On the afternoon of March 19, he was led across the crowded jail yard to the scaffold, preceded by Father Serda and carrying a small crucifix. The trap was sprung at 1:35 P.M.

The days of Mexican outlawry that had bedeviled California for twenty years were over. Although the state granted the reward of $8,000 to Sheriff Rowland of Los Angeles, for the capture of Tiburcio Vasquez, Harry Morse had done more to break up the Mexican gangs than any other lawman. In a gun duel he had killed Juan Soto, an even more vicious renegade than Vasquez, and dealt a similar fate to Narrato Bartola. Over the years and without fanfare, he had run down Jesus Tejada, Bartola Sepulveda, and half a dozen others of their kind and hustled them off to long prison terms.

The hanging of Vasquez did not mean the ending of lawlessness; a new type of banditry, perhaps less violent but equally spectacular, was ready to take over.

VI

Black Bart—California's Premier Road Agent

ALTHOUGH by the 1860's Wells, Fargo dominated the banking and express business of California, it owned no stage lines (with one exception), preferring to continue a close working arrangement with the California Stage Company with its hundreds of coaches and thousands of horses. More often than not, wherever a wheel turned in the state, it belonged to the California Stage Company.

Notwithstanding the competition, a score of short-haul independent lines managed to survive. Their coaches did not escape being stopped and robbed, some of them transporting Wells, Fargo treasure and the mails. But these were not included in the confidential list of twenty-eight robberies the company had suffered and with which Wells, Fargo supplied its agents in 1888, all of them attributed to California's most masterful road agent, the ubiquitous Black Bart.[1,2]

Stage drivers became well acquainted with him over the years, either from personal experience or through the tales they exchanged with their fellow drivers at the end of a run. They were agreed that he was a rather smallish man and, judging from his resonant voice, perhaps in his fifties. He had a routine he followed in all his holdups. First, he chose a spot at the head of a steep grade that would slow the stage team to a walk. As the sweating horses topped out on level ground, he would step out of his concealment and cover the driver with his double-barreled shotgun. In his long linen duster and a flour sack with eyeholes over his head, he was a menacing figure. So was the business end of his shotgun. Without being ordered to do so, the driver pulled up his team and waited for the four words that always followed: "Throw down the box!"

Although a score of sheriffs, deputy sheriffs, and Wells, Fargo detectives were continuously snapping at his heels, it took them eight years to run him to earth, and then only by accident. Long before then he had become a California legend—the gentleman bandit, who consistently outwitted his pursuers and harmed no one. While it was agreed that any form of outlawry was deplorable and must be put down, a considerable segment of the populace entertained a grudging admiration for the singular highwayman.

It was the policy of Wells, Fargo to make good the losses its customers suffered and to minimize its own, company theory being that by so doing it might discourage would-be road agents from taking up that profession. For that reason, among others, it was, and still is, impossible to say what the take of Black Bart's many robberies amounted to. Estimates range all the way from $4,000 to $40,000. A safe estimate would place the minimum at not less than $8,000. Very likely it was twice that figure. If it appears to be a trifling sum, considering his many holdups, it must be remembered that the days of big gold shipments of the sixties were a thing of the past when he was active. Even the speedy *Antelope*, which had brought so many millions of gold down the Sacramento to the Wells, Fargo vaults in San Francisco that she had been nicknamed The Gold Boat, had been towed across the Bay to Oakland Slough and turned over to the junk dealers to be broken up.

On July 26, 1875, the Sonora-Milton stage was stopped and the treasure chest handed over to a lone bandit. A few months later the San Juan–Marysville stage suffered the same fate. Early the following June, the Roseburg-Yreka stage lost the treasure it was carrying. In each instance the holdup had been made by a lone road agent wearing a linen duster and the familiar flour sack of his trade. The series of robberies created no great commotion, such things being more or less expected on lonely mountain roads.

At high noon on August 3, 1877, the stage moving over the hills between Duncan's Mills on the Russian River and Point Arena was stopped by a man in a long linen duster, with the inevitable flour sack over his head. The driver, understanding the significance of the double-barreled shotgun pointed at him, pulled up his two-horse team. He had no shotgun messenger at his side and no passengers. When the road agent motioned for him to throw down the box, he complied with alacrity, and when the man in the duster motioned for him to drive on, he cracked his whip and got away.

The sheriff from Ukiah and a deputy found the shattered box that afternoon. It was empty, save for a waybill on the back of which was written, each line in a different hand, a poem:

> I've labored long and hard for bread,
> For honor and for riches,
> But on my corns too long you've tread
> You fine haired sons of bitches.

It was signed "Black Bart, the PO8." To the meanest intelligence it was obvious that "PO8" was the writer's impish way of spelling POET.

The message was sent to San Francisco, where Wells, Fargo's Chief of Detectives Jim Hume and his assistant John Thacker made what they could of it. Obviously Black Bart entertained a personal grievance against Wells, Fargo. It was also clear that he had a waggish streak in him, as evidenced by the different "hands" in which he had written his poem. As for the name Black Bart, Hume attached no significance to it. Experience had taught him that men living outside the law did not foolishly disclose their identity. To the contrary, they went to great lengths to conceal it. Black Bart might not be any great shucks as a poet, but obviously he was a man of more than average intelligence.

The Express Company informed inquiring newspaper reporters that $305.52 in cash and several pieces of jewelry had been taken in the Point Arena robbery but could supply little further information about Black Bart. It was enough; leaving the rest to their imagination, they created a character for Black Bart, the gentleman bandit. He did not fail them, for on July 25, 1878, the Quincy-Oroville stage was held up, the loot amounting this time to $359, a diamond ring valued at several hundred dollars, and a silver watch. It was an authentic Black Bart robbery, for in the shattered treasure box the sheriff of Plumas County found another poem:

> Here I lay me down to sleep
> To wait the coming morrow,
> Perhaps success, perhaps defeat,
> And everlasting sorrow,
> Let come what will I'll try it on,
> My condition can't be worse;
> And if there's money in that box
> 'Tis muney in my purse!
> (signed "Black Bart, The PO8")

In the last line Bart had deliberately misspelled "money," further evidence of his waggishness.[3] William Irwin, governor of California, announced a reward of $300 "for the capture and conviction of the bandit known as Black Bart." Wells, Fargo supplemented that figure with another $300 and the Post Office Department added another $200. Black Bart was now worth $800 to the party or parties who could put him behind bars.

It did no good, for only a week later the Laporte-Oroville stage was robbed by a lone bandit attired in a linen duster and a flour sack; and a number of gold specimens valued at several hundred dollars were taken from the box.

Two more stage robberies occurred in the northern part of the state that October. In both instances they were the work of a lone bandit who struck twice within ten miles of Ukiah on succeeding days. There was no poetry, but such daring could only be attributed to Black Bart. By now his name was appearing so frequently in the newspapers that most Californians were familiar with it. Feature writers poured out columns of trash about Bart, picturing him fighting single-handedly against the giant corporation (Wells, Fargo) that somehow had wronged him.

Hume was becoming desperate. He didn't even know what the bandit looked like. Certainly drivers and passengers whose journeying had been interrupted could not describe the appearance of a bandit whose head and shoulders were hidden beneath a flour sack. Hume packed a bag and set out for Ukiah, hoping he might be lucky enough to find someone who had actually seen Bart. He had no luck in Ukiah, but in the Eel River country he found a widow and her daughter who recalled that on October 4, the day following the second robbery, a stranger—they called him a tourist—who was on his way to San Francisco had stopped at their house and asked if they could give him dinner, for which he would gladly pay.

He carried a canvas bag slung over his shoulders (doubtless in which reposed a miner's pick, pry bar, and his unbreeched shotgun, wrapped in a blanket—the tools of his trade).

Mother and daughter described for Hume a man in his late fifties, about five feet ten inches tall, wearing a trimmed grayish moustache and small goatee of the same shade. His cheekbones were high and his forehead wide and slightly wrinkled. His eyes were blue, piercing, and deep set under heavy brows. He told them he neither drank nor smoked.

"His hands were slender and well kept," said the daughter. "It was easy to see that he was a gentleman."

Hume now had a picture of the man firmly planted in his mind and was convinced that he was Black Bart. Hume and his assistants looked long and hard for him; for five years, to be exact. But the little man avoided the traps they set. On occasion he would remain inactive for four or five months, then suddenly, in quick succession, two or three stage robberies would take place. Always it was a small man in the linen duster and the flour sack who got the treasure chest. There must have been times when Wells, Fargo brass wondered whether Black Bart robbed because he needed the money or just for the hell of it.

There was a reminder of the past, in the years before lawmen realized that there were two Tom Bells and could not understand how he could appear almost at the same moment in two places a hundred miles apart, in the incredible distances Black Bart covered on foot between holdups.

There is an old saying, and a true one, that the pitcher that goes to the well too often will eventually get broken. Usually it results from carelessness. In this instance that was not true. Now that we know the details and can put the pieces together in their correct order, it becomes obvious that the robbery of the Sonora-Milton stage on Saturday, November 3, 1883, at Reynolds Ferry, which ended so disastrously for Black Bart, had been carefully planned every step of the way. We do not know why or how he came to be at the Patterson Mine in the environs of Tuttletown on the day previous to the holdup, but he was there, passing himself off as a prospective investor looking for a profitable opening. The manager of the Patterson Mine recalled having had a lengthy talk with him.

Before leaving, Bart learned some salient facts, most important of which to him was that on the following morning the Nevada Stage Company's Sonora-Milton down stage was to pick up a sizable shipment of amalgam and a small quantity of gold dust. In due course the shipment was to be turned over to the California Navigation Company at Stockton and forwarded downriver to the Wells, Fargo coffers in San Francisco. He was also informed that the treasure box would not be in its accustomed place, under the driver's seat, but securely fastened inside to the floor. He had dealt with that difficulty before and was not unduly annoyed.

To refresh his memory of the country, he followed the road partway to Reynolds Ferry. Back in 1875 he had begun his outlaw career—so far as the record goes—by holding up the Sonora-Milton stage four miles from nearby Copperopolis.

This afternoon on leaving the road he cut across the hills to

Angel's Camp, where he bought a bagful of groceries, it evidently being his intention to sleep out for the night. But it was November and cold in the open. Accordingly, he put up at Madame Rolleri's roadside inn at Reynolds Ferry. With the help of her son, nineteen-year-old Jimmy, she operated the ferry as well as the inn. Ironically, young Jimmy Rolleri, a back-country boy, was to have a hand in the undoing of Black Bart, the illusive, masterful road agent who had been thumbing his nose at lawmen for eight years.

After Jimmy had got Reason McConnell, the driver, and his stage across the river, the two of them sat down at the inn for a cup of coffee. There were no passengers, and McConnell was making the run without being accompanied by a shotgun messenger. He and Jimmy were well acquainted, and when the young man asked McConnell to let him hitch a ride as far as Copperopolis, about ten miles, the latter said, "Sure! Fetch your new rifle along. Mebbe you'll be lucky and bag a deer."

When they got to Funk Mountain, Jimmy got down. He knew the team had a stiff climb ahead of it.

"It'll take twenty-five minutes to git up and around the mountain," he said. "I'll be waiting for you down below."

Bart was watching. He saw Jimmy get down but was too far away to recognize him. As he watched, the boy disappeared into the brush, his rifle at the ready in case he flushed something. Bart went to a place of concealment behind a big boulder and settled down to await the reappearance of the stage.

The road around Funk Mountain descends to the valley beyond in a series of ups and downs usual to such thoroughfares. Bart heard the stage coming. Having chosen a spot for the holdup where McConnell was most likely to pull up his team for a breather, he stepped out of concealment and quickly had the surprised and unarmed driver covered with his shotgun. He remembered having seen someone who was carrying a rifle get down from the stage before it started up the mountain. It bothered Bart.

"He asked me who the man was," McConnell recalled when questioned by Ben Thorn, the aggressive sheriff of Calaveras

County, on the evening of the holdup. "I told him it wasn't no man, just young Jimmy Rolleri, who hoped to get a shot at a deer or a fox with his new rifle. He [Bart] told me to unhook the team and take it down the road a few yards. I did, after chocking a wheel so the rig wouldn't roll down on me. When I had gone thirty, forty yards, he motioned that that was far enough. He got into the stage and I could hear him smashing the box with an ax."

When McConnell repeated his story to Wells, Fargo detective John Thacker and special detective Harry Morse, former Alameda County sheriff, the details were the same. He had caught sight of Jimmy waiting below and motioned for young Rolleri to join him. Jimmy confirmed it. "When I saw McConnell standing in the road with the horses, I knew something was wrong," Jimmy stated. "I made my way up to him, keeping out of sight as much as I could, and was in time to see the robber getting out of the stage, carrying a heavy bag. He took off at once down the mountain. McConnell took my rifle and fired two shots at him and missed. I took the rifle and fired once. It didn't stop him, but I must have drawn blood."

He had. Ben Thorn, several deputies, and Wells, Fargo detectives Thacker and Morse combed Funk Mountain the morning after the robbery. Among other items, they found a bloodstained handkerchief in which were tied a number of buckshot. It was an expensive handkerchief and had not been exposed to the elements for long. In one corner, in indelible ink, was what was unquestionably a laundry mark—F.X.O.7. A mile from the scene of the holdup the searchers found the cabin of a market hunter, known locally just as Old Martin. Had he seen any strangers in the past twenty-four hours? Yes, he had. A man had stopped at the cabin and asked directions to Jackson, and of course he would recognize the man if he saw him again.[4]

Thacker, Morse, and Sheriff Thorn went down to San Francisco with their accumulated evidence and presented it to Chief of Detectives Hume. You may believe or disbelieve the published newspaper accounts of what transpired at that conference and the others that followed, including the charge by the San Francisco *Examiner* that the Express Company had instructed Hume to make a "deal" with the notorious bandit. The proposed arrangement, as spelled out by the *Examiner*, was that if Black Bart surrendered himself, acknowledged the robbery of the Sonora-Milton stage, and enabled the Express Company to recover the missing loot, it would drop all other charges and guarantee him a minimum sentence.

That any such scheme could have been given serious consideration until Black Bart was taken into custody is unlikely. But Lucius Beebe, the Wells, Fargo historian, who was fiercely loyal to the company, once had occasion to say, "Wells, Fargo did many things that do not appear on its books." [5]

One thing young Mr. Hearst, editor of the *Examiner*, dredged up was that Harry Morse, the supersleuth, had not been hired by the Express Company but was in the personal employ of Chief Hume. Morse had insisted on that arrangement, which left him eligible to receive his share of the reward money, if and when Black Bart was taken into custody. Hume had hired him for that exclusive purpose.

Instead of continuing to look for his man in the foothills of the Mother Lode, Morse confined his activities to the streets of San Francisco. Being convinced that the origin of the laundry mark on the bloodstained handkerchief that had been picked up on Funk Mountain would reveal the identity of the man he sought and lead to his capture, he settled down to the wearisome task of checking and interviewing every laundry and laundry agency in the city, a hundred or more in all.

After a week of getting nowhere, Morse struck pay dirt at Ware's Bush Street tobacco shop, which was also an agency for the California Laundry. Mr. Ware, the proprietor, recognized the laundry mark. His books disclosed that it belonged to C. E. Bolton, a retired mining man who lived at the nearby Webb House on Second Street.

The garbled newspaper accounts that appeared some days later say that Mr. Bolton came up the street as Morse was talking with Ware and that the latter introduced the two men. After a pleasant conversation concerning mining investments, Bolton allegedly accompanied Morse to Superintendent Hume's office, where Bolton was grilled. There is nothing in the record to confirm this. But Morse is credited with the following description of the dapper little man he had met at Ware's tobacco shop:

"He was elegantly dressed, carrying a little cane. He wore a natty little derby hat, a diamond pin, a large diamond ring on his little finger, and a heavy gold watch and chain."

Obviously Morse realized that Bolton was the man he wanted. At his request, his friend Captain Stone, of the city police, had the Webb House staked out. Bolton walked into the hands of the waiting detectives and was taken to the Central Police Station and locked up.

A search of Bolton's room at the Webb House revealed that his true name was Charles E. Boles, that he was originally from Decatur, Illinois, and he had a wife and children, whom he had not seen in years, residing in Hannibal, Missouri. Despite the evidence, the prisoner insisted vehemently that his name was not Boles, nor did he ever acknowledge it.

evening. What transpired has never been disclosed; but if the

Hume, Thacker, and Morse had a long conference with him that Express Company ever made any deal with Black Bart, it was consummated at that meeting. The San Francisco *Examiner* declared with screaming indignation that Wells, Fargo had indeed made a bargain with Black Bart. It spelled out the terms: After full restitution of the gold taken from the Sonora-Milton stage ($4,000) he was to plead guilty to the robbery and receive a light sentence. In return, Wells, Fargo would drop all other charges against him.

Perhaps that was the way it was, or, as Joseph Henry Jackson, always violently anti-Hearst, put it, "The honors here rest with the *Examiner*."

Bart was taken up the river to Stockton. A small crowd was gathered at the landing. Sheriff Thorn was on hand with Old Martin, the hunter, at whose cabin Bart had stopped on the day of the robbery. "That's him!" he told Thorn when he caught sight of the prisoner. "That's him!"

They spent the night in Milton and went on to San Andreas, the county seat of Calaveras County, in the morning. After the arraignment, Bart was taken back to Funk Hill (or Mountain). He led Morse and the other members of the party to a hollow log and, after removing the leaves and dirt that covered it, pulled out the sack containing the gold.

On November 17, he was brought before Superior Court Judge Gottschalk, entered a plea of guilty, waived trial, and asked the court to pronounce sentence. He was given six years in state prison. With time off for good behavior, that meant only four and a half years. If Wells, Fargo had made a "deal" with him, it was holding up its end.

Black Bart must have been a well-behaved prisoner, for on January 21, 1888, he was back on the streets of San Francisco and soon looking as dapper as ever, wearing the curly-brimmed bowler and satin-faced Chesterfield in which he liked to be photographed. The city was overflowing with newcomers and changing rapidly. To them he was just a name. As for the old-timers, they did not ostracize him; he had given them too many chuckles in the past (at the Express Company's expense) for that.

It was remarked that he was often observed on Montgomery Street. Wells, Fargo's general offices were located at the north-east corner of Montgomery and California streets. He was seen entering and leaving the building on different occasions. If anyone wondered about it, it was to speculate on the nature of the business he had with the Express Company. Then he disappeared and was not seen on Montgomery Street again or, in fact, in California.

Several holdups occurred in the northern part of the state that seemed to have the authentic Black Bart touch. Mr. Hume thought so, or at least pretended to think so, for it was at this time that he compiled the secret list of Black Bart robberies and circulated it among Wells, Fargo agents. The two stage robberies that occurred in November, 1888, were solved with the capture and conviction of the man who committed them.

Regretfully, those Californians who entertained a lively regard for the gentlemanly little P.O.8 realized that he was not back, after all. The state was never to see him again. From time to time, stories appeared in the San Francisco newspapers that he had been seen in Mexico City, in New Orleans, or in St. Louis, living a life of luxury. Whether true or not, these accounts gave rise to the charge that the Wells, Fargo Express Company had purchased immunity by putting him on its payroll. The *Examiner*, depending on sensational news stories to increase its circulation, tried to make something of it. Unable to produce anything in the way of substantiating evidence, Mr. Hearst's witch hunt was called off. It was a victory for Wells, Fargo but does not prove that Black Bart was not living on the Company's bounty, however unlikely that may have been.

If Black Bart, wherever he was, was able to keep up with the San Francisco newspapers, it must have pleased him to see the prominence still given him in California.

VII

Sagebrush Bonanza

OF THE thousands of Argonauts who arrived in California in Forty-nine and the following three or four years, as many, if not more, came by land as by sea. Of the overlanders, the great majority reached their destination by way of the Overland Trail, which meant they had to cross the three hundred uninhabited (save for Indians), semidesert miles of Nevada before they were confronted by the dangerous mountain passage over the Sierra Nevada.

As they rested in the fertile valleys along the eastern slope of the Sierras and took account of what they had before them, a few of the westering emigrants decided against going farther and became the first white settlers in the Washoe Valley Truckee Meadows. They could not have numbered more than several hundred, for as late as 1854 the white population of all of Utah Territory lying west of Great Salt Lake and largely near today's Carson City, was fewer than five hundred.

In 1854 the Utah Legislature established the western half of the Territory as Carson County and attempted to colonize it, but with very little success. It was a political arrangement that did not please Nevadans (non-Mormons), and in 1861 they succeeded in establishing Nevada Territory. Three years later the State of Nevada, already world famous for the vast amount of treasure its mines were producing, was officially organized and entered the Union as its thirty-sixth state on October 31, 1864.

In California, in 1859 the mining fraternity was aware that across the Sierras prospectors were working the streams along the eastern slope but not making more than poor to fair wages. A man could still do that good placering on the Mother Lode. So they were not tempted to gather up their tools and set out for the Washoe Valley. Quartz miners were pretty much of the same opinion. They recognized that the lush days of the early 1850's were gone, but a hard-rock miner never knew what he would find when he blew out a quartz facing. The chance was always there that he might uncover a jewelry store. If you were lucky, you still could win big. It was enough to keep the miners anchored where they were. But they were not lightly dismissing the tales that filtered back to them from across the mountains, for they knew, despite what they professed, that if news of a big strike suddenly broke, they would be the first to join in the stampede back across the Sierras to the Nevada diggings.

The big news came, of course—late in July, 1859—and the "great rush to Washoe," which saw thousands of Californians backtracking across the Sierras to Nevada, was under way. But first the story of what brought it about is in order.

Over the crest of what was then Sun Mountain (today's Mount Davidson), where incredible Virginia City, the capital of the Comstock Lode, was soon to rise, was the small, struggling mining camp of Gold Hill, from which a score of men were patiently exploring Six-Mile Canyon and the gulches to the north. They didn't know it, but they were treading what was to become the richest discovery in mining history.

Who actually discovered the Comstock Lode is questionable. Certainly it was not windy Henry Comstock, "Old Pancake," who always claimed everything in sight and ended up by committing suicide or being killed on his way to Montana. Very likely the honor belongs to the Grosch brothers, Hosea and Ethan Allen Grosch, young Pennsylvanians who had been prospecting the Gold

Hill region for five years and supported themselves by their mining. They were not mineralogists, but they were educated men with some knowledge of minerals. They knew that the "damned black stuff" that they—as well as others—found clogging their rockers was sulfurets of silver. Why it did not interest them remains an unanswered mystery, for Hosea accidentally stuck a pick into his foot and died from gangrene in a few days. Only a few weeks later, Allen Grosch had his feet frozen so severely that they had to be amputated. He failed to recover from the shock of the operation. So the reason for their silence went to the grave with them. It remained for the curiosity of August Harrison, a Truckee Meadows rancher, to lead to the discovery. Bundling up a few samples of the blue-black ore his friends Pete O'Riley and Pat McLaughlin had found on their claim, he sent them to a Grass Valley, California, assayer.

The Grass Valley assay showed the Comstock ore to run as high as $4,790 a ton in silver, with $200 in gold.

Judge James Walsh of Grass Valley and his friend Joe Woodworth were the first to learn of the Mount Davidson bonanza. "They barely had time to pack a pair of mules and set out for the new diggings before half the population of Nevada, Placer, El Dorado, and Sierra counties were on their heels, bound for the Washoe." [1]

The great Rush to Washoe not only emptied California of its miners but swept along with it a small army of thugs, thieves, gamblers, and other undesirables. In San Francisco, dozens of notorious characters disappeared from the Barbary Coast and other underworld strongholds. A message scrawled on the door of a closed Kearney Street brothel—"Gone to Washoe"—told the story. Although every steamboat that could turn a wheel was pressed into service, they could not accommodate the hundreds of San Franciscans clamoring to get up the river to Sacramento. Sacramento River steamers had an unpleasant habit of burning and exploding, but with the stage now set for a major tragedy, miraculously none occurred.

From Sacramento the Nevada diggings could be reached either by the northern stage road through Grass Valley or by the shorter and easier Placerville–Carson City route. The latter soon got most of the traffic, and in 1860 brought Wells, Fargo into the stageline business for the first time, the company purchasing Jared Crandall's run-down Pioneer Line for a song. It proved to be one of the most profitable investments Wells, Fargo ever made. Within the year it put twelve new Abbott and Downing thoroughbrace stages on the Sacramento–Washoe run, six-horse hitches, with drivers whose expertise equaled their recklessness handling the reins; beside each driver rode a gimlet-eyed express messenger with a shotgun cradled in his arms.

But Wells, Fargo didn't stop there; in specially built, canvas-roofed wagons that moved only a little slower than its fancy stages, it transported as much as five hundred tons of freight a week from California into Washoe.

In September, 1861, three masked bandits held up a Pioneer Line stage at Strawberry Station, a relay point east of Placerville, as the team was being changed. They ordered the passengers down from the coach and, after lining them up, relieved them of their valuables. Baldy Green, the driver, the express messenger, and the hostlers, hands raised, looked on helplessly as the road agents smashed the treasure chest and took from it an estimated $3,000 in gold coin. When they were ready to make their getaway, a signal shot was fired that brought a fourth member of the gang dashing up the trail with the horses he had been holding back in the brush.

According to Baldy Green, who, having survived a score of such encounters, could speak with an expert's opinion, it was a professional job. It differed from past holdups only in the ease with which the express company's men had been taken by surprise. But for Wells, Fargo it had to be recorded as the first time one of the company's stages had been robbed.

Although the story of how Virginia City, the Queen of the Comstock, got its name has been told a thousand times, it rates another retelling. Jim Finney, a Virginian, was known up and down

Six-Mile Canyon as "Old Virginny" because of his incessant boasting about the wonders of his native state. One night, well along in his liquor, he was stumbling back to Gold Hill when he accidentally dropped the bottle of Mountain Dew he was carrying. As it crashed on the rocks, he threw up his hands in a fervor of alcoholic delight and cried, "I christen this place Virginia Town!" He didn't have it quite his way. But Virginia City was close enough.

There was never another place like it. From a gaggle of tents in 1859 it had grown to a city of twenty thousand four years later (local boosters claimed forty thousand). But beneath its crust of gaudy sophistication it was raw frontier, wicked, largely lawless, where today's millionaire might be tomorrow's pauper, depending on whether Gould & Curry, Belcher, Ophir, or whatever bonanza stock he owned, skyrocketed to even dizzier heights or plummeted to the depths.

The establishing of the spectacular pony express in 1860 and the Central Overland California and Pike's Peak Express a year later, provided the Comstock with what was considered fast mail, passenger, and freight service between the East and California, and further guaranteed the growth and prosperity of Virginia City, Carson City, Gold Hill, and other blossoming Nevada mining camps.

As a town, Virginia City had character. It accurately reflected the character of its conglomerate population, mostly strangers to one another, the overwhelming number of whom were in Nevada for the single purpose of getting rich as quickly as possible, either by honest endeavor or otherwise. No mining district was ever more sorely beset by the activities of its criminal scum than the Comstock. Robbery, holdups, killings were almost a daily or nightly occurrence. Law-enforcement agencies, city police, sheriffs, and the courts could not cope with the situation. But Virginia City not only tolerated the rampant lawlessness but pretended to enjoy it. Everybody seemed to have money; wages in the mines were high; every few days the Hale and Norcross, Consolidated Virginia, or another of the big bonanzas reached new bodies of rich ore and sent mining stocks soaring. The Pacific Telegraph Company had connected the Virginia City stock exchange with the San Francisco Board of Trade. With nine men out of ten playing the market, the most exciting spot in Virginia City was the C Street Exchange.

Before the discovery of the Comstock Lode, mining activity in the Territory had been limited to the Washoe Valley and Pioche region, far to the southeast. Other than a few scattered stage stations, open to more or less constant Indian attack, north-central Nevada was an uninhabited sand and sagebrush wasteland. Now, suddenly, a score of mining camps sprang into existence, obviously fostered by the conviction that the whole region was highly mineralized, a theory which proved to have some substance.

Some of those boom camps, such as Austin, Ely, Eureka, Pioche, Hawthorne, blossomed into permanent, prosperous towns; others, like Hamilton, Bodie (across the line in California), Aurora, Candelaria, were to wither and vanish again. The stage roads that connected them became the favorite hunting grounds of an army of road agents. It was accounted a rare day in the Virginia City office of Wells, Fargo when it was not alerted by news of still another holdup or an attempted holdup of one of its own stages or a leased stage on which it held the express privilege.

Although California is popularly believed to have suffered most at the hands of road agents, largely due to the publicized exploits of Black Bart, Nevada topped it and all Western states, including Montana. Baldy Green, one of Wells, Fargo's most famous drivers, acknowledged that he had been stopped thirty-one times before he wearied of responding to the summons to "throw down the box" and retired to ranching at Winnemucca on the Humboldt River.

A brief application of vigilante law, followed by a purgative fire that leveled the town, resulted in most of the blacklegs taking up residence in other camps. But they were soon back, among them popular Big Jack Davis, a successful road agent and all-around crook. He had been charged and prosecuted three or four times for his crimes, but was never convicted. The bizarre feat of making off with a wheelbarrow-load of amalgam from the Hale and Norcross mill had given him local status. He was back with an even more spectacular stroke in mind.

Estimating that six cool-headed men would be required to bring it off successfully, Big Jack began recruiting them. They included John Squires, an accomplished hand at stage robbery, Ed Parsons, a Virginia City gambler, Bill Cockerell, Dave Jones, Henry Gilchrist, and a young thug named Buck Chahman.

During the evening of November 3, 1870, they slipped out of town in pairs, Big Jack bringing up the rear, without attracting attention, and headed north, well armed and with grub enough in their saddlebags to last them two or three days. Their destination was the little sawmill town of Verdi (pronounced Ver-di in Nevada) on the Truckee River. By daylight they were safely hidden in the aspens on the mountainside above Verdi.

They had a long wait ahead of them, for what they were about was nothing less than robbing the Central Pacific's crack eastbound No. 1 Express, which was not due to come through until early evening. Time must have dragged as the hours ticked away; there was so much that could go wrong, with nothing in their own experience or the experience of others to guide them. Remember that another two years were to pass before the James-Younger Gang was to make robbing the steam cars its principal business. Back in Indiana, the Reno brothers had tossed a treasure safe off a moving train on two occasions, only to be quickly apprehended.

A scant eleven miles down the tracks to the east of Verdi stood the thriving little railroad-made town of Reno, the funnel through which passed untold tons of supplies and machinery for Virginia City and from which, in return, came vast amounts of silver and gold bullion on its way to San Francisco and the world market.[2]

In the heart of the little town a toll bridge spanned the Truckee River. Before the coming of the railroad the settlement had taken its name from the bridge and was known simply as Lake's Crossing, for the man who owned the bridge. On the evening that the train robbers waited on the slope above Verdi, Nels Hammond, Reno agent of Wells, Fargo, nervously paced the office floor in the Central Pacific depot as he awaited the arrival of the eastbound express, knowing it was carrying more than $40,000 in minted coin. A company wagon stood by, with armed guards in attendance, to move the shipment quickly to the Wells, Fargo office and its steel safe.

He, too, was to have a long wait, for when the No. 1 Express slowed as it was passing the Verdi depot, seven men swung aboard the moving train. Two of them, armed with pistols, confronted Conductor Mitchell, on the platform of the second car, and quickly convinced him that he would be happier and more comfortable inside. They ran forward through the car and joined their companions on the front platform of the express car, next to the tender. Scrambling over the cordwood, they quickly subdued the engineer and fireman and forced them to leap off into the darkness. After the train had proceeded a quarter of a mile, Big Jack seized the throttle and cut off power.

In those days of primitive railroading, so little thought had been given to protecting the contents of the combination mail-and-express car that, for the convenience of the train crew, it could be entered by a door at either end. These doors could be locked but seldom were. It was not until after the Verdi robbery that measures were taken to safeguard mail and express cars and their contents. When molesting the steam cars became the highest level of professional outlaw activity, a bolted door did not stop them; the threat to place dynamite under a car and blow it skyward invariably brought results.

Although the various accounts of the Verdi robbery may differ, even to the date—Beebe, Drury, and many others say it was November 5, but in its "Robbers Record" Wells, Fargo has it as November 6—all agree that Davis and his desperadoes made off with a haul in excess of $40,000 without a shot being fired. Returning to their tethered horses, they made a quick getaway and were back in Virginia City before daylight, apparently beyond suspicion. But there were seven of them, too many to keep a secret for long.

Almost lost sight of in the furor aroused by the Verdi robbery was the startling news that the Central Pacific's crack eastbound express had been stopped a second time some ten hours later at Independence, a flag stop in eastern Elko County. Nothing remains of Independence, but the story of what happened there in the early morning hours of November 6, 1870, has been preserved.

About all there was at Independence was a water tank and a pile of ties. As No. 1 was taking on water, six men, deserters from the United States army post at Fort Halleck, ran out from behind the tie pile and took charge of the train crew. In the express car they found $4,490 that Big Jack Davis and his gang had overlooked. They didn't have it for long. Elko County officers and a troop of cavalry followed the trail of the robbers into the desert. The fugitives were well mounted, but the posse overtook them in the Ruby Mountains and recovered the stolen money. The amateur bandits were brought to trial at once and were sentenced to ten years of hard labor in the state prison at Carson City. They were paying in part for the Verdi robbery as well as for their own.

The State of Nevada, the Central Pacific, and Wells, Fargo were unanimous in agreeing that looting the express cars could not be tolerated. To prove it, rewards totaling more than $25,000 were posted for the apprehension and conviction of what had become known overnight as the "Verdi car robbers." The size of the rewards unleashed an amateur manhunt such as the West had never known. Posses scoured the valleys and mountains, but without finding any trace of the culprits. No one enjoyed the excitement more than Big Jack and his fellow conspirators as they made the rounds of their favorite C Street haunts, their pockets stuffed with gold eagles and double eagles.

It couldn't last; they were taking it too high, wide, and handsome, squandering money on their favorites down the slope on Sporting Row. Whiskey unloosened Ed Parsons' tongue. He let something slip to the wrong man, Charlie Williamson, sheriff of Storey County, where the robbery had occurred. Within four days, Big Jack and his six accomplices were in jail.

They pleaded guilty and asked for the mercy of the court.

Davis gave a novel reason for the railroad robbery, stating that Wells, Fargo, by putting two shotgun messengers on its coaches, with a pair of armed guards following behind, had put him out of business as a road agent and that he had been forced to turn to something new.

Strangely, when sentence was pronounced, he, the leader of the Verdi robbers, was given only ten years; the others, fifteen.[3] Davis was pardoned after serving five years and was soon back at his old trade of sticking up stages, restricting his operations to the camps in the eastern part of the state. On September 3, 1875, he was killed in the attempted robbery of the Eureka-Tybo stage at Willow Station.

It was just after nightfall when the stage, with Jimmy Brown driving and Eugene Blair riding guard, pulled up at the stable. From its darkened depths came the familiar summons to "throw down the box," followed by the persuasive crack of a .45. The slug struck Brown in the calf of his left leg, inflicting a painful wound. Gene Blair, an old hand at such confrontation, leaped to the ground on the far side of the coach. A mighty blast of buckshot from his smooth-bore ten-gauge shotgun almost decapitated the bandit.

The station keeper came running with a lantern, and in the flickering light they recognized the slain bandit. It was Big Jack Davis, the once-famous "Verdi train robber."

VIII

Wells, Fargo Is Harassed

ONE OF the most painful and persistent thorns in its side that Wells, Fargo had to contend with in its Nevada years was a big, rough, tough, brawling thug named Jack Harris. He claimed to be a State-of-Mainer, but there is some evidence that he hailed from Massachusetts. A deep-water sailor, he arrived in San Francisco on a square-rigger from Boston in 1851 and deserted his ship at the first opportunity. For something less than a decade, he bounced around from one Mother Lode mining camp to another. Wherever he went, he seemed to leave a trail of minor robberies behind him. The sheriffs of Yuba and Nevada counties pooled what evidence they had, and it pointed to Jack Harris. He was arrested and brought to trial, charged with the robbery of the general store at Nevada City. But the jury could not agree on a verdict and he went free.

That was to be the story of his repeated appearances before a judge and jury in the years that followed. Prosecutors found it difficult even to impanel a jury to weigh the evidence against Harris; men who had seen him demolish his opponents in his frequent saloon brawls had no desire to draw his enmity by sitting in judgment on him.

In the so-called great rush to Washoe of 1859 or the following year, Jack Harris transferred his activities from California to Nevada, settling in Carson City, where he married and established himself as a saloonkeeper. It must have been a profitable business, for he stayed with it for three or four years. To catch the news and gossip of the district, there was no better listening post than the convivial atmosphere of a saloon, where men gathered and liquor freed their tongues. The record shows that Harris kept his ears open.

He couldn't have chosen a better spot to gather the sort of information in which he was interested. The Comstock's principal outlet to California was the heavily traveled road that curled over the Sierra from Sacramento to Placerville and from there on eastward until it descended into little Carson Valley and Carson City.[1]

Coming and going, the commerce of the Comstock had to pass through Carson City. To take advantage of its water supply (the sluggish Carson River) and the adjacent stands of timber, a number of reduction mills were built there, but in a strict sense, Carson City was never a mining town. With its wide tree-lined streets, gardens, and brick or stone houses and business buildings, it was a beautiful, pleasant little place, quite in contrast with Virginia City, which, even with its six-story International Hotel (equipped with an elevator, the only one west of the Mississippi at the time), its Piper's Opera House, and other signs of great wealth, was always an ugly-looking town.

Being the state capital, Carson was a gay place whenever the Legislature was in session. Perhaps the little town of four thousand was proudest of the fact that a branch of the United States Mint was located in its midst. But as Sam Clemens (the future Mark Twain) of the *Territorial Enterprise* observed, Carson had another attraction that received more attention than the mint. He was referring to the state penitentiary at Warm Springs, two miles east of town.

Jack Harris pursued his dual role of successful saloonkeeper and road agent until the summer of 1864. Operating on both sides of the invisible line that separated California from Nevada, he plundered the stages of the Pioneer Line seemingly at will, always working without accomplices, who might turn state's evidence against him if caught.

If, after 1864, he confined his activities to the Nevada side of the line, it was largely because Jim Hume, deputy sheriff of El Dorado County, was riding hard on his trail. This, of course, was years before Hume went to work for Wells, Fargo in 1871.

Late in June, 1865, acting on a tip that a valuable shipment of minted coin to meet the payroll of the Hale and Norcross mine ($14,000) was coming through, which proved to be accurate, he broke his rule against using accomplices and induced Al Waterman, an experienced desperado, and an unknown whose alias was Red Smith, to throw in with him.

Early on the morning of June 29, the stage in which they were interested, with ubiquitous Baldy Green handling the ribbons, was rolling along below Silver City, when the masked bandits stopped it. Finding three ten-gauge shotguns pointed at him, Baldy pulled up and pushed the treasure chest off into the road, the impact splitting it open as it struck the ground. Harris and his partners made off with the $14,000. It was one of the easiest touches he had ever made.

No doubt spurred by the feeling it was Harris who had punished them again, Wells, Fargo offered a reward of $5,000 for the arrest of the bandits. The size of the reward alerted every peace officer in the state. Jack Harris and Red Smith were taken into custody in Austin a few days later; Al Waterman was captured in Sierra Valley. When arrested, the thieves had only several hundred dollars on them. Obviously they had buried the proceeds of the robbery in a safe place. Since the robbery had occurred in Lyon County, the prisoners were lodged in the county jail at Dayton.

Wells, Fargo was more interested in getting its money back than in securing the conviction of the three men. The most likely of the trio to cave in under pressure was Smith. Wells, Fargo detectives went to work on him, offering immunity if he turned state's evidence and revealed where the loot was cached. The man confessed and, fearing Harris' vengeance, lost no time in getting out of Nevada.

But that was not the end of it. The Express Company had Harris behind bars and with the evidence it possessed could send him away for at least ten years, yet it twice secured a postponement as he and Waterman were about to be brought to trial.

The Express Company's reluctance to prosecute the case aroused some sharp editorial criticism throughout the state, to the effect that Wells, Fargo was making a deal with Jack Harris. In this instance the charge was unquestionably true; Harris had information concerning other crimes against it which the firm felt would aid in putting down highway outlawry; in return for divulging what he knew, Wells, Fargo was ready to go light on Harris—provided he agreed to get out of Nevada. Proof of this is revealed in the fact that he was sentenced to only five years for the Silver City robbery, while Waterman received twelve years. That Wells, Fargo could get about what it wanted from Nevada courts became evident when Jack Harris walked out of state's prison two months later, a free man.

Keeping his part of the bargain, Harris disappeared from Nevada and was heard of next in Washington, D. C., where he is said to have served in some capacity in the District's police department. There is nothing in the record to confirm it. He was back in Nevada in 1867 and, in partnership with the notorious cattle thief and highwayman Nicanor Rodrigues, opened a saloon in Austin.

Why Nevadans insisted on calling Nicanor Rodrigues "Nickamora" cannot be explained. He was either the Silver State's foremost thief and all-round outlaw, or at least its second.

More so than most desert mining camps, Austin's mercurial history was one of boom and bust. Jack Harris and his partner caught it at a time when it was entering one of its periodic slumps, which became more painful when word was received of several rich strikes that had been made at Hamilton and Treasure Hill in White Pine County, less than a hundred miles to the east.[2] Harris joined the exodus to the new camp, and his canvas saloon was open for business two hours after he arrived.

In the high noon of its brief prosperity, Hamilton—Hamilton City, its boosters renamed it—was madness, with thousands of people rushing in by stage, buckboard, muleback, and on foot. The point of arrival and departure for the Concords was the Main Street corner, where Wells, Fargo shared a building with the Red Light Saloon.

Staging had never been more profitable or competitive. Every day half a dozen or more competing coaches could be seen lined up at the Red Light corner, ready to take off for points north, south, east, and west. The boots of Gilmer and Salisbury stages, the Eureka, Tybo, and Belmont Staging Company, Woodruff and Ennor, and the Gilmore and Hamilton Line carried the treasure chests of Wells, Fargo.

For reasons that the record does not reveal, Harris did not prosper in Hamilton. He moved to Eureka, but that camp was small and he could not have found anything there to interest him, for he was back in Hamilton two months later. There, on election day 1872, he became embroiled in a street duel with an old enemy and received a bullet in his right, or gun hand, permanently disabling it. After the first great fire that leveled Hamilton and left eight thousand persons homeless, he moved downstate to Pioche, where the claim-jumping war was raging. He may or may not have got into it. In any event, the Pioche *Record* recorded his death there from natural causes in May, 1875. In Austin, where Harris had been unfavorably known, the *Reese River Reveille* in a rather lengthy obituary refrained from mentioning the wife he had taken in his Carson City days and subsequently deserted.

After Jack Harris and Nicanor Rodrigues had disposed of their saloon at Austin, they appear to have had no further contact. At least there is no evidence that they subsequently engaged in any joint activity, legal or otherwise. When Harris arrived in Pioche, where Rodrigues, the so-called Spanish King, and his gang of Mexicans had been stopping stages and stealing horses at will, it may have been with the expectation of joining up with him. But by then the celebrated Nickamora had left the United States and was on his way to Mexico with the proceeds of his years of outlawry.

To Nevada's Mexicans, Nickamora was something of a folk hero, a legendary Robin Hood who took from the rich and gave to the poor. There is very little in his record to justify the high admiration they had for him. At best, he was a robber baron, cruel, relentless, and a known killer. But a disarming aura of culture and romance enabled him to go unsuspected of his crimes for several years.

"He was a handsome young fellow, who was born in the mountains of old Spain," comments Wells Drury, a careful reporter, in *An Editor on the Comstock Lode.* "His father held some kind of a government job—an army officer, I think—and started Nick out early with a few hundred pesos and his wits to make his way in the world. Nobody knows what brought Nick to California, but he used to tell about when he lived in Rome, Paris, and the City of Mexico."

He was only sixteen when he was arrested in Tuolumne County, California, for his part in robbing a stage, and sentenced for ten years. On account of his youth he was pardoned after serving several months. He was next reported in Nevada, where for some time he made a business of stealing amalgam from the quartz mills. That soon became too dangerous and, nearly having been caught in the act on several occasions, he left western Nevada for the camps in White Pine County. Some time later he was in Pioche, where he organized his first gang, all Mexicans. When this was cannot be determined, but it must have been soon after the great prison break from the Nevada State Prison in 1871, in which twenty-nine convicts escaped, for two of them joined Nickamora's band.

Pioche was booming; hundreds of Mexicans were being imported to work its mines. Not only had the more or less permanent population doubled in the past four months, but the town itself was taking on a metropolitan look with its new deluxe saloons and fancy French restaurants. How to feed the growing town became a problem. Suddenly there was a crucial shortage of beef. Prices soared. Nickamora came to the rescue; he had cattle to sell on his terms, steers that his gang had rustled in Utah and driven across the state line to Pioche. Butchers surmised as much, but they did business with him and asked no questions.

From rustling cattle Spanish Nick turned to the more lucrative and safer business of highway robbery. The Gilmer and Saulsbury State Lines, on which Wells, Fargo had the express privilege, became his favorite target. Soon the roads of eastern Nevada, north from Pioche all the way to Battle Mountain on the transcontinental railroad, became unsafe, with two and three holdups a week being reported. Unmistakably the bandits were Mexicans who had become so bold that they disdained masking their faces with a bandanna or paint.

Although passengers were robbed and treasure chests rifled with annoying frequency, Nick did not bother the shipments of silver being shipped out of Pioche and other camps; the bullion bars were heavy and awkward to handle.

The Express Company was the heaviest loser. Superintendent Valentine dispatched his best detectives to eastern Nevada. But even with the aid of local and county lawmen, Well, Fargo was unable to stop the depredations. Nickamora and his men were expert riders, and with so much country to work in, they were in one place today and a hundred miles away on the morrow.

By the early 1870's, various tales in the modern cops-and-robbers tradition were in circulation regarding the exploits of the "Spanish King." No matter how absurd, they have been accepted as factual by some commentators, including the most incredible of all, namely that to protect its shipments Wells, Fargo agreed to pay Nick $2,000 a month for ending his marauding. The truth is that Nick finally stubbed his toe and was lodged in the county jail, charged with robbery. The judge set his bail so high that he could not meet it.

Facing a long term in state's prison, he engineered a jail break with the assistance of two of his fellow prisoners. When the jailer made his nightly round of inspection, they jumped him and escaped. Some of Nick's followers were waiting with fast horses. The whole party got away without a shot being fired. After crossing Spring Mountain, they are known to have reached Jim Maxwell's ranch on the Sevier River, in Utah, two days later.

Nickamora's trail ends there; the rest is just supposition or fiction. The bodies of the two convicts who had escaped the Pioche jail with him were found fifty miles south of Maxwell's. The conjecture was that, determined to cut his back trail, Nick had killed them.

A miner returning to Nevada from Mexico some years later claimed to have seen Nickamora in Sinaloa, where he was living in luxury on his rancho near Mazatlán, which may well have been true. Certainly his years of banditry must have enabled Nick to put by a snug fortune.

IX

Milton Sharp,
the Gentlemanly Bandit

IN THE late 1860's and early 1870's, the conviction that a pistol or shotgun provided a man with more independence than he was likely to find in the Constitution was so widely held that Nevada was ablaze with gunfire. But although a tremendous amount of powder was burned in the commission of crimes and the settling of personal feuds, the results were not always lethal, the 1870 United States Census placing the population of the Silver State at 42,491. Despite this amazing growth, there had always been a shortage of labor on the Comstock.

Disastrous fires occurred in the mine workings. On one occasion the charred bodies of twenty-nine miners were brought out from the Crown Point. But after a stoppage of work of several weeks, production was resumed. A more serious interruption came when the deep workings of the Chollar and Potosi and several other big producers were flooded by so much subterranean water that the pumps could not cope with it. Hundreds of miners were laid off; as production fell, so did the value of Comstock shares. This was the beginning of the long battle that was to continue until completion of the controversial Sutro Tunnel, one of the great engineering feats of all time, solved the problem.

When the *Territorial Enterprise*, which was usually abreast of and often ahead of what was happening, coined the phrase "Nabobs of the Comstock" to distinguish the wealthy mine owners who had made their millions or were about to—John R. Jones, George Hearst, John Mackay and his partners Jim Fair and Jim Flood, and half a dozen others—any C Street regular could identify them by name.

But it was the powerful Bank of California and its triumvirate of financial wizards, William Ralston, Darius Ogden Mills, and his scandal-prone satellite, William Sharon, who dictated the ups and downs of the Comstock. Their greatest achievement for its advancement was construction of the Virginia and Truckee Railroad, connecting Virginia City with Reno and the Central Pacific by way of Carson City.[1]

In 1869 a thousand Chinese were put to work digging and blasting a roadbed. By 1872, the Virginia and Truckee, a standard-gauge railroad, was in operation and was soon to become the most profitable railroad in the world. Its sleek, yellow-painted cars and brass-bound locomotives were things of beauty that still quicken the pulse of those who remember them in their days of glory, when as many as forty trains a day were chugging back and forth between Carson and Virginia City.

It was painfully obvious to the proprietors of the stagelines that the Concords could not compete with the steam cars. But instead of going out of business, they shifted their routes to the booming camps to the south—Aurora, Bodie, Candelaria—where the iron horse was not yet ready to make its appearance. Presently holdups were occurring so frequently on the Bodie-Carson City run as to make it obvious that road agents had changed bases as well as the stage lines. It set the stage for the appearance of Milton Anthony Sharp, Nevada's premier highwayman.

"Sharp in a modest way, did what he could to reduce the wealth of Wells, Fargo," says Wells Drury. "He robbed stages whenever he wanted to, and with great thoroughness, never making a mistake and never finding an empty treasure-box."

He was a rather handsome man, somewhat on the lean side. In numerous photographs he is seen wearing a neatly trimmed moustache and a goatee. When holding up a stage it was his custom, after securing the treasure chest, to invite the passengers to get down and line up at the side of the road and drop their money and other valuables into a grain sack. All accounts agree that if there were women among the passengers, he treated them with gentlemanly consideration, circumstances permitting.

Sharp was a Missourian, and in the great War Between the States he had fought for the Rebel cause. He must have seen a considerable amount of combat, for Wells, Fargo in its *Robbers' Record* lists no fewer than five rifle and bayonet scars on his body. Shortly after his arrival in Nevada in the summer of 1869 he was working in the mines at the new, booming camp of Aurora, ten miles east of Bodie, in what was generally known as the Esmeralda country. It was there that he began his dual career of miner and highwayman.

How many holdups he committed in the eight years that followed, without coming under suspicion, is not known. The Bodie-Carson road became his favorite hunting ground, the flour sack, à la Black Bart, his only disguise.

There was nothing spectacular about these holdups. He stopped the stages of Dorsey and Company, the Bodie Stage Lines as well as C. Novacoveich's Concords. The latter carried the treasure shipments of Wells, Fargo.

Milton Sharp did not drink, smoke, or gamble. To make splurging impossible and to maintain an appearance of frugality, he buried the proceeds of his robberies, obviously planning to recover them when he had stashed away enough to make him comfortable for life. It didn't always work out as he planned. From one holdup he made away with $13,000 in gold notes issued by a Sacramento bank. He buried the money temporarily in what he considered to be a safe place, but when he returned a few days later to pick up the bank notes and remove them to a more secure hiding place, they were not there.

Wells, Fargo detectives working on the case did not uncover sufficient evidence against Sharp to charge him with the robbery. However, when they learned that a rancher living in the area had paid off a $12,000 mortgage on his property, using gold notes of the Sacramento Bank as collateral, they had him arrested, charging that he had found and misappropriated the money for his own use. The evidence against the man was strong, but the jury, composed of his neighbors, found in his favor, and the case was dismissed.

Although Wells, Fargo exercised a near monopoly of the Nevada express business, a score of independent stage lines, largely restricted to the passenger trade, were in operation. Their coaches were stopped and travelers compelled to hand over their valuables. But no record was kept of such robberies, and the details soon became lost in folklore, as, for instance, the holdup on the outskirts of the little town of Genoa, when a small keg filled with gold coin was removed from a stage and allegedly buried at the foot of a certain pine tree and never recovered.

On the other hand, the careful record kept by Wells, Fargo of the depredations it suffered is both precise and illuminating. It reveals that in 1880, on six different occasions, Milton A. Sharp held up a stage carrying Express Company treasure and made off with the contents of its strongbox.

Sharp had been pursuing his career of lone highwayman for so long and with such success—never having been found guilty of a major crime—that it is difficult to suggest why, in the winter of 1879–1880, he teamed up with W. C. (Bill) Jones, alias Frank Dow, an accomplished bandit who had served a sentence or two in San Quentin before showing up in Bodie, where Sharp became acquainted with him.

Dow (to give him his alias) appears in photographs as a short, muscular, tough-fibered man, the opposite of sleek Milton Sharp. He was better acquainted with California than Nevada, and he evidently persuaded Sharp that stopping the Forest Hill–Auburn stage would be an easy touch, which it proved to be.

Here is a page from the Express Company's *Robbers' Record* under the heading of M. A. Sharp:

> Robbed W.F. & Co.'s Express on stage from Forest Hill to Auburn, May 15, 1880, with W. C. Jones, alias Frank Dow.
>
> Robbed W.F. & Co.'s Express on stage from Carson City to Bodie, June 8, 1880, with Jones, alias Dow.
>
> Robbed W.F. & Co.'s Express on stage Carson City to Bodie, June 15, 1880, with Jones, alias Dow.
>
> Robbed W.F. & Co.'s Express on stage from Auburn to Forest Hill, August 6, 1880, with Jones.
>
> Robbed W.F. & Co.'s Express on stage from Carson City to Bodie, September 4, 1880, with Jones.
>
> Robbed W.F. & Co.'s Express on stage from Bodie to Carson the morning of September 5th. At time of halting the stage Jones fired two shots, killing one of the stage horses. Mike Tovey, W.F. & Co.'s guard, then fired, killing Jones. Sharp then fired, seriously wounding Tovey in the right arm.[2] Tovey being disabled, started for a neighboring farm-house to have his arm dressed, when Sharp returned to the stage, demanded the box from the driver, and robbed it of $700, while Jones was lying dead on the road, and the stage being detained by the dead horse still attached to the team.

Six holdups in less than four months! Small wonder that Wells, Fargo's Chief of Detectives Hume and his men, as well as Nevada peace officers, swarmed in to end the lawlessness.

The first robbery on the Carson City–Bodie road charged to Sharp and Dow occurred within a few yards of the wooden bridge across the East Fork of Walker River near Desert Creek. Billings, the Wells, Fargo route agent, reasoned with much justification that when the road agents struck again it would be anywhere but at the East Walker River bridge. He was mistaken, for Sharp and Dow were back again a week later. They got so little on their second try that Billings was convinced he could forget about the East Walker River bridge for sure this time. For a few weeks that appeared to be true, but on the night of September 4, and again on September 5, the East Walker River bridge was the scene of a double holdup.

There is some reason to believe that Milton Sharp had decided to quit Nevada and go below to San Francisco, where he could lead a life of luxury on the proceeds of the robberies he had stashed away. If true, it would explain why it appealed to his peculiar ego to end his Nevada career of banditry in spectacular fashion. The record shows that other outlaws, more famous than he, met their downfall by entertaining similar vainglorious ideas.

Sharp was acquainted with the schedule of the north- and southbound Wells, Fargo stages on the Carson City–Bodie run and knew they would pass each other at the bridge a few minutes before midnight. He and Dow cut across country in the early evening and left their horses a half mile east of the bridge. With an hour to spare, they were in position, first to intercept the southbound stage and then the other.

It was a bright, moonlit night. In the tangle of willows and cottonwoods that lined the road, the shadows were black and impenetrable. The bandits, wearing face masks, saw the Bodie stage coming and waited until it crossed the bridge before stepping out into the road.

Hank Chamberlain was on the box, handling the ribbons. Sharp and his accomplice, covering him with their guns, ordered him to pull up. Chamberlain obeyed with alacrity, smarting with indignation at being stopped again by the same pair in a matter of weeks.

James Cross, a prominent Candelaria businessman, and Colonel T. W. Davies of Carson were seated up on the box beside the driver. Cross called out to the bandits, "You don't have to do any shooting. There are no messengers on board."

Taking him at his word, Sharp and Dow lowered their shotguns. When Chamberlain was told to throw down the treasure chest, which for some reason was not chained to the floor, he kicked it off. It contained $3,000 in bank notes. Delighted with their unexpected good fortune, the highwaymen, wasting no time on the passengers, motioned for Chamberlain to drive on, which he did. When he heard the northbound stage rumbling toward him, he pulled up and waited for it to draw alongside.

The northbound stage carried no passengers, but in addition to the driver, route agent Billings, Mike Tovey, and Tom Woodruff, Wells, Fargo's most celebrated shotgun messengers, were aboard. It took only a few minutes for Chamberlain to acquaint them with what had occurred. Billings took charge, ordering Chamberlain to continue on to Bodie with his passengers and instructing his own driver to whip up his team and reach the scene of the holdup as quickly as possible. As they neared the bridge, the two messengers kept their eyes fastened on the side of the road. "There it is," Tovey exclaimed on catching sight of the shattered treasure chest. He, Woodruff, and Billings got down as the driver applied the brake and brought the heavy coach to a grinding stop. Tovey, Woodruff, and Billings leaped to the ground and had no difficulty picking up the trail of the bandits in the heavy dust. Tovey took one side of the road and Woodruff and Billings the other.

Mike Tovey had been in so many tight corners in his years with Wells, Fargo that he hadn't bothered to pick up his sawed-off shotgun when he leaped down from the stage. Intent on following the tracks in the dust, he was a few feet ahead of the standing stage when two shots flamed at him from the inky blackness of the trees. They missed him but killed the near leader of the six-horse team. Running back to the stage, Tovey caught the gun that the driver tossed down to him.

When one of the bandits emerged from the shadows—it was Dow—Tovey fired, killing him instantly. He saw Sharp then and was about to fire again, but he was a split second too slow; the blast from Sharp's gun mangled Mike's right arm.

The three Company men huddled behind the coach. After a look at Tovey's arm, which was bleeding profusely, Billings realized that if Mike's life, if not his arm, was to be saved, they had to get him to the nearest farmhouse so that something could be done for him.

ABOVE: Sutter's mill on the South Fork of the American River, where James Marshall discovered gold.

LEFT: An unknown artist's conception of Joaquin Murrieta, the legendary bandit.

Stagecoach with two shotgun messengers aboard, 1852.

The steamer *Antelope*, which transported vast amounts of gold down the Sacramento River for Wells, Fargo.

LEFT: Tiburcio Vasquez, the most formidable of all California outlaws.
RIGHT: Sheriff Harry Morse of Alameda County, who led the hunt for Vasquez.

Juan Soto, bandit and savage killer, known as the Human Wildcat.

LEFT: Black Bart, the gentlemanly road agent.

BELOW: Wells, Fargo's first office, San Francisco.

LEFT: James B. Hume, Wells, Fargo's remarkably efficient chief of detectives.
RIGHT: William G. Fargo in 1878.

Henry Wells.

The main stage road from Sacramento to Virginia City via Placerville, scene of frequent holdups.

Here, on the Truckee River, where the first transcontinental rails were being laid in 1869, the great Verdi train robbery was to occur ten months later.

Milton Sharp, Nevada's premier road agent.

Wells Fargo Bank History Room

The great express company's C Street headquarters in Virginia City, Nevada.

Wells Fargo Bank History Room

James Butler (Wild Bill) Hickok.

Deadwood's first jail.

Deadwood Gulch in 1877.

Henry Starr, last of the horseback outlaws.

Jim Reynolds (left) and John Reynolds (right), Colorado road agents.

RIGHT: Captain Theodore G. Cree, whose company of the Third Colorado Cavalry massacred the Reynolds Gang.

BELOW: Kenosha Pass in South Park, where the hunt for the buried treasure of the Reynolds Gang continues.

Jesse Woodson James, age thirty-one.

Frank James when he was nearing sixty.

Cole Younger after his release from the Stillwater penitentiary, where he had served twenty-five years.

The Samuel homestead, where the Pinkertons tossed the bomb through the
window.

Aftermath of Coffeeville, which spelled the end of the Dalton Gang.

Emmett Dalton, 1928.

Judge Parker, when he was named to the Fort Smith Court.

Judge Parker's courtroom as it appears (restored) today.

Marshal Heck Thomas.

Marshal Chris Madsen.

Bill Tilghman, Marshal of
the Last Frontier.

Sharp watched them leave. The driver, left to his own resources, took the harness from the dead horse, tied the other lead animal to the rear of the stage, and with his makeshift four-horse hitch was ready to drive on when Sharp, who had been watching him for some minutes, stepped out into the moonlight and requested the startled driver to toss down the box.[3]

When the slain bandit was identified as alias Frank Dow, it left little doubt that his missing accomplice had been Milton Sharp. Local, state, and Express Company rewards totaling $3,000 were posted for his capture. In addition to the amateur sleuthing that was aroused, Wells, Fargo detectives descended on Aurora, Bodie, Candelaria, and the other mining camps in the Esmeralda country. They not only failed to pick up any trace of Milton Sharp's whereabouts but discovered that a considerable number of men admired him for his daring and were disinclined to peach on him.

Chief of Detectives Hume became convinced that Nevada was not the place to look for Sharp. Leaving his men there to continue the search, he returned to California, believing that sooner or later the famous highwayman would show up in San Francisco and that, with the cooperation of the city police department, a net could be spread to entrap him. Sharp was already in town, and on October 3, 1880, Police Captain Lees trailed him to his lodgings on Minna Street and took him into custody. Sharp waived extradition and was taken back to Nevada in irons and lodged in the Aurora jail to await trial. Half a dozen indictments were brought against him. He was found guilty of one—the first robbery at the East Walker River bridge—and returned to jail to await sentencing.

To discourage any attempt at escape, an "Oregon boot," a fifteen-pound steel shackle, was locked to Sharp's right ankle. But even that handicap did not deter him for long, for on a frosty November morning it was discovered that he was gone. He had removed a number of bricks from the outside wall of the jail and crawled through the opening. Tools found on the ground indicated that he had had help from the outside.

Again rewards were posted, and another widespread manhunt

began. But no trace of the missing bandit was discovered until the cumbersome Oregon boot was found in a ravine five miles south-east of town in the direction of Candelaria. Obviously he had managed to pick the lock and remove the shackle from his ankle. Bets were made that he would never be captured now. But his suspected friends were being watched and could not come to his aid. A week later, unarmed, freezing and starving, he walked into Candelaria and gave himself up. A few days later he was sentenced to twenty years in state's prison.

Nevada changed with the passing years; the great Comstock mines began to wallow in their first serious decline; the Carson mint suspended operations; Virginia City began to fade as the world's premier mining camp. Milton Sharp, languishing in prison, was largely forgotten. But the loot of his many robberies remained safe where he had buried it. It is not unlikely that he offered to share his hidden wealth with someone in return for his liberty. However that may have been, on August 15, 1889, he disappeared from the state prison, and this time he was gone for good.

The state made no great effort to return him to custody. In fact, the following year, with Milton Sharp still legally a fugitive from justice, Governor R. K. Colcord pardoned him. If this was a radical departure from the established rules covering executive clemency, most Nevadans couldn't have cared less.

X

Panamint City—
Toughest of the Tough

THE BLEAK, forbidding Panamint Range lies well within the borders
of California and forms the rocky western barrier that holds back
the alkali plains and fiery furnace that is Death Valley. In 1874,
rich outcroppings of silver were found in the Panamints. Immediately, and without evidence to support it, the story was put in
circulation that the fabled Lost Gunsight Ledge, for which men
had been searching since 1850, had been rediscovered. There was
something electric about news of a new strike. But this was over-
powering: "Richer than the Comstock," rumor had it. Twenty-
four hours after word reached Virginia City, the stampede to the
Panamints was under way.

Not many knew how to get there and lost a day or more
floundering around on the desert until they reached the Cerro
Gordon mine on the shoulder of Mount Montgomery and got their
bearings. Converging on Surprise Canyon, they began the long,
wearisome climb to its head, some on foot, others by mule or on
horseback. Senator John P. Jones, the silver millionaire and superintendent of the Crown Point, and Senator William M. Stewart, the
Virginia City potentate, who had driven the three hundred miles
by wagon, found the canyon so narrow in spots that they had

difficulty getting the vehicle through. Jones and Stewart were there for the understandable purpose of adding to their millions.

Dick Jacobs, Bob Stewart (no relation to William M.), and W. T. Henderson, the discoverers, had organized a mining district in jig time, and had laid out a townsite two miles above the desert floor and named it Panamint City. Six months later it had a population of three thousand and was a stronghold for robbers, outlaws, and assorted desperadoes. It was also a thriving camp, with tons of silver ore being crushed and smelted into bullion.

Holdups in Surprise Canyon were of such frequent occurrence that treasure had to be shipped out of the Panamints under heavy guard. Wages were so high that it was a standard joke in Dave Neagle's [1] Oriental Saloon and similar places of liquid refreshment that it was almost as profitable and somewhat less dangerous to ride guard than to stick up a wagon carrying bullion.

Of all the good men and bad who arrived in Panamint City in its earliest boom days, none had a better reason for holing up there, beyond the reach of the law, or nearly so, than a pair of mediocre road agents, Smith and McDonald. Having failed in the attempted stopping of a Concord on its way north from Eureka to Battle Mountain because of a shotgun blast from an alert messenger, they had walked into Wells, Fargo's Eureka office the following noon, killed the agent, and extracted $4,500 from the Company safe. Hume put several of his best operatives on the case and they soon were convinced that the wanted men were in Panamint City. Could they be taken out of that citadel of lawlessness?

Senator Stewart, with his stamp mill and smelter and the purchase of half a dozen leases, had become not only the camp's biggest investor but had induced such wealthy friends as Lloyd Tevis, president of Wells, Fargo, Ben Ali Haggin of its Board of Directors, and immensely wealthy George Hearst to come in with him. Equally important, he had won Darius Ogden Mills' promise to extend his narrow-gauge Carson and Colorado Railroad southward to the Panamint mines. It never got there, but the promise of a railroad to the mouth of Surprise Canyon induced many hesitating investors to get aboard the bandwagon. Due to the senator's maneuvering, Panamint mining stocks were being traded on the San Francisco Exchange. When General Superintendent Valentine informed him that Wells, Fargo was coming for Smith and McDonald, Senator Stewart, after some fast thinking, called them to his office.

The two men had invested their stolen funds in several leases that were already worth twice what they had paid for them and were very likely to triple in value in a few weeks. Stewart wanted those leases.

"You can run if you want to," he told them. "But if you do, Wells, Fargo will track you down. Undoubtedly, if you're taken back to Eureka, you'll be hanged. The best I can do is to make you a deal. I'll give you $14,500 for your leases, less $4,500 I'll hold back to hand over to Wells, Fargo if they agree to drop the matter. In the meantime you can make yourselves scarce."

It was better than the two culprits expected. Stewart had the money waiting when Valentine and his men arrived, accompanied by two Inyo County deputy sheriffs. With face-saving reluctance Valentine accepted the proffered money and the matter was closed.

The occasion marked Wells, Fargo's last appearance in Panamint City. Stewart had hoped to arrange an express service to the north, but Valentine said no; the Company was not interested in engaging in an unprofitable battle of Winchesters. The lawless camp, in which the saying "a dead man for breakfast" was more fact than fiction, had to settle for Remi Nadeau's freight line across Panamint Valley and southward through the Argus Mountains to Los Angeles.

For some reason, historians have given Nadeau scant attention. Actually his achievements as road builder, desert and mountain freighter were second to none. A French Canadian, he arrived in California in 1861 and began long-distance hauling as soon as he accumulated money enough to purchase a wagon and horses. In his time he made and lost two fortunes and still managed to die wealthy. At the peak of his affluence he owned five hundred horses, countless wagons, and his own relay stations, a dozen or more.[2]

No canyon road was impassable or impossible to Nadeau. He went to work in Surprise Canyon, and when he got through blasting, filling, and widening it, he had a trail that bore a reasonable likeness to a road, over which wagons could move without snapping their axles.

Traffic increased at once. So did the number of holdups. Wagons carrying out ore were not molested; it was a different story when the load was in silver bars, which, at a big discount, could be readily converted into cash in Panamint City.

Senator Stewart and Senator Jones, able partners in floating mining stock, soon wearied of having the cream skimmed off their shipments of precious metal. They stopped the practice by casting their silver into 700-pound cannonballs, which were loaded on open express wagons with great difficulty and sent off on the long haul to the Carson City Mint without armed guard.

Borax, the "white gold of Death Valley," was not to become a factor in the economic life of that desolate region for another twenty years; but deposits of it were known to the wandering Indians who inhabited the region, the Cocopahs and a few Shoshones, remnants of the once powerful Paiute tribe. They recognized gold and silver for what it was when they chanced to find it. Folklore credits them with having made many discoveries only to be done out of them for a few dollars, a bottle of whiskey, or a white man's bullet.

Such tales are mostly fiction. "If an Indian who had made a discovery had to be killed to get his secret out of him, it didn't happen very often," Shorty Harris, the most famous of the Desert Rats, declared when being interviewed by a Los Angeles *Times* reporter. "Fact is, Indians made mighty few finds. I recall only one or two, including Indian George. There wasn't much to that story; the two shysters who did George out of his claim for a pair of overalls, ten dollars and a bottle of whiskey, never took a dollar out of the ground."

If the social life of Panamint City was somewhat limited, it was not due to any restricting city ordinance. On the contrary, its forty-odd saloons and gambling parlors never closed, and the several hundred painted frails who pursued their profession in Catfish Gulch, had the freedom of the town. There was no Main Street establishment whose doors were not open to them. In the late afternoon, responding to the urging of a boozy crowd of males, it was not unusual for one of the girls to submit to being lifted to the top of the bar to perform what passed for a lewd dance. Although the Jezebels of Panamint City were the overage, worn-out rejects of the Barbary Coast and similar centers of vice, the tough, lawless camp was not critical of them.

One of the women was robust Della Ryan, who gained notoriety in the folklore of Panamint City as "Fighting Della Ryan." She was feared not only by her scarlet sisters but by the town's saloonkeepers. Customarily she went armed, and when she went on one of her rampages and marched into a saloon to settle a fancied grievance, the saloonkeeper and his bartenders, fearful of the havoc that might be wrought on the glassware displayed on the back bar, did their best to placate her.

Jimmy Bruce, Dave Neagle's inoffensive faro dealer, a little, pale-faced individual, was Della's "man." Misunderstandings occurred at the faro table, but no one wanted any trouble with Jimmy, knowing they would have to settle with Della.

But eventually one of Panamint's unhanged killers who had been humbled by Fighting Della picked a quarrel with Jimmy as a means of getting back at her. One night in Neagle's bar he walked up to the faro layout, and after calling Jimmy a stinking, white-livered coward, started to draw his gun. Neagle and his bartenders ducked as a shot crashed. They looked up as the smoke cleared, expecting to see Jimmy Bruce stretched out lifeless on the floor. To their surprise it was the bad man who lay there. Jimmy was coolly lighting a fresh cigar.

It having been demonstrated that Jimmy had a fast gun, the prestige to be won by killing him moved the dead man's pals to have a try at it. Not until five of them had been interred on the slope above the town cemetery in what came to be called "Jimmy Bruce's Graveyard" was he left alone.

There was not much of the Death Valley region with which Frank (Shorty) Harris was not familiar. He was not only that country's foremost "single blanket, jackass prospector" but a truthful reporter when, in his words, he "didn't have too much 'Oh, be Joyful' aboard." He coined Panamint City's most fitting epitaph when he dubbed it "the last stop on the road to hell."

Other mining camps harbored known road agents, killers, and assorted outlaws, but they were held in some restraint. Not so in Panamint City, where they preyed on the business community and no man was rash enough to suggest that what the town needed was a strong dose of vigilante law. Bill Stewart and John Jones, his fellow-promoter, were more interested in getting their mines into production than in the future of Panamint City.

Stewart had tried one innovation, and it had been such a fiasco that he was not inclined to try another. With labor being in short supply, he had announced that he was importing a hundred Chinese to speed work in his Wonder mine. When the first wagon-load of yellow men arrived at the mouth of Surprise Canyon, they were greeted by a fusillade of gunfire. Three or four were killed, and the rest stampeded back in the direction from which they had come.

Boom and bust—from bonanza to *borrasca*—are the two great periods in the life-style of every mining camp. None escape it. When a producing mine becomes exhausted, the best thing to do is to walk away from it. That was exactly what the well-informed in Panamint were preparing to do in June, 1877, two years after Stewart and Jones had crushed the first Panamint ore.

In the beginning, the Panamint excitement had been touched off by the widely held belief that what had been found was the legendary Lost Gunsight, so rich that it could not be exhausted for several decades. That now, only three years later, evidence was accumulating of approaching *borrasca* was proof enough that the Panamint find was unrelated to the fabled Lost Gunsight.

No tale of Death Valley disaster has had a wider circulation nor more versions than the passage from east to west of the starving Bennett-Arcane party in 1850. They had burned their wagons, slaughtered the last of their oxen, and discarded all personal belongings save their rifles. They had left Salt Lake City as members of a party of two hundred Argonauts bound for the California Mother Lode. Dissension arose over the direction their guide was taking. Twenty of their number—hereafter known to history as the Bennett-Arcane party—split off from the main party and headed directly west, determined to get to California as quickly as possible.

On New Year's Day they straggled into White Sage Flats, starving and without water. It snowed for an hour. They scooped up snow and quenched their thirst. Ahead of them they saw the two-mile-high Panamints blocking their way to the west. When he was somewhat refreshed, As (Ashael) Bennett seized his rifle and set out, hoping to sight a deer. He saw one, but when he raised his gun to fire, he found that the bead sight had been knocked. Picking up what he thought was a sliver of black quartz, he fashioned a crude sight and inserted it in the empty slot. He succeeded in killing the deer and it gave the group a respite from starvation.

Reduced to skin and bones, they managed to reach old Fort Tejon ten days later. When fully recuperated from their ordeal, they headed north and at the Mariposa mines Bennett asked a gunsmith to make him a proper sight for his rifle. The man saw at once that the improvised sight was a piece of solid silver. Asked where he had found it, the best answer Bennett could give was that it was on a mesa—"The ground was black with the stuff and there was a dike of it three feet high."

Lost mines have been found with less information than that to guide searchers. Certainly, Panamint was not the mesa that was black with silver.

When a mining camp begins to disintegrate, the whores and the gamblers are the first to leave; saloonkeepers, the last. Otto Yager, proprietor of the glamorous Dexter Saloon, with its crystal chandeliers and ormolu champagne buckets, had taken the play away from Dave Neagle's Oriental and was anxiously awaiting the arrival of a barroom fixture that would definitely make the Dexter the toast of the town. It was nothing less than a thirty-foot-long back-bar mirror, rolled in Pittsburgh, Pennsylvania, the mightiest piece of plate glass west of St. Louis. By steamboat it had been shipped down the Ohio and Mississippi and by steamboat around the Horn and up to Wilmington, the Los Angeles seaport. Under Remi Nadeau's personal supervision, a monster truck had been built to transport the costly and fragile mirror over California's rocky desert roads to Panamint. It was now on its way, having passed Mojave, Little Lake, and was nearing Olancha.

Yager posted daily bulletins reporting its triumphal progress. Panamint City responded with mounting excitement. Bets were made on the hour of arrival of Otto Yager's costly mirror. When at last Nadeau's cumbersome vehicle began ascending Surprise Canyon, the little Frenchman rode ahead, clearing the way and shouting instructions.

Without mishap the crated mirror reached its destination. The waiting crowd cheered as it was removed from the wagon and turned over to the crew Yager had recruited to install it. Then it happened: the mirror slipped out of their inexperienced hands and crashed to the ground with a shattering impact.

The incident had momentarily diverted the camp's attention from the gloomy realities facing it. A greater crash came when Stewart and Jones, the sponsors of the Panamint mines, closed up shop and withdrew. They had invested $2 million in the promotion but had recovered that much or more from public stock sales.

The exodus from Panamint City began almost at once; the bawds and their masters took off for distant Nevada boom camps. The gambling fraternity followed them. The outlaw element—road agents, bank robbers, killers—who had enjoyed the safety of

Panamint City, were loath to leave it. Gravitating to regions of least restraint, they faded away into the sagebrush vastness to the north. Again, booming Austin and turbulent Pioche got most of them.

In their absence, things had changed in north-central Nevada. Austin had built its own narrow-gauge railroad, the Nevada Central, connecting it with Battle Mountain and the transcontinental Central-Union Pacific. It had changed the staging pattern in that part of the state, no fewer than ten lines making Austin their joint terminus. Holdups occurred with annoying frequency. To protect the treasure, Wells, Fargo transferred some of its most reliable drivers and shotgun messengers to the Austin runs. Stages continued to be stopped, but no treasure chests were surrendered. In a matter of ten days, on the Reese River run three road agents, refugees from Panamint, were killed, and two others taken into custody. It convinced many of their kind that highway robbery in Nevada was no longer profitable, and they pulled up stakes for the greener fields of Idaho.

In the ordinary course of events, Panamint City would have become just another in the long list of ghost towns that mark the Death Valley region. For thirteen months it had stood silent and deserted, when the elements combined to spare it that ignominy. In September, 1878, a cloudburst and flash flood swept down Surprise Canyon, carrying away every trace of it. Today, out in Panamint Valley, only a few whitened timbers remain to remind one of the past.

XI

Lawless Boise Basin

BEFORE what was to become the territories—and eventually states—of Washington, Idaho, Montana, and part of Wyoming was lopped off from the original Oregon Territory, Idaho was the most inaccessible section of the American Northwest. Walled off along its eastern frontier by the Bitterroot Range and the Rockies, to the south and west by the hostile Snake River Plains and the Blue Mountains of Oregon, its only contact with the world beyond its borders was by way of the Oregon Trail, which crossed it, east to west, from Fort Hall to the Boise Basin.

Far to the north the Army had hacked out a trail connecting Fort Benton on the upper Missouri with Fort Walla Walla near the confluence of the Snake and Columbia rivers. This was the famous Mullan Road, over which pack trains moved from mid-April until the early snows of winter blotted it from sight. In 1856 a number of prospectors, less than a hundred, who had been placering the streams of Washington and Oregon Territories with little success, followed the Mullan Road eastward into northern Idaho and spread out over the Coeur d'Alene region. The only "values" they found in their pans was a color.

After a profitless summer they moved southward, out of the heavily forested pine and spruce country, and began working the tributary streams of the Clearwater. They had had no difficulty with the Palouse Indians, but were now among the Nez Percé, who resented the presence of white trappers on their hunting grounds; the Indians widened their animosity to include the prospectors, two of whom were attacked and wounded on the St. Maries River.

At the confluence of the Clearwater and the Snake, where the town of Lewiston (named for the famous explorer Meriwether Lewis) now stands, the trappers had established their strongest rendezvous.[1] They began gathering there as it became evident that an Indian war was in the offing, the Palouse and Bannock having been induced by the Nez Percé to join them in driving the whites out of the territory. Prospectors picked up their tools and headed for the trapper stronghold at the mouth of the Clearwater. By the first of November, at least three hundred white men were gathered there.

The Indians soundly defeated the first punitive expedition led against them by Colonel Edward Steptoe, but in April, 1857, a large force of regular troops, commanded by Colonel George Wright, crushed the uprising. Save for several minor incidents, it marked the end of Indian hostilities in Idaho.[2]

John Hailey, the recognized authority on early Idaho, places its white population at no more than three thousand in 1858, mostly located in the southeastern Fort Hall area and the north-central Boise Basin. He includes in this figure the several hundred Mormon sheepmen who had moved in from Utah, as well as those who were making salt in the Bear River marshes.

Idaho had witnessed the passing of thousands of pioneers bound for the Oregon country with little profit to itself. Now, a decade and a half later, it was stagnating in its remoteness. To the north its great stands of virgin timber, potentially worth millions, remained untouched, for without a market for forest products, there could be little interest in logging. Its great, fast-flowing, mountain-born rivers—the Clearwater, the fabled Salmon, the "river of no return," and the mighty Snake, flowing for eight hundred miles in its deep, rocky canyon—in their natural state could not be regarded as a boon to agriculture. As for mining, two years of placering on various creeks and mountain streams had proved so unprofitable that only a few ingrained optimists still dared to believe that Idaho would take its place with California and Nevada as one of the great mineral-producing regions of the American West.

And then it happened. In the summer of 1860, Ed Pierce, an Indian trader from Walla Walla who had camped for the night in Boise Basin, found gold in quantity on a sand bar in Orofino Creek. Greater still was the subsequent discovery that all, or mostly all, of Boise Basin was highly mineralized.

Because the Boise Basin was figuratively "a thousand miles from nowhere," without roads or other convenient means of travel, news of the discovery was a long time reaching the outside world. First to hear it were the Columbia River towns. The reaction was swift; within twenty-four hours it became impossible to get even deck passage on any boat bound upriver. The lucky ones left the Columbia at Umatilla and proceeded across country on foot or horseback for a hundred miles. When they reached the new and booming town of Lewiston they were greeted with the exciting news that gold had just been found in the Salmon River country; that a camp, named Warren for the discoverer, had been established and already had a population of two hundred.

If the rush to Idaho was slow in getting started, it was tremendous before it was over, second only to the great rush to Washoe. Official estimates place the number of men and women residing in Idaho in 1863 at between 25,000 and 30,000—the year it was organized as Idaho Territory, which included all of Montana and part of northern Wyoming. A score of towns had sprung into existence in Boise Basin, including Idaho City (first named Bannack City), Florence, with a population of 4,000, Placerville, Orofino, Newsome, Pioneerville, Warren, and many others.

With public funds a road was established across eastern Oregon to the head of the Sacramento Valley, connecting Idaho City with Sacramento. When it was completed it brought Wells, Fargo and its civilizing influence to Boise Basin, its treasure being shipped out via the Oregon State Coach Line's weekly Concords.[3]

The old, established settlements of Payette on the Snake River and Boise (no longer Boise City) began to grow and prosper. Boise, due to its central location and historic past, became the center of the political life of the Territory. Its adherents, who stood to profit if they were successful, launched a campaign to move the Territorial capital from Lewiston to Boise. Thousands of miles away the War Between the States was being fought to its bitter conclusion, and it was the war that was the real issue in Idaho, pitting Rebel sympathizers against Union supporters.

Boise won the contest, but Lewiston refused to hand over the Territorial archives, and it was not until the autumn of 1865 that W. C. McConnell, recently appointed United States marshal, on orders from Washington seized the books and removed them to Boise.[4] It was a Rebel victory that cost the lives of four men and the destruction by fire of the business district of Florence.

The crime and violence that had beset the gold and silver camps of California and Nevada were duplicated in Idaho. In fact, among the desperadoes were a score or more who had fled the Nevada camps with a price on their heads, including the soon to become notorious Henry Plummer, a suave, merciless killer with the deceiving façade of a gentleman.

But it was not only the outlaw element with which the Territory had to contend; its officials, from the governor down, were corrupt. As Big Bill McConnell, Payette's fiery grass-roots historian and organizer of Idaho's first vigilance movement, put it succinctly, "Disorder was in fact better organized than order. It was impossible to impanel a jury that was not composed of thugs and gamblers. Prior to 1865, about sixty deaths by violence had occurred without a single conviction for murder."

Stealing horses in Idaho and driving them across Oregon to a rendezvous with Mexican horse thieves and exchanging them for animals stolen in California became a profitable and reasonably safe outlaw activity. Made bold by success, the rustlers rounded up a bunch of horses in the Payette Valley and drove off with them. It was then that McConnell and his neighbors resorted to vigilante law. Taking after the thieves, they hanged all four and recovered their property. Cronies of the dead men sought to have the vigilantes brought to trial and charged with murder. But the outlaws had gone too far; the aroused public had had enough.

By 1867, four years before Black Bart and other notorious road agents made their appearance in California, Idaho City, although twice destroyed by fire, had become the recognized mining capital of the Territory, with an estimated population of 12,000. After the second holocaust of 1867, substantial buildings of brick and stone replaced the flimsy wooden structures of the past. The semiweekly *Idaho World* boasted that the town had 250 thriving mercantile establishments, including four breweries and four theaters, the Idaho, Temple, Forrest, and the Jenny Lind. "There is reliable express service to all parts of Boise Basin and the southern Owyhee district."

The War Between the States was over, but the animosities it had spawned in Idaho were still very much alive. It was not until Idaho City had been rebuilt after the second fire, that the two political factions joined hands in a campaign to rid Boise Basin of its thugs and outlaws. Without the secrecy that usually attends the formation of such organizations, the vigilance committee, composed of businessmen and other leading citizens, among them W. C. McConnell, came into being. The committee published a list of twenty-one men it had marked for deportation, placing them on forty-eight hours' notice. More than half of the designated blacklegs heeded the warning and disappeared from their favorite haunts.

In its July 27, 1867, issue the *Idaho World* noted that the two Williams brothers and the Stuarts, father and son, working adjoining claims in Thomas Gulch, have "cleaned up about $13,000 since the clean up of $24,000, noted two or three weeks ago." That they would be coming to town to deposit their gold with the Express Company for safekeeping was a foregone conclusion.

On a Friday afternoon the Williamses and Stuarts, traveling together for safety, were stopped by Yank Kinney and his gang of desperadoes within several miles of town. It was widely believed that Kinney and his thugs had been involved in a score of robberies and killings that had occurred in Boise Basin within the past two years. The spot they had chosen for the holdup that afternoon was well suited to their purpose, a dip in the trail cutting through high brush for a hundred yards before it emerged into open country. Lying concealed, they permitted the four miners to advance to within a few yards of them before leaping out with guns raised.

But the Williamses and the Stuarts were not disposed to hand over their gold without a fight. Dashing into the brush, they began firing at anything that moved. Although they were outnumbered two to one, they put the bandits to flight. Several of them, including Kinney himself, were in need of a doctor. The prospectors' only casualty was young Stuart, who was seriously wounded. They got him to town as quickly as possible.

As news of the attack spread, the reaction was swift and violent. Under the auspices of the vigilance committee, a mass meeting was held that evening. Without a dissenting voice it was agreed that the moment had come to crack down on the thieves and murderers who were terrorizing Boise Basin. "You know who the leaders are," Big Bill McConnell cried. "Round them up and show them no more mercy than they have shown their innocent victims!"

That was what the angry crowd wanted to hear. Men were appointed to various tasks, and the roundup began. They worked quickly, but news of what was under way ran ahead of them and enabled a score of undesirables to make a hasty exit from Idaho City. Even so, ten blacklegs, including Yank Kinney, were dragged out of the saloons and marched up the gulch to the cottonwoods.

Yank did not cringe when his turn came and the noose was dropped over his head. Hands tied, he was lifted to the back of a horse. "To hell with you!" he snarled as the animal was driven out from under him and he was left dangling in the air.

The night's action was more the work of an infuriated mob than of a vigilance committee. It could be justified by the knowledge that no man had had the life jerked out of him who didn't doubly deserve hanging. But, though it didn't mark the end of all violence, it broke the back of outlaw domination of the trails.

The Owyhee mines were located seventy-five miles southwest of Boise in the region where the Owyhee River spills over from Nevada into Idaho. With the discovery of both gold and silver in 1865, a minor rush to the Owyhee mines got under way. Before it was over, Silver City prospered for years and became the center of a ranking silver-producing region, second only to the Comstock.

Wells, Fargo's Idaho banking and express business was singularly free of molestation by the desperadoes whose robberies and crimes of violence were almost a daily occurrence. It can be explained in part by the fact that the stages carrying its treasure chests, with outriders ahead and a shotgun messenger on the box with the driver, were not exposed to surprise attack as they rolled across the open plains of Oregon. Then, too, it was obviously far less dangerous to hold up a miner on his way to town with a poke filled with gold on his person.

It is generally acknowledged that between 1862 and 1886, when mining practically ceased, the Boise Basin produced $300 million in gold. If we add to that imposing figure the millions recovered in the Owyhee region, at Warren and other placers in the Salmon River district, as well as the much later finds in the Idaho panhandle, then Idaho emerges as one of the richest gold-producing fields of the world, dwarfing the more publicized Alder Gulch (Montana) and Pike's Peak discoveries.

It was not until long after the placers were worked out that silver and lead were discovered in the Coeur d'Alenes. Today, a century later, silver and lead mining still play an important role in Idaho's economy.

With the exception of the Nez Percé, the Indian tribes had no qualms about selling their young women to white men. Indeed it was regarded as a profitable business. Young Lapwai girls, who were more attractive in white men's eyes than most of their Indian sisters, were readily salable. Since they were regarded as valuable merchandise, their fathers and husbands guarded against their being stolen. Every mining camp had its handful of unscrupulous men who made a living by supplying Indian women to the brothels. They bought them when they had to but stole them whenever possible. Even among otherwise lawless men they had no standing.

When Henry Plummer, in response to the glad tidings from Alder Gulch, left Lewiston and crossed the Bitterroots into what only a year later became by President Lincoln's ukase Montana Territory, he left behind him an assortment of low-class thugs and murderers of little consequence. Among them were Deb Grimes and Arch Walters. Needing some quick money, they rode out of Lewiston one September morning and headed up the Clearwater. What they had in mind was obvious, for their saddlebags were filled with beads, small mirrors, and other gewgaws that Indian women craved.

On reaching the Potlatch River, some twenty miles up the Clearwater, they turned up the lesser stream and came to a small encampment of Nez Percé who were harvesting their winter supply of trout, cleaning the fish as they yanked them out of the water and hanging them up on willow racks to dry. The braves gave the two men a cool reception, but the women swarmed around the white strangers to receive the presents they handed out. When Grimes and his partner were satisfied that the trap had been set, they said "No more!"—making sure that some of the women saw that the saddlebags were far from empty.

Mounting their horses, the two would-be procurers doubled back down the Potlatch a short distance and made camp, lighting a fire and cooking their supper. While thus engaged, two Nez Percé girls appeared on the trail, hands outstretched, begging for more presents. Grimes and Walters seized the women, bound their hands and, putting them in the saddle, got up behind them and started down the river at once.

They didn't get far. A trapper found the men's mutilated bodies a few days later. There was no investigation, the general verdict being that it was "good riddance."

Mining camps and prostitution were as inseparable in Idaho as they were elsewhere. In 1864 the *Idaho World* reports, "There are more than 3,000 Chinese in Boise Basin. Every camp has its Chinatown, Chinese shops, wash houses and slave girls."

In such remote and hard-to-reach camps as Warren, lost in the rocky wilderness of the Salmon River Valley, no white woman was seen during the first thirty years of its existence. Half a dozen slave girls, brought in over the mountains by pack train by their Chinese owner, and an unknown number of Lapwai and Sheep-eater Indian women catered to the needs of Warren's rutting males.

XII

Alder Gulch and the Road Agents

SINCE Granville Stuart [1] is revered not only as the "father" of Montana's range cattle industry but for his other major contributions to the shaping and advancements of that state, it is relatively unimportant whether he and his brother James were the first to find flake gold within the present borders of Montana or whether François Finlay, known as Benetsee, a Scottish half-breed from the Red River of the North had found it. Certainly, if the Stuarts were not the first, they were a close second. However, it appears that Granville Stuart felt the honor rightly belonged to him and his brother. On July 4, 1876, he wrote:

> François Finlay, better known as Benetsee, perhaps did find a few colors of gold in Benetsee creek in 1852, but his prospecting was of a very superficial nature and he was never certain whether he had found gold or not. I first became acquainted with him in November, 1860. I asked him if he had ever dug a hole and he said, "No, I had nothing to dig with, and I never cared to prospect." I am certain that this was true, because although we (James and I) prospected in all the gulches and streams leading into the creek . . . we never found any trace of prospecting being done.

Over the years, Benetsee partisans have contended that because he was a mixed-blood, who lived and hunted with the Flatheads, and had a Salish Indian wife and was more Indian than white in his ways, he received less than his due. No evidence to that effect has been presented unless it is found in the fact that Benetsee had a small quantity of gold in his possession and traded for it at Fort Connah, the Hudson's Bay Company post. He was warned to say nothing about his discovery lest it result in a stampede into the country that would ruin the fur business—a circumstance that soon came to pass, whether Benetsee had anything to do with it or not.

The Stuarts were traders and storekeepers as well as prospectors. One does not gather from Granville Stuart's journal, *Forty Years on the Frontier*, that their mining enriched them, although they prospected up and down the Beaverhead and the Deer Lodge country with dogged determination. Their repeated failure to make a rich strike led James Stuart to organize a prospecting party to explore the headwaters of the Stinkingwater and the Beaverhead in what is now the Yellowstone National Park area. In a left-handed way the Stuart expedition was to lead to the discovery of Montana's great bonanza, the incredibly rich Alder Gulch diggings.

Just a little back-tracking will reveal how a series of seemingly unrelated events led to the great discovery. It began in 1862, when John White found a handful of flake gold in his pan as he washed away the gravel he had just dug up on what was then Willard's Creek, in the valley of the Beaverhead. At that time there were perhaps as many as five hundred men in what is today western Montana. Within a week, two thirds of them were on their way to Willard's Creek. There wasn't a town within eighty miles of the place for which they were headed. But they got there, and after several days of picking hoppers out of their gold pans, they re-named the little stream Grasshopper Creek.

The good claims were soon staked off, but as news of the discovery continued to spread, newcomers arrived daily, many of them men who had had no luck in the Idaho camps. They made their way through the Bitterroots by way of Monida Pass to reach

Grasshopper Creek. By the time snow blocked the trails, upward of a thousand men were gathered in the raw camp, among them thieves, gamblers, outlaws, whiskey peddlers, and traders. The straggling cluster of log cabins, tents, and wickiups was named Bannack City—soon to be, if briefly, the territorial capital. Robberies and killings were a commonplace. There was no law other than that dispensed by the ex officio miners' courts. Their decisions were harsh, brutal, and often prejudiced, but they were the only deterrent to crime.

In the spring of 1863, seven men who had claims on Grasshopper Creek were doing so poorly that they decided to pull out and join the prospecting party James Stuart was organizing to explore the Yellowstone country. They had placered together on the Clearwater in Idaho and were men of some substance. Stuart was glad to have them along. He and his party were to be the first to leave. A date was named on which they would rendezvous with the Bannack City men at the junction of the Stinkingwater and the Beaverhead.

Bill Fairweather was the leader of the Bannack City group. With him were Tom Cover, Henry Edgar, Barney Hughes, Mike Sweeney, Harry Rodgers, and Lew Simmons—all destined to become famous in Montana history. They were several days late in reaching the appointed rendezvous and discovered that Stuart and his party, after tarrying there for a day, had gone on. Fairweather and the others decided to push on after Stuart and overtake him.

They had not gone far when they found themselves surrounded by a large party of marauding Crow Indians, who appropriated their horses, guns, and whatever else struck their fancy. The prospect of being set afoot, unarmed, without grub, 125 miles from the nearest settlement, was grim but seemingly unavoidable until Lew Simmons walked aside with the chief and began a long powwow. He had lived with this band of Crow for a year, liked them, and seemingly they liked him. The chief, Bull Bear, relented when Simmons agreed to return to the tribe if his friends were supplied with ponies and enough food to get them home.

The run-down ponies the Indians gave the prospectors were a poor substitute for their own good horses. Even so, they were glad to get them. A sack of jerky (dried venison) and parched corn were also given them. They knew it was useless to ask for the return of their guns.

"Git goin'," Simmons advised Fairweather. "These fellows are like the wind; they change their mind every time it shifts."

Moving stealthily by day and concealing themselves in the buckbrush by night, the men followed the valley of the Beaverhead for days. They encountered no one. Food was their main concern now, and that was solved when they discovered the partly devoured carcass of a deer that a wolf had dragged down. They skinned and butchered the animal and feasted that night for the first time in days.

They were now back in a country in which one or another of them recognized landmarks. When a mountain range reared up ahead of them, they knew it was the Tobacco Roots. Once they had crossed it they would be within a day's traveling, two, at the worst, of Bannack City.

Still wary, they were careful not to skyline themselves as they topped the crest of the Tobacco Roots and began the long descent to the tree-choked gulch below. Before they were halfway down, the sound of rushing water reached their ears, informing them that they would find a mountain stream of considerable size flowing down the gulch. What they were hearing was the impatient grumbling of Alder Creek on its hurried downhill flight to the headwaters of the Stinkingwater. Breaking through a dense growth of young alders and chokecherries, they reached the creek and picked out a sheltered spot for their night camp. After a scanty supper, with an hour of daylight left, four of the group took their gold pans and went up the creek to prospect, leaving Fairweather and Edgar to scrape the dishes and stake out the horses.

A few minutes later they heard the men who had gone upstream shouting with joy, a sure indication that they had found something. It was too much for Fairweather and Edgar. The tin plates and the ponies could wait; snatching up picks and gold pans, they rushed to the creek. An outcropping caught Fairweather's eye and they went to work on it. At first, they couldn't believe what they saw in their pans. But there it was! They had struck it rich. By the time darkness stopped them, they had recovered fifteen dollars' worth of gold at Bannack City prices. The others had been almost as lucky. Throwing caution aside, they built a campfire, a luxury they hadn't allowed themselves in weeks.

There was no thought of sleep. They knew they had made a major discovery. It was May 26, 1863. They were not likely to forget it.

"Bill, what are we going to call this place?" asked Barney Hughes.

"I christen it Alder Gulch!" Fairweather declared soberly. "We'll stake our claims tomorrow, take out enough gold to buy us an outfit, and head for Bannack."

They pledged each other to say nothing about the great discovery they had made, but when they reached town and began spending outside gold, the cat was out of the bag; they were watched, every move they made.

Although they succeeded in stealing out of town unnoticed, they soon were followed. The great rush to Alder Gulch was under way. Bannack City was deserted. Within a week there wasn't a foot of ground up and down Alder Creek for twenty miles that wasn't staked off, with armed owners prepared to fend off claim jumpers.

The Alder Gulch diggings were to produce many millions in gold, change the face of Montana, and take its place as one of the great mineral discoveries of all time, comparable to the Mother Lode of California and the Comstock. Granted that, sooner or later, it could not have escaped being discovered, does not make its discovery any less remarkable. Consider the "ifs." If Fairweather and his friends had kept their rendezvous with the Stuart party . . . if they had not encountered the roving band of Crows . . . if they had not found the slaughtered deer when they were at the point of starvation . . . what logical conclusion can be reached other than that, like most great bonanzas, Alder Gulch was discovered by outrageous accident. There was nothing accidental about the crime and violence that soon distinguished the Gulch and the brawling, lawless camp that blossomed into existence on Alder Creek.

It was Territorial mining law that a claim could not be more than a hundred feet wide and no man could own more than two such claims. Because it was equitable, and the alternative chaos, this law was observed. It did not do away with disputes, many of which ended in gunfire, but it was the backlog on which miners' courts leaned in trying to produce some semblance of law and order.

Alder Gulch was completely isolated from the outside world by mountains and distance. There were only several tiny settlements to the north; Salt Lake City, 400 miles to the south, was the only sizable town from which it could be reached; Fort Benton, head of steamboat navigation on the Missouri River, was 180 miles to the northeast. There were no roads or trails over which a wheeled vehicle could move. And yet hundreds of men were reaching the diggings on foot and by pack train, having avoided roving bands of Plains Indians and swum or forded rushing mountain streams.

By midsummer the Alder Creek diggings had been cut up into separate districts—Fairweather, Nevada, and several more.[2] Fairweather district elected its own officials by acclamation at a hilarious miners' meeting, made notable by the amount of whiskey consumed. A president, recorder, and judge were elected, all nonpaying jobs. But nothing was done about electing a sheriff, who would have to be paid a salary, it being the consensus of the meeting that they could supply all the law enforcement needed without paying a man to do it.

Now that they had got their second breath, the miners declared it was time to locate a permanent townsite. A quarter of a mile downstream from the point of discovery they preempted several hundred acres of rocky, down-hill ground, through which Daylight flowed to its Junction with Alder Creek, and staked off what was to be the thoroughfare.[3] Tents, brush shelters, and log cabins began to dot the selected location for the town that was to be. Giving it a name presented the Fairweather Mining District with its first problem. As in the Idaho camps, the Alder Gulch diggings was sharply divided between Union and Confederate sympathizers. The latter were slightly more numerous and decidedly more vociferous. They decided that the town should be named Varina City, in honor of the wife of the Confederate leader Jefferson Davis. Dr. Bissell, judge of the Fairweather District, was elected mayor. When the first official documents were presented for his signature, he confounded the electorate by declaring, "I'll be damned if I'll sign any papers naming a town for the wife of Jeff Davis." Scratching out Varina City, he renamed the town Virginia City.

Purloining the name of the other Virginia City, capital of the Comstock, aside from its lack of originality, was to plague the town until it sank into obscurity, not to mention the burden it placed on the United States Post Office.

Six months after the discovery, more than twelve hundred human beings were scattered up and down Alder Gulch and Daylight Creek, including a few Chinese, silk-vested gamblers, whiskey dealers, a multitude of whores, and the usual run of mining camp scum, in this instance largely composed of refugees from Idaho City and Boise Basin. A sawmill was in operation, cutting timber for the stores and cabins that were being hammered together. On Wallace Street, the three-story Idaho Hotel was under construction. At the corner of Wallace and Jackson streets, Content's general store and the establishments of Dance and Stuart and Paris Pfouts were well stocked with groceries, hardware, and clothing. A road pointing north from Salt Lake City had been hacked out and improved to permit the passing of bull trains drawing heavy freighters. Day and night they rumbled into Virginia City. Andy Oliver, Montana's pioneer expressman and stageline operator, was managing to get a stage through from Fort Benton on a weekly schedule, the fare an even hundred dollars. Passengers found the three-day journey a horrendous experience. They went hungry unless they had had the foresight to provide themselves with food before leaving Fort Benton. If a river that had to be crossed was running high, passengers put their lives in jeopardy in fording it. As yet there wasn't a bridge or ferry between Fort Benton and Virginia City.

The fear that when the gold had been washed out of the surface gravel the Alder Gulch diggings would be exhausted had long since been dispelled. Numerous shafts had been sunk to a depth of eight to twelve feet, and they revealed that treasure was to be found a foot or two above bedrock. It meant that a man had to have a partner, taking turns, one down in the shaft, digging, and the other operating the windlass. It was hard, grueling work, a man often toiling in ice-cold water up to his waist for hours at a time. But it was rewarding and the best proof that Virginia City was a permanent camp.

On a warm October afternoon, Henry Plummer, having been recently elevated to the position of sheriff of Bannack Mining District, rode into Virginia City, a handsome, even elegant figure on his high-stepping sorrel. He had an ingratiating manner, and was neat and better educated than Bill Fairweather, Mayor Doc Bissell, and other men of their status. His carefully tended black moustache emphasized rather than concealed the whiteness of his teeth. As befitted his position of sheriff of Bannack, he wore a heavy Navy Colt on his hip. He was a young man, still in his middle thirties.

Usually the reader is introduced to a master villain in terms so black and melodramatic as to make one wonder why men of goodwill were not warned against him on sight. That was not the case with Henry Plummer. He was shrewd and affable (when it was to his advantage to be affable). Although prior to leaving Lewiston, Idaho, in the fall of 1862, he had served time for robbery in the California penitentiary and was wanted in three states for complicity in the killing of five men, no taint of suspicion attended him when he reached Bannack and the Grasshopper Creek excitement. Proof of it is found in an entry in James Stuart's diary of September 18, 1862:

> On our way to Hell Gate at Beaver Dam hill we met two fine looking young men. One of them said his name was Henry Plummer, the other was Charles Reeves. Woody (Judge F.H. Woody) and I told them who we were. . . . They rode two good horses and had another packed with their blankets and provisions. We liked their looks . . . and asked them to return to Hell Gate with us and we could all go up the canyon together.

Plummer had come to Virginia City with a definite mission in mind. He liked what he saw and persuaded Bill Fairweather and his associates that what the district needed to preserve law and order was a man with a fast gun, and that he was the man. They agreed.

As he rode for home, Plummer could congratulate himself: he was the law in both Bannack and Virginia City. All that remained to be done now was to put together a gang of desperadoes and raise armed robbery to the level of an organized business—directed by himself.

Recruiting a number of thugs, sufficient to guarantee the success of the enterprise, presented no problem. In Cyrus Skinner's rowdy log saloon in Bannack—the same Cyrus Skinner who had ridden with Rattlesnake Dick's gang in California—he had renewed acquaintance with a choice band of cutthroats including, among others, George Ives, Haze Lyon, Whisky Bill Graves, Bill Hunter, Frank Parrish, Ned Ray, Bill Moore, and Red Yeager. Charlie Reeves, his companion from Lewiston, was there, as were Buck Stinson, Bill Carrhart, and Club Foot George Lane. When their drunken revelries turned sour, the thugs fought among themselves. Only their poor marksmanship could account for the fact that when the smoke cleared there were so few lifeless on the floor.

It was out of such crude material that Plummer welded together his supergang of road agents and assassins. He knew that Ives and the others feared him, largely because they realized that his cunning and intelligence were superior to theirs.

There was no time to lose if advantage was to be taken of the fall exodus from Bannack and Virginia City, when several hundred miners who had made a comfortable stake would be getting out of the country with their gold before winter snows came to block the trails and roads. Plummer had Ives set up a corral and stock ranch at Rattlesnake Creek on the Bannack–Virginia City road. This became the infamous Rattlesnake Creek Ranch, where the gang held many of its meetings and from which miners leaving the area were killed and robbed. Dempsey's Cottonwood Creek ranch became another gang outpost, and Daly's saloon at Ramshorn Creek Crossing a third.

Club Foot George Lane, a cobbler by trade, was dispatched to Virginia City, where he rented space for his cobbler's bench in Dance and Stuart's store, so he could gather information about who was leaving camp and the amount of gold they were packing out. The information he collected enabled him to mark the Oliver and Company stages that were worth stopping. When gang members, usually a pair, waiting concealed a mile or two from town, saw the cryptic marking, they couldn't go wrong.

If a departing miner refused to hand over his gold, they shot him. Savage George Ives shot men for no better reason than that they were unfortunate enough not to have any gold on their persons.

It has been said that at top strength the gang numbered at least forty men. But that is as unprovable as the number of its victims, which may have equaled that figure. Certainly no like amount of bloodletting had ever been witnessed in any other mining camp. The gang had a secret password—"I am innocent"—by which a member could always identify himself to another member. They tied their neckerchiefs in the road agent's knot and shaved their beards.

In Bannack, Sheriff Plummer had a gallows erected as a manifestation of his own uprightness and continuing battle against lawlessness. The town was impressed. In Skinner's saloon he shot and killed a new arrival in camp, who called himself Jack Cleveland.[4] In miners' court he testified that Cleveland had followed him from California to Bannack, seeking revenge for having been sent to prison on evidence he (Plummer) had presented. Bannack believed him, and the killing was dismissed as a justifiable homicide.

Plummer must have smiled to himself; men were so easily fooled. Robberies were being reported every day or two, but he was always forty miles away and then rushing to the scene to investigate. Above suspicion, he was the very picture of a hard-working, hard-riding lawman.

XIII

Vigilante War

THE ANNUAL freeze-up virtually put an end to mining operations until the following spring. On November 18, a foot and a half of snow blanketed the frozen ground and was quickly swept into drifts that made the trails and roads impassable. A few late starters, determined to get out of the country at any cost, attempted to get through. A few made it; others failed. Naturally, with so few travelers on the move, the number of robberies and killings decreased.

Although the Alder Gulch diggings had had a fantastic growth, with the population now nearing five thousand, the camp was well provisioned to see it through the long winter ahead. As the pace of life slowed, a small group of Virginia City's leading businessmen began holding secret meetings around the stove in Pfouts' and Behm's general store in the evening, their purpose being to devise ways and means of combating the road agents who had terrorized the diggings for the past few months. Paris Pfouts, a fighting gamecock, brushed aside as inadequate various suggestions that were made and declared that only a vigilance committee, taking the law into its hands, would suffice. Fighting Jim Williams, of Nevada City, not only agreed with him but demanded that Henry Plummer be removed from office. "I believe he's one of them," he said.

This was the first time Plummer had come under suspicion. But no action was taken.

In the middle of December, at first a seemingly unrelated incident set the wheels in motion. Bill Palmer, a Nevada City man, and his son set out by wagon to hunt grouse on the sagebrush flats east of the Ramshorn Mountains. On reaching the area where he wanted to hunt, Palmer and the boy got down from the wagon and proceeded on foot. They had gone only several hundred yards when a bird got up. Palmer shot it and his son went on ahead to recover the grouse. The lad found that it had plummeted to earth on the body of a dead man.

Palmer recognized the remains of his friend Nicola Tbalt, a popular young German. He had been killed by a bullet through the head. Tbalt had been missing for over a week, having been last reported on his way to Rattlesnake Ranch, George Ives' headquarters, to dispose of a pair of mules. The mules were not in evidence, nor was the money he should have received in payment for the animals in his pockets, circumstantial evidence enough to convince Palmer that there had been foul play.

His first concern was to take the dead man to Nevada City, but when he had brought up his wagon, he found he could not lift the body over the wheels. There was a brush wickiup a half mile to the west, and the smoke rising from the vent in the roof told him it was occupied. Seeking help, he drove over to it and found two men, Long John Franck and George Hilderman, there. They refused to leave their fire to help him. Palmer returned to the dead man and with the help of his son managed to load the corpse and bring it to town, where it was viewed by an angry throng. The gawking crowd shouted its approval when Jim Williams said, "We'll go out there in the morning and grab those two gents and bring them in and try them for murder. While we're about it, we'll pay George Ives a visit."

The posse found Ives at the wickiup, along with Long John Franck and a young thug who answered to the name of Tex. Ives pretended to take it as a joke when he was told that he was under arrest to be tried for murder.

Hilderman was unlucky enough to ride into the posse as it was returning to Nevada City. He was arrested and disarmed. On reaching town, he, Ives, Hilderman, and Long John Franck were placed in a makeshift jail under armed guard. Williams informed them that they would be brought to trial in the morning. As the day wore on, a number of suspicious characters began drifting in. They were under orders to disrupt the trial and howl down any move to find the prisoners guilty. They were taking orders from one of Plummer's lieutenants, very likely Frank Parrish. At least it was he who hastily dispatched Club Foot George Lane to Bannack to acquaint Plummer with what was taking place.

Jim Williams realized that an attempt might be made to free the prisoners. He prepared for it by doubling the number of armed men guarding them. That the blacklegs gathering in Nevada City were acquainted with one another and were members of an organized outlaw gang could hardly be doubted. Knowing it was going to require a strong man to preside over the trial, he induced Judge Byam of Nevada City and Judge Wilson of Junction Mining District to conduct it. Naming a prosecutor who would not be cowed by the rabble was even more important. Colonel W. F. Sanders, of Bannack, chanced to be visiting in Nevada City. He was a young, accomplished lawyer, courageous and fearless. When he acceded to Williams' request to handle the prosecution, the battle was half won.

No building in Nevada City was large enough to hold the hundreds of miners from every district who trudged into town for the trial. Most of them were present not only for the purpose of striking a blow for frontier justice but also for the excitement of the occasion. The open-air "court" was set up on the main street, handy to the saloons. Two wagons were wheeled into position to serve as the judges' bench and witness box. Since it was a cold day, a log fire was kept burning throughout the trial, which the men replenished from time to time by raiding the stacked piles of woodcutters. In the meantime, there was a continuous movement of the noisy, jostling crowd back and forth to the saloons, for whiskey provided a quick, if temporary, antidote against the cold.

Ground rules for the proceedings were agreed on by noisy acclamation before the trial proper began. Georeg Ives was to be tried first and by himself; he was to be permitted counsel (which Frank Parrish or one of his cohorts had already provided); a jury of twenty-four men was to sit in judgment, and the verdict they rendered was to be accepted or rejected by voice vote of the crowd.

Little else was accomplished during the rest of the morning, and it was midafternoon before Colonel Sanders put his first witness on the stand. Doubting that he could get a conviction against Ives on the charge that he had murdered young Tbalt, Sanders broadened his attack on him as a known criminal, robber, murderer, and member of the outlaw gang that was terrorizing the country. He called up miners, freighters, and stage drivers who had been held up, robbed, and pistol-whipped by George Ives.

Sanders climaxed his case by calling up a little man on crutches. One of the guards had to help him as he made his way to the witness box. Several weeks back, on his way from Deer Lodge to Virginia City, he had been stopped by two bandits who had shot and robbed him. When Sanders asked him if he could identify the man whose slug had lamed him, he pointed to Ives.

The angry crowd had heard enough and demanded that a vote be taken. When Judge Byam had brought the court to a semblance of order, he announced that the trial would continue.

For the first time the four prisoners and their lawyers realized the seriousness of the situation. The verdict of a make-believe trial might have no standing in law, but it could make little difference to a man whether he was hanged legally or by the fiat of a half-drunken mob. Ives had not given up hope; he still expected Plummer to appear and claim the prisoners as legally belonging to him.

Long John Franck conferred briefly with Colonel Sanders, offering to talk if given immunity. Sanders agreed. What he learned is not known, but he already had evidence enough to convict.

The defense lawyers had their turn. There was little they could do beyond stalling for time, hoping to have a recess called to the following morning. Judge Byam listened until darkness was falling before he called a halt and charged the jury. Half an hour later the twenty-four men were back with a verdict: guilty as charged. With only a handful of dissenting votes, the crowd shouted approval.

Judge Byam instructed Jim Williams to proceed with the execution. A five-foot-high packing box was placed beneath the projecting beam that was used for raising hay to the loft of a livery barn. A rope was draped over the beam. Ives was lifted to the top of the box and the hangman's noose dropped over his head. Someone threw fresh logs on the fire. The leaping flames cast weird shadows across his strained face. He knew he had only minutes to live and he winced as the growling crowd, there to see him die, hurled its abuse at him.

Without warning the packing box was kicked out from under him and he made his drop. Death was instantaneous, the fall breaking his neck.

The hanging of George Ives has often been cited as a victory for law and order; actually—save for the effort of a handful of earnest men—it was as much a victory for rotgut whiskey as for civic-mindedness. Carried away by the sight of the lifeless body dangling in the air, a movement started in the crowd to rush the cabin in which Long John, Hilderman, and Tex were being held and to string them up. Williams and his armed guards stopped the mob before it got beyond control.

Later that evening Ives was buried on the same hillside where Tbalt lay. The jury reassembled in the morning and passed sentence on the other three prisoners. Since there was no specific charge against Tex, he was given his freedom. Hilderman was banished from the Territory under penalty of death if he was seen after

New Year's, only ten days away. Long John was judged to have purchased immunity by testifying against Ives. The court disbanded, and Alder Gulch appeared to settle down to the enforced complacency of winter.

Actually it was only the calm before the storm, for Colonel Sanders, Jim Williams, and others who had been behind the successful prosecution of Ives were agreed that the time had come for organizing an army to make war on the road agents. Somewhere—very likely in Virginia City—a score of leading citizens met in a secret meeting to settle on ways and means of proceeding. They issued the following pronunciamento and affixed their signatures:

> We the undersigned uniting ourselves in a party for the laudable purposes of arresting thieves and murderers and recovering stolen property do pledge ourselves and our sacred honor each to all others and solemnly swear that we will reveal no secrets, violate no laws of and never desert each other or our standards of justice so help us God as witness our hand and seal this 23 of December A.D. 1863.[1]

Among the signers were James Williams, elected executive officer, Paris Pfouts, president, and John S. Lott of Nevada City, treasurer. Twenty-one other men affixed their signatures. Colonel Sanders was present but he did not sign, believing that as a resident of Bannack he should become a member of the committee that was to be formed there.

How many men, all substantial citizens, either joined or aided the vigilance committee, in addition to the twenty-four signers, is not a matter of record—perhaps as many as fifty. Having agreed to take action, they wasted no time in palavering. Long John Franck had named Alex Carter as the man who had killed young Tbalt. Upon learning that he was living in Deer Lodge with a fellow thug who went by the name of Whisky Bill, the vigilantes set out in the frosty morning on the long ride to apprehend them, determined to hang both. Somehow, word of their destination and purpose leaked out, and Red Yeager, a gang messenger, was dispatched to Deer Lodge to warn Whisky Bill and Carter. Yeager rode two horses to death on his mad ride. He was in time, however, with the result that Jim Williams and his party found that their birds had flown.

But they had not made their long ride for nothing. Williams had recognized Yeager as he passed, and when he learned that he had been in Deer Lodge that afternoon, he was certain Yeager had carried the warning.

The posse was still twenty-five miles from home when word was passed to stop and eat the last of their grub. As they huddled around, cold and disgruntled, they noticed a thin spiral of smoke rising from a wickiup on Rattlesnake Creek, a mile away, which meant that someone was there. The crude shelter had long been suspected of being a way station for road agents.

Anxious to learn who it was, they approached the shelter carefully. There was a horse in the corral. It was still warm, proof that it had not been there long. The place was quickly surrounded, and whoever was inside was ordered to step out, hands up.

The buffalo robe that served as the door was raised. Red Yeager came out. He was there alone. He admitted that he had carried the warning to Whisky Bill and Alex Carter. Questioned further, he confessed that Frank Brown, the barkeep at Dempsey's stage station on the Stinkingwater, had written the message.

Yeager was taken to Dempsey's station. Realizing that the vigilantes had already decided to hang him, he not only identified the bartender as his accomplice but gave Captain Williams the names of twenty-six members of the road-agent gang, including Henry Plummer, the leader, so that they might meet the same fate that awaited him.[2]

Without delay, Red Yeager and Frank Brown were strung up from the branch of a convenient cottonwood. It chanced to be New Year's Day. The committee could congratulate itself, for it now had the information it needed to complete its work.

Faithless Henry Plummer, the arch villain who had betrayed

their trust, was their first consideration. Without losing time, Williams and a group of Virginia City vigilantes rode to Bannack to execute him and his lieutenants Ned Ray and Buck Stinson. Reinforced by Colonel Sanders and his friends, they took the three condemned men into custody and marched them to the crude gallows Plummer had had erected, little presuming, one must imagine, that he himself would be one of its victims.

Three ropes were tossed over the overhead beam. Plummer, his nerve deserting him, wept and begged for mercy as a noose was dropped over his head. Since no box could be found to provide a good drop, the three condemned men were lifted to the shoulders of the executioners and tossed into the air.

The drop was insufficient to cause instant death. "Hold on, you sons of bitches," Ned Ray gasped as the noose tightened about his throat, "you're choking me!" Stinson died cursing; Plummer screamed in terror as he flailed the air with waving arms.

The work of the vigilantes was far from over. But they had made a good beginning. As news of the lynchings spread, it became obvious that an organized campaign was being waged to eliminate thugs and road agents. It was rumored that the committee had a secret list of over fifty men who had been tried secretly, found guilty and condemned to be hanged. This was an exaggeration, but a man who had reason to believe that his name might be on that list was faced with a choice: he could stay put and take his chances, or get out while there was still time. Getting out of the Territory in midwinter was difficult. But some did, for they were heard of later in the Idaho camps. Some went only as far north as Missoula, and that proved to be not far enough.

Without Plummer they were leaderless. Without anyone to take his place, they were just a disorganized gang of second-rate desperadoes.

On Sunday evening, January 10, the vigilantes hanged Dutch John Wagner, whose name was on Red Yeager's list, before returning to Virginia City. Four days later, the town awakened to discover that it had been sealed off from the outside world; a ring of armed men had it surrounded, making it impossible for anyone to leave. Shortly after eight o'clock, a massive search began for the six outlaws who were known to be somewhere in Virginia City. They had been tried in absentia, found guilty and sentenced to death. By early afternoon five of the six—Club Foot George Lane, Jack Gallagher, Frank Parrish, Haze Lyon, and Boone Helm—had been taken into custody. The sixth man, Bill Hunter, had escaped by crawling through a drainage ditch.

Business came to a standstill as the prisoners were marched in a hollow square to an unfinished building at the corner of Wallace and Van Buren streets. Five ropes were looped over a second-floor rafter. Packing cases had been brought up from Pfouts and Behm's freight yard and placed in position. With a thousand men watching, nooses were placed about the necks of the condemned. With false bravado they flung back the jeering taunts of the onlookers. In quick succession the packing cases were kicked out from under them and they made their drop. The bodies were left hanging until early evening, when they were cut down and buried by acquaintances. Virginia City had something to talk about over its supper table.

The vigilance committee had jerked the life out of a dozen blacklegs, including George Ives. But they were not yet halfway through the list Red Yeager had given them. Had they not had a much higher sense of responsibility than motivates a lynch mob, they might well have rested on their oars and left it to others to finish the work they had begun. Instead, having learned that at least half a dozen of Plummer's old gang were holed up at Hell Gate (Missoula), they set out after them.

It was two hundred miles from Virginia City to Hell Gate. To embark on such a journey in the dead of winter, with the temperature twenty degrees below zero, sleeping in the snow and dependent for sustenance on the rations they carried in their saddlebags, was enough to test the hardiest of men.

Their score at Hell Gate was eight men hanged. On February 1, the vigilantes were back in Virginia City and on the third they strung up Bill Hunter, who had previously escaped through the drainage ditch.

His death marked the twenty-first hanging in little more than a month. The vigilantes took down their ropes once more on February 14 and hanged a man for the shotgun murder of a miner. The hanging of notorious Jack Slade, the former Overland Stage Company agent of Julesburg fame, some time later, was not a vigilante lynching.

The committee did not disband. In fact, two years passed before it went out of existence. There were no more lynchings, but offenders against law and order were flogged. Virginia City appointed a city policeman. The town was becoming almost as safe, if not as quiet, as Battle Creek, Michigan.

On May 26, 1864, that part of Idaho east of the Bitterroots was chopped off Idaho and became by President Lincoln's signature Montana Territory. A meeting was held at Bannack to organize it. Virginia City delegates were there in great number and succeeded in having the town named the first capital of Montana.[3]

While the politicians were still engaged in various skulduggeries, a discovery was made in Last Chance Gulch (Helena) so rich that Alder Gulch was forgotten in a wild stampede that swept half of Virginia City over Boulder Hill to the new diggings. In Nevada City, a "For Rent" sign appeared on almost every building.

Virginia City had the capital and the business of the Territory, but Helena was booming, growing fatter and richer by the day.

It was a blow from which Virginia City was never to recover. Up and down Alder Gulch, Chinese miners had moved in and were working the piles of old gravel, surest sign in the world that the days of bonanza had passed.

XIV

Lawless Deadwood

THE Black Hills were sacred to the Sioux, and in the Treaty of Laramie, of 1868, the government of the United States solemnly guaranteed them that white men would forever be barred from entering or settling in them. That the United States thus obligated itself in good faith must be doubted, if for no better reason than that it had violated or ignored its treaty obligations with the other tribes of Plains Indians. In this instance it resorted to subterfuge, labeling the strong military force it sent into the Black Hills in 1874, under command of Brevet Major General George A. Custer, "a scientific and geographical" expedition. It was accompanied by a group of naturalists, topographers, mineralogists, and newspaper correspondents.

For several years reports had been reaching the outside world that in the Black Hills gold had been found at the grass roots. Unmistakably the real purpose of the Custer expedition was to discover whether the tales were true or false. They were true; gold was being found in so many streams and outcroppings that in the exaggerated reports that went flashing across the country, the whole Black Hills region was said to be richly mineralized. Overnight the news ignited the greatest gold rush since Alder Gulch, with thousands of men and women taking off for the new bonanza. The War Department thundered that it would stop by force of arms any invasion of the lands of the Sioux. It might as well have threatened to turn back Niagara.

By midsummer of 1875, upward of twelve thousand gold seekers, gamblers, whiskey peddlers, prostitutes, and criminals, all scenting easy pickings, were spreading out over Deadwood Gulch and its environs like an infestation of swarming ants. Back in St. Paul, General A. H. Terry, commander of the Department of Dakota, threw up his hands in disgust, realizing that the situation was beyond his control, and turned to the more pressing problem of learning what the Sioux were doing about the invasion of their lands.

What the infuriated Sioux were doing was quitting their reservations in defiance of regulations and gathering in the Badlands, preparing for war. Their fiery orators had whipped them to a fighting pitch, and the big drums were going night and day. Soon their number exceeded five thousand. Whether one chooses to regard them as bloodthirsty savages or patriots ready to sacrifice themselves in an unequal struggle to drive the white invaders out of their sacred homeland—that injustice was done them cannot be questioned.

The brief struggle is often said to have culminated in the Indian victory—or massacre—in the Battle of the Little Big Horn on June 25, 1876. Actually it was the prelude; the end came when the Sioux, apparently shocked by the temerity they had exhibited, began surrendering, and Sitting Bull and his followers fled to Canada.

Deadwood City and the neighboring camps of Crook City and Elizabeth City were too concerned with their own affairs to be seriously affected by the debacle on the Little Big Horn. Forty miles to the southeast, Rapid City had come into existence and showed signs of amounting to something. In all, in as many as ten widely separated camps, gold had been found and prospectors were flourishing. But Deadwood Gulch was the big producer, and Deadwood City (it soon dropped the "city" from its name), at the head of the gulch, quickly became the capital of the Black Hills goldfield.

Located at the very head of the long, narrow canyon, beyond which a road could not go, Deadwood was a one-street town, its only thoroughfare studded with unpulled stumps. For half a mile or so, as it twisted and curved down the gulch, it was lined with crude, jerry-built, false-front buildings, constructed with green lumber and already beginning to warp. They housed the usual assortment of frontier enterprises—groceries, hardware stores, barber shops, "eating houses," honky-tonks, and an abundance of saloons.

Property owners had laid a plank sidewalk in front of their buildings, but at different levels, to suit themselves, which gave the pedestrian the uneasy feeling of going up or down stairs. The planks were slippery after a rain, which made negotiating the sidewalk a precarious undertaking, especially after dark or if the passerby had been imbibing too freely.

In no other western mining camp had so many men been constricted to such a small space. By day the street was a tangle of mules, bull trains, and wagons; by night the scuffing of boots as the nightherd moved up and down the sidewalks became a dull undertone to the laughter and profanity emanating from the saloons. Shootings were an almost nightly occurrence. If a man went down, his friends carried him to a doctor or undertaker, whichever was needed. There were no arrests, for Deadwood was completely lawless. All men went armed, even the few who were above reproach.

The easiest way to reach Deadwood was either from Sidney, Nebraska, on the Union Pacific Railroad, 225 miles to the south, or from more distant Cheyenne, by way of Fort Laramie. Both routes presented road agents with an opportunity for enriching themselves. They were not interested in anything bound for Deadwood; they were concerned with what was going out—gold on the person of a miner leaving the country or an express shipment of treasure.

New strikes were reported every few days, and in the temporary excitement they caused, little attention was paid to the progress the Manuel brothers, Mose and Fred, and their partner Henry

Harney were making on their rich quartz claim at Lead, which they had named the Homestake. They erected a small stamp mill to break up the hard rock, and by midsummer had taken out $5,000 in gold. Encouraged, they bought the adjoining Old Abe and Tera claims.

They knew their claims were rich, but by the first of the year realized that it was going to take "big" money to develop them. So they sold, receiving $70,000 for the Homestake, $40,000 for Old Abe, and $35,000 for the Tera. The purchasers were J. Haggin, Lloyd Tevis, president of Wells, Fargo, and the ubiquitous George Hearst. The latter soon bought out his partners, and the great Homestake Mine laid the cornerstone of the vast Hearst fortune. It was still producing in 1972, and ranks as the richest of all American gold mines.

Before Deadwood was a year old, millions of Americans were devouring the lurid, hairbreadth adventures of the mythical *Deadwood Dick* and his host of imitators. They were trash, but the uncritical audience they reached was convinced that it was learning what life was like in the wild Black Hills of Dakota.

Deadwood is said to have attracted more famous Western characters than any other gold camp. Wild Bill Hickok was there; so were his friends "Colorado Charley" Utter and his brother Steve; California Joe; Calamity Jane; Belle Siddons, the Confederate spy; Sam Bass, the outlaw; Wyatt and Morgan Earp; and Charles Goodnight, the famous Texas cattleman. That is as far as the record goes. Of the road agents who swarmed along the Deadwood trails, none were famous when they arrived in Dakota. As for Sam Bass, he was an ignorant, blundering cowpuncher who had come north with a trail herd and is remembered only because he and five companions stopped a Union Pacific train at Big Springs, Nebraska, and made off with $60,000.[1] They were run down and Bass was killed at Round Rock, Texas.

Hickok busied himself locating a claim and renewing old friendships with acquaintances he met in the saloons. He did a little work on his claim but gave up when he found it would not even produce what he termed "wages." Gambling was more in his line. Charlie Shingle, who ran the Number Three saloon, was an old friend, and Wild Bill spent much of his time there, or in Carl Mann's place, where there was always a game going.

Charlie Storms and Jim Levy, known outlaws, had drifted into Deadwood. Shingle and Mann, who were coining money, were afraid that the two men might try to take over. They didn't want the status quo disturbed, and they suggested to Hickok that he become town marshal. Wild Bill agreed to think it over, but nothing came of it.

In Deadwood, at approximately four o'clock on the afternoon of August 2, 1876, William Butler Hickok, the famous scout and plainsman, was assassinated in Carl Mann's Number Ten saloon by Jack McCall, a town bummer and two-bit gambler. Possibly no incident in frontier history has had more coverage. Countless writers have told it in minutest detail, the majority, unfortunately, embroidering their accounts with romantic fiction.[2]

In all, Wild Bill had been in Deadwood only twenty days when he was killed. There is not a whit of evidence that in that time he ever saw Calamity Jane. She was living in one of the cribs on Gold Street and between her whoring and gambling was managing to support herself. By her own admission she did not attend Wild Bill's funeral, her excuse being that "she didn't dare to attend, because her emotions were far from under control."

Wells, Fargo reached Deadwood in August and installed its safe and gold scales in a rented corner of Shingle's Number Three saloon, while the small brick building next door, which was to be its permanent headquarters, was being completed. To the rear, a wagon yard and stables were ready for service. With the Sioux returning peaceably to their reservations, the fear of further Indian difficulties seemed to be disappearing. Nevertheless the trails were becoming more hazardous, holdups more frequent. A southbound Cheyenne–Black Hills Stage and Express Line coach was held up at Hat Creek Crossing and two passengers were killed.

Knowing it faced the same harassment that its chief competitor was receiving, Wells, Fargo brought in veteran personnel from California and Nevada to operate the Deadwood run. Its fears were quickly realized when a stage headed for town and, though carrying no treasure, was attacked within a mile of Deadwood by three masked road agents. Abe Simmons, the driver, instead of stopping, whipped up his team. One of the bandits killed him, and as he pitched to the ground, the team ran away. The masked attackers tried to kill one of the horses to stop the stage; but they failed and the coach roared into Main Street and was not halted until a wheel locked on a stump.

It was a bungled job, obviously the work of amateurs. Suspicion pointed to Sam Bass and the young Texans in whose company he was always to be found. Their criminal proclivities peaked a year later when they—Joel Collins, Bill Heffridge, Jack Davis, Jim Berry, Tom Nixon, and Bass—robbed the Union Pacific Express at Big Spring.[3]

Of all the characters who came to Deadwood, none was as beautiful, charming, and sophisticated as Lurline Monte Verde, the proprietor of the camp's most popular and profitable gambling casino.

Little wonder that her casino was popular. Lurline was still in her early thirties, always carefully groomed. Win or lose, as she dealt *monte* or black jack, her sloe-eyed smile never deserted her. She had come to Deadwood from Denver where, calling herself Madame Vestal (one of her many aliases), her tented casino of chance had been so highly profitable that the sporting crowd wondered why steely-eyed Ed Chase, the gambling czar of the town, did not crush her as he had crushed other competitors. Perhaps he knew her story and respected it.

She was the once famous Confederate spy Belle Siddons, a graduate of the Missouri Female Seminary at Lexington, Missouri, and the niece of Claiborne Fox Jackson, the last elected governor of that state prior to the War Between the States.

Eventually she came under suspicion, and her arrest was ordered. She fled St. Louis on horseback. At war's end she returned to Missouri from Texas and spent several years as a lobbyist at Jefferson City, the state capital. There she met and married Newton Hallett, an army surgeon from Kansas City. When he was ordered to Fort Brown, at the mouth of the Rio Grande, she accompanied him. In that forlorn, sunbaked post, garrisoned by two companies of black infantrymen, Hallett taught her how to deal *monte, vingt-et-un,* and black jack. For relaxation they crossed the river to the Mexican town of Matamoros and its gaming tables.

Hallett died in the yellow fever epidemic of 1869. As for Belle, about all that is known of her subsequent wanderings is that she was in New Orleans a few months later dealing black jack and *monte* in a St. Charles Street gambling establishment.

In Denver her Blake Street tent was directly across the way from the Palace, Ed Chase's little kingdom of chance. Undoubtedly he often crossed the street to confer with "Madame Vestal." The two had at least one joint problem that was troubling them: the steady exodus from Denver to the Black Hills. An estimated two thousand men had already left, and more were leaving every day. Chase was confident that the Mile-High City would weather the storm and continue to be the mining capital of the Rockies. To his drinking companions he ridiculed Madame Vestal's pessimistic predictions. That she had already reached a decision and was quietly preparing to pull up stakes and head for Deadwood soon became apparent, as the following excerpt from *Notorious Ladies* [4] indicates:

> After several weeks of planning and preparation, she avoided breaking up her organization by taking her staff with her. (Counting dealers, spindlemen, bartenders and bouncers she had a dozen men in her employ.) Instead of entraining for Cheyenne, the expedition covered the entire distance to Deadwood by trail, and it was a caravan the like of which the Cheyenne-Deadwood Trail was never to see again. She had purchased a second-hand yellow omnibus and remodeled it into a comfortable home on wheels, with

bed, alcohol stove for light cooking, curtained windows and a shelf for books. When she tired of riding inside, she rode up on top with the driver. Her maid traveled in the wagon that followed, along with her staff. Behind it rolled a sort of commissary wagon, which also transported the personal effects of the party. In a fourth wagon were stowed the large tent and gambling paraphernalia.

Not more than ten days after the killing of Wild Bill, Lurline Monte Verde (to give her her new name, which she had very likely filched from one of Laura Jean Libbey's romantic novels, of which she was an omnivorous reader) opened her Deadwood establishment.

Of course, as the days passed, she encountered a number of men who recognized her as the woman they had known in Denver as Madame Vestal. She could have expected no less, which makes it difficult to understand why she had assumed still another alias—unless she fancied that it would add to the aura of mystery with which she chose to surround herself.

Knowing that in her business she would have to face a world of men, she had established some rules for herself, the most inflexible of which—no doubt born of some past experience—was never to become involved romantically with one of her patrons. But such resolves are made only to be broken when Fate steps in and shuffles the cards.

On the night that young, handsome Archie McLaughlin, with his reckless smile, sat across the table from her and lost game after game until he went broke with a laugh, she realized that the promises she had made herself were suddenly meaningless. She offered to stake him, but he said no and assured her that he would be back.

There were over a hundred men in Deadwood and the neighboring camps who passed themselves off as prospectors as a cover-up for their real profession, which was robbery. In addition to the thugs and common thieves were the gangs of road agents who infested the Cheyenne and Sidney trails. Smiling, unsuspected

Archie McLaughlin rode at the head of his own gang of bandits: Billy Mansfield, Alex Casswell, Jim Brown, and Jack Smith. Under his leadership they were so uniformly successful that the Cheyenne–Black Hills Stage and Express Line as well as Wells, Fargo had posted rewards for their capture dead or alive. A week after bidding Lurline good-night, he and his gang held up the Sidney stage and made off with $9,000.

McLaughlin saw Lurline the following evening. He was gay, carefree, and plentifully supplied with money. Answering the un-asked question in her eyes, he told her he had made a little strike—always a valid explanation in a mining camp. His luck was better that evening, perhaps because her mind was not on the cards.

In the weeks that followed he dropped in almost every evening. Lurline soon realized that she was in love with him. McLaughlin sensed it, and knowing he was succeeding in his conquest flattered his ego. Sure of his ground, he invited her to have dinner with him at the Tivoli, where the best food in Deadwood was to be had. She said no. But he was insistent, and they dined together in the intimacy of a private room.

Word of their rendezvous quickly reached the ears of Art Donovan, her head bartender. He felt it his duty to inform her that Archie McLaughlin was the leader of a gang of road agents. Lurline had surmised as much. Now that she knew the truth, she realized that it came too late to make any difference to her.

With the approach of winter and men leaving the diggings with their gold, the number of holdups increased. Lurline very likely was supplying McLaughlin with information that he turned to good account.

In the spring of 1877, with the snows melting and the Cheyenne-Deadwood trail becoming passable again, Wells, Fargo had $200,000 in its coffers awaiting shipment. To make sure that it got through safely, the Express Company sent Chief of Detectives Hume to Deadwood. According to the often-repeated tale, he was standing at the counter in the Deadwood office, conversing with the local agent, on the day before the treasure coach was to leave, when Wyatt Earp and his brother Morgan came in to purchase passage to Cheyenne. The Earps had been prospecting around Spearfish for some months with discouraging luck and were on their way back to Dodge City.

Hume was acquainted with the much-publicized Wyatt, at least by reputation. According to the late Lucius Beebe, the piquant Wells, Fargo historian, Hume spoke up at once. "Wells, Fargo will give you and your brother free transportation to Cheyenne and fifty dollars in gold if you'll ride shotgun for us tomorrow." The deal was made, and within the hour a sign appeared in the office window.

> The spring cleanup will go out on tomorow's stage, with Wyatt Earp, of Dodge City, riding shotgun.

The treasure coach went through unmolested. Beebe says, "Earp told me it was the easiest fifty dollars he ever earned." [5]

As the first wild mining excitement leveled off and a semblance of law and order came to the Black Hills, a level-headed man or two realized that a Longhorn steer could be bought in Texas for ten dollars, driven north, butchered, and sold to the meat-hungry miners for $125. The venture was foolproof, and soon thousands of Longhorns were being driven north to the Black Hills. It also marked the beginning of the range cattle business in Dakota, soon second only to mining. Charles Goodnight brought in the first big herd over what became the Texas-Goodnight Trail, and later the Texas-Montana Trail, entering Wyoming east of Cheyenne, passing Lagrange, crossing the North Platte east of Fort Laramie, and on north through Lusk to the Cheyenne River.

On the evening of July 2, 1878, the passengers who boarded the Wells, Fargo night stage for Rapid City and Sidney had no reason to suspect that they were being used as puppets to convince the McLaughlin gang that they had caught the Express Company detectives napping again and could get away with another holdup with little difficulty. During the afternoon Wells, Fargo had let the news slip out that the night stage south would be carrying in excess of $100,000 in gold bars from the Homestake mine. This was a reversal of Company policy. What it was doing was baiting the trap, for it had been tipped off that McLaughlin and his desperadoes intended to stop the stage somewhere in Whoop-Up Canyon, a few miles before it reached Rapid City.

A short distance out of town, a second coach was waiting. In it were half a dozen armed Company deputies. They got out at once and changed places with the passengers. The scheduled stage with its treasure chest aboard proceeded on its way after the brief delay. The trail followed Box Elder Creek for the better part of the way to Rapid City. When it began to dip down into Whoop-Up Canyon, the driver pulled up his six-horse team momentarily and two of the guards got out on top with him and the man riding shotgun. The others fingered their Winchesters. If there was to be a holdup, they were ready for it. Whoop-Up Canyon, with its pines and cottonwoods and high brush crowding close to the trail, was admirably suited for a surprise attack by road agents. In the past two years, in a five-mile stretch, four robberies had occurred. The McLaughlin gang was responsible for three of them.

As the armed stage swung around a curve, Alex Casswell broke from cover. Seizing the bits of the lead team, he ordered the driver to pull up. Archie and Billy Mansfield leaped out from one side of the trail, Jim Brown and Jack Smith from the other. A blast of gunfire greeted them.

Casswell went down, his head literally torn off. A slug in the groin doubled up Jim Brown, but he managed to stagger off into the brush. McLaughlin was struck in the shoulder. Miraculously, Smith and Mansfield survived the blast untouched. They picked up Brown, reached their horses, and got away. The attempted holdup had not taken more than a minute or two.

Safe in their mountain hideout above Deadwood, McLaughlin, his superficial wound dressed, and the others did what they could to relieve Brown's suffering. By the end of the week his condition was critical. Convinced that he was in urgent need of a doctor if he was to survive, Archie talked it over with Billy Mansfield and the latter volunteered to go to Deadwood and ask Lurline to do what she could.

That McLaughlin expected her to induce a doctor to come to the bandit camp is unlikely. He had his own safety, as well as the safety of the others to consider, for their identity was now known, and rewards had been posted for their capture. Undoubtedly Lurline had told him that when she was married to Dr. Hallett she had assisted him in his operations. What Archie was asking was that she come herself and do what she could for Brown.

When Mansfield acquainted her with the purpose of his errand, she said no; she couldn't afford to risk letting it become known that she was associating with outlaws. He then played his trump card. "Archie is asking you to help him; there's no one else he can turn to."

Of the doctors practicing in Deadwood, the majority patronized her casino. From which one she borrowed a wire loop, used in extracting an embedded bullet, or what excuse she gave for needing it, remains a secret. But sometime before dawn, on a horse supplied by Mansfield, she rode out of Deadwood with him, bound for the outlaw camp.

With great patience and what little surgical skill she possessed, she succeeded in removing the offending slug. Brown recovered, and three months later, when taken into custody for his part in the attempted Whoop-Up Canyon holdup, repaid her for saving his life by implicating Archie, Smith, and Mansfield. The three men fled the country before the net closed in on them, but they were captured north of Cheyenne several weeks later. Shortly after leaving the Hat Creek station, the coach in which the prisoners were being returned to Deadwood to stand trial was stopped by a group of masked men, posing as vigilantes. McLaughlin, Smith, and Mansfield were taken off, marched to a grove of cottonwoods, and hanged.

It was promptly alleged that the bogus vigilantes were in reality the paid employees of the stage lines; that the express companies, forgetting their petty differences, had joined hands and meant the lynchings to serve as a warning to all road agents that they would meet the same fate if they continued to harass the stages.[6] Whether true or not, it had a salutary effect; the fall gold shipments out of Deadwood got through unmolested.

Undoubtedly among her associates there were some who surmised what the lynching of Archie McLaughlin meant to Lurline. She confided in no one, but the town had become hateful to her. Determined to get away, she disposed of her business and left, hoping once more to leave her memories behind her.

No detailed account of her subsequent wanderings has ever appeared, but it is known that some time after leaving Deadwood she was employed as a dealer in a Bennett Avenue gambling house in booming Leadville. After that she was seen in El Paso, then in Tombstone, in Virginia City, Nevada, and finally in San Francisco, where, known only as Lurline Monte Verde, she died in October, 1881, her passing scarcely noticed by the press.

Back in Deadwood, the *Daily Pioneer* missed the item in its exchanges, and so it went unreported. The town had lost its edge and was lagging far behind rival Rapid City, which was eagerly awaiting the arrival of the Fremont, Elkhorn and Missouri Valley Railroad, then building up from the south. When the first locomotive chugged into town on July 4, 1886, to be greeted by waving flags and a great celebration, Rapid City became the capital of the Black Hills, leaving Deadwood to its memories.

XV

Robbery in the Rockies

IN 1857 gold was discovered on Cherry Creek (Denver) and other nearby tributaries of the South Fork of the Platte. Within twelve months a dozen mining camps sprang into existence, such as Black Hawk, Golden, Central City, and Nevadaville. Breckenridge, Georgetown, and Gold Hill were established a bit later. Until then Colorado was practically unknown beyond its own borders, which were still more or less a matter of guesswork. In fact, it remained to be determined whether Colorado was Colorado or Jefferson Territory or Arapahoe County, a part of Kansas Territory.

However, as word went flashing across the country that gold was being washed out of the gravel on a score of mountain streams, and veins of the precious metal were discovered every day in quartz outcroppings, the rush to Colorado got underway. By covered wagon, the canvas tilt daubed with the legend "Pike's Peak or Bust," or partners on foot, pushing a handcart—thousands of men crossed the Kansas prairies, bound for the new bonanza.

Although the quantity of gold recovered from the sands of Cherry Creek was of no great consequence, it marked the beginning of Colorado's rise to preeminence as the greatest producer of precious metals in the United States. However, gold had been found within its present borders long before the Cherry Creek discovery. Back in 1801, a party of Frenchmen, mostly former bushrangers from Canada, who were as much at home in the wilds as the Indians, set out from New Orleans and ascended the Arkansas River in the hope of finding gold in the mountains at its headwaters.

They did not come as trespassers, for all of present Colorado east of the Continental Divide lay within the borders of Louisiana Territory. On the east fork of the San Juan, somewhere between Wolf Creek Pass and today's mountain town of Summitville, rich ore was found. They mined the gold and cached it until some way could be found of getting it out of the country. With the coming of winter they went down the Rio Grande to the Spanish-Mexican settlement of Taos. The following year they wintered in the Bayou Salado (South Park) with a band of friendly Utes, which was their undoing, for it led the fierce Arapahoes, deadly enemies of the Utes, to regard them as allies of the enemy. When the Frenchmen decided to leave the mountains with the coming of spring, they were attacked and slaughtered.

According to the meager records, only one man, Remi Ledoux, made his way back to New Orleans. In 1842, a young man claiming to be Ledoux's grandson arrived in Taos and organized an expedition to search for the treasure his grandfather and companions had buried. Young Ledoux failed to find any trace of the cached gold. His funds exhausted, he induced Don Archuleta, the wealthy cattle baron for whom Archuleta County was named, to continue the search. Ledoux was accidentally drowned in the San Juan River several years later. Don Archuleta grew old, and his son José finally wearied of continuing the fruitless search. But that wasn't the end of it; always there was someone to carry on the hunt for the buried hoard.

Modern-day Colorado folklorists have embroidered the tale of the Frenchmen's golden cache with titillating so-called "newly discovered facts," born of the imagination and designed to quicken the pulse of the rainbow chasers. They have even given the mountain on which the lost gold is supposedly buried the name of Treasure Mountain.

There was nothing legendary or make-believe about the gold strikes being reported every few days in the early 1860's. Seemingly, ledges of silver-bearing ore could be found almost anywhere. But the gold hunters were not interested in silver. Lawlessness was widespread, the only hint of government being the provisional legislature of the Territory of Jefferson, set up at Golden. But in 1861, the United States moved in and organized the legal government of Colorado Territory, naming Golden the capital, which it continued to be until 1868, when it was removed to Denver.

Soon after the establishment of Colorado Territory in 1861, the United States was in urgent need of Colorado's gold, for the nation's ability to survive was about to be tested by the long and costly Civil War. While sentiment in the Territory was largely favorable to the Union cause, frequent clashes with Confederate sympathizers occurred.

As yet, there were no railroads in Colorado—in fact, there were none west of the Missouri River. The Territory's only contact with the East was the triweekly Leavenworth and Pike's Peak Express, 687 miles up the valley of the Smoky Hill River to Denver. As for roads, they were no better than treacherous, narrow trails hacked out of the rocky mountainside. They were dangerous even in the best of weather; a false step by a mule or horse, and over the coach (seldom a heavy Concord), driver, and passengers went, to end up a mangled heap at the bottom of a canyon. But they were heavily trafficked nevertheless, and, miraculously, accidents were few. The almost constant proximity of danger made speed impossible. Perhaps that explains why Colorado, of all the Western states, ranks second in the number of recorded stage holdups by road agents.

With very few exceptions, highwaymen are interesting subjects to recall only as long as they were successful; when their audacity failed them or their luck ran out, and they were either shot down, hanged, or bundled off to prison, the aura of glamour that had surrounded them faded, and they were quickly forgotten. If they were believed to have buried a vast amount of loot somewhere, that was a different story; searching for the cached treasure began, and with the passing of years it was carried on by men who knew little or nothing about the bandit gang which, supposedly, had buried it.

"The Lost Gold of the Reynolds Gang," to quote a recent Denver newspaper headline, is a case in point. Today, more than a century later, weekend adventurers of both sexes are still digging in Handcart Gulch and other places, undismayed by the failure of the generations of treasure seekers who preceded them. Most of them are well acquainted with the lore that had grown up about the legendary Reynolds gold, but they are only mildly interested in the early history of Bold Jim Reynolds and his brother John.

The Reynolds brothers, Texans by birth, are known to have been in the South Park region as early as 1862. They soon hooked up with Owen Singleterry, Charlie Harrison, and Cap McKee, fellow Texans who shared their aversion to hard work. Being always on the move from one mining camp to the next, they became as well acquainted with the Bayou Salado as any white man. Although they led a life of leisure, they rode good horses and always had money to spend in the saloons, which aroused the suspicion that they were the masked bandits who were waylaying travelers and robbing the stages.

When the road agents took possession of McLaughlin's stage station, within a few miles of Fairplay, and robbed the west-bound stage when it rolled in and not only relieved the passengers of their valuables but made off with the mail, Fairplay decided it was time to take action. A posse was hurriedly organized and left at once to scour the country to the north. Although the men were out until after dark, they returned to camp without having caught sight of the highwaymen. But the following noon Adolph Guiraud, a nearby rancher, raced into town with word that the bandits were at his place and had ordered his wife to cook their dinner.

A score of armed men left for the ranch at once and were in time to catch the bandits at the table. They were packed off to the Denver jail, from which Jim Reynolds and his cellmates—his

brother John, Owen Singleterry, Charlie Harrison, and Cap McKee
—escaped the next evening. Helping themselves to the best horses
they could find on the street, they headed south. Swinging off to
the east of Old Fort Wise, they made their escape without incident.

According to Jim Reynolds' story, he returned to Texas. It was
the spring of 1864, and the fortunes of the Confederacy were
brighter than they were ever to be again. But the treasury of the
Confederate States was bare. Reynolds says he agreed to lead a
small guerrilla force into Colorado, seize its gold, and turn it over
to the C.S.A., and that his offer was accepted. This is nonsense.
Had he made such a proposition to tough, stalwart General Henry
McCulloch, former Texas ranger and commanding general of the
Department of Texas for the Confederacy, he would have been
thrown out on his ear. Reynolds did return to Colorado with a
small force, fewer than thirty men, and not all Texans, and gave
himself the rank of colonel. Needless to say, the War Records of
the Confederate States of America do not show that he was ever
granted a commission.

By calling themselves guerrillas they gave themselves a decep-
tive quasi-military status. Actually, they were outlaws, frontier
brigands recruited by Jim Reynolds in Las Vegas, the most lawless
of all New Mexican settlements. Most accounts agree that they
numbered twenty-three men. In a notebook subsequently found
on Reynolds there occurs a copy of the oath of loyalty they supposedly swore to the Confederacy and each other. As Eberhart
points out, Reynolds, with his limited education, could hardly
have written it.

The gang made its first big haul when it intercepted a wagon
train bound north from Chihuahua for Santa Fe and the States
and made off with $60,000 in minted gold. They eluded pursuit
and lost themselves in the Sangre Cristos, where Reynolds proposed
to bury the loot temporarily and turn it over to the South later,
along with other accumulations. Many of his followers did not see
it that way; they wanted their cut now. Reynolds had to accede to
their wishes. The gang split up and with only eight men—his

brother John, Owen Singleterry, Jake Stowe, Tom Holliman, John Bobbitt, John Andrews, Jack Robinson, Tom Knight—remaining loyal to him, he led the way into Colorado. Their share of the wagon-train robbery was buried somewhere in the vicinity of the Spanish Peaks. It has never been found.

Reynolds led his remaining followers back to his old haunts in South Park, and the gang made its more or less permanent camp in the mountains above the headwaters of the South Platte. It wasn't long before the Bayou Salado knew that the Reynolds brothers were back. Throughout what is now the central counties of Colorado, east and west of the Divide, holdups began occurring with increasing frequency. The Reynolds gang was not responsible for all of them, but they were charged with the majority.

Organizing a posse to run them down became a popular pastime; groups of as many as thirty men, armed to the teeth, setting out to run the outlaws to earth, became a common sight. Always they returned from their labors empty-handed. It was said, half in jest but with some truth, that the leaders were careful to keep out of the way of the men they were chasing. That the Reynolds gang appeared to lead a charmed life was due in part to the fact that many outlying ranchers, running a few cattle and doing a little farming in some remote mountain valley, were in the pay of the gang. On the other hand, the fortune that Jim, allegedly, had sworn to gather in for the South, was disappointingly slow in materializing, for the average stage holdup seldom netted more than a thousand dollars. Disgusted with such picayunish business, he decided to make a bold play for really big money. After talking it over with his brother John and the others for a few days, he convinced them that there was no reason why they couldn't ride into Denver and loot the Territorial Treasury.

They left the Bayou Salado at sunrise the following morning and, avoiding the main trails where possible, headed for the capital. On the night before they were to ride into town, they stopped to sup at the Omaha House and talked too much. A young man overheard enough to learn whither they were bound and what their mission was. Riding through the night, he reached Denver in time to inform the authorities. Police Captain Maynard swore in a large posse and rode west to intercept the bandits. Instead of turning tail and running as posses usually did, Captain Maynard and his men charged the gang. After a sharp exchange of gunfire, the latter disappeared into the timber and fled.

Safely back in their stronghold, they lay quiet for a month or more, giving Singleterry and several others who had been wounded time to recover. When the gang was ready to ride again, it went back to stopping the stages, extending its marauding across the Divide to Alma and Breckenridge. When they eventually struck the jackpot, it was much nearer home. Again it was to be Fairplay and McLaughlin's station.

No one has satisfactorily explained why between $30,000 and $60,000 in gold had been permitted to accumulate in Fairplay, awaiting shipment to Denver. Obviously it was a loosely kept secret, for someone working in Jim Reynolds' interest learned when the shipment was to go out and passed word to him.

There were several places where it might be intercepted. McLaughlin's station was familiar ground; the gang had been successful there once before. That settled it; win, lose, or draw they'd make their play at McLaughlin's.

They took possession of the station and the crew an hour before the stage was due. When it rolled in, the road agents seized the team and ordered the passengers to get out. Riding up on the box with the driver was Billy McClellen, one of the owners of the McClellen and Spottswood Stage Lines. He was armed, but he tossed his gun to the ground and was herded inside with the passengers. The treasure chest was smashed open. What it contained no one will ever know. Some commentators say the amount was as low as $3,000; others place the figure as high as $60,000. Whatever it was, it is with the loot they made off with that afternoon at McLaughlin's station that the living legend of "the buried gold of the Reynolds Gang" began.

Following the robbery at McLaughlin's station, the Reynolds

gang discovered that public indignation against them had been aroused; that from every direction a massive hunt was under way to run them down. It kept them on the move, for their old hideouts were no longer safe. Avoiding one posse threw them into the way of another. A large posse, led by Jack Sparks, came over the Divide from Swan River. Camped one night above the headwaters of the North Fork, they caught sight of a distant campfire below them. Sparks, thinking at first that it might be another posse, decided to investigate, only to discover that he had stumbled onto the bandits' camp.

As the posse was moving in to surround the camp, one of the possemen lost his head and fired a shot. Immediately the outlaws kicked out the fire and retreated into the trees, from where they began blazing away at anything that moved. Owen Singleterry was killed; [1] the others made their getaway and scattered. Holliman was captured at a ranch near Canon City where he was hiding; John Reynolds, Jake Stowe, and John Andrews eluded pursuit and escaped into New Mexico. Meanwhile, Jim Reynolds, John Bobbitt, Tom Knight, and Jack Robinson were hunted down and were captured a few miles east of Canon City.

The five men, Holliman and the others, were taken to Denver and lodged in jail overnight. In the morning a detachment of the Third Colorado Cavalry, under command of Captain Cree, left town with the prisoners for the announced purpose of escorting them to Fort Wise and turning them over to the military on the flimsy pretext that they were Confederate guerrillas and as such were properly prisoners of the United States.

Toward evening Captain Cree and his troopers returned to Denver with the fantastic tale that at the old ghost town of Russelville the prisoners had attempted to escape and it had been necessary to shoot them. Some credence might have been placed in the tale had Reynolds and the other four been armed, but that Colorado troops, even though only volunteer militia, had found it necessary to shoot down unarmed men, even if they had been trying to escape, which is doubtful, was a transparent lie. Any doubt that

the five men had been foully murdered was dispelled when Uncle
Dick Wooten, the famous frontiersman, found the bullet-riddled
bodies lashed to trees. In a way, it was as black a page in the history
of Colorado troops as the Sand Creek Massacre of Chief Black
Kettle's Cheyennes.[2]

If the Reynolds gang had been bundled off to prison to pay
for their crimes, they very likely soon would have been forgotten.
But the great newspaper coverage given their grisly demise awakened public interest in them, and soon the digging for their buried
treasure was in full swing. If you had some reason to believe that
it would be found in Geneva Gulch—and a lot of people thought
so—you didn't divulge it to anyone. Whether you fancied Handcart Gulch, Webster Pass, Shafer's Crossing, or any other place,
you were tight-lipped about why you were digging there.

What none of the little army of treasure seekers was willing to
face up to was the possibility that John Reynolds had returned to
Colorado and recovered the buried gold. Even when faced with
the indisputable fact that John Reynolds and a companion were
in South Park in 1871, stealing horses, and were killed there, they
refused to admit that he might have dug up the Reynolds' gold.
Of course, if you are a dyed-in-the-wool rainbow chaser, you don't
permit facts to get in your way; you believe only what you want
to believe.

A new era dawned for Colorado when the Kansas Pacific Railroad and the Denver Pacific put their rails into Denver within a
few weeks of each other in 1869. The Territory had expected to
get the transcontinental, but it had been bypassed a hundred miles
to the north, and where General Grenville Dodge, chief engineer
of the Union Pacific, had driven a stake into the prairie sod on
Crow Creek in 1867 and named the spot Cheyenne, there was now
a town of twelve thousand inhabitants, not counting the several
thousand parasites, gamblers, criminals, whiskey peddlers, and
prostitutes who fattened on the construction crews.

Not by way of apology but because it needed the business,
the Union Pacific took over the still trackless but partially graded

Colorado and Clear Creek line and built a standard-gauge (4 feet 8½ inches) railroad, the Colorado Central, from Cheyenne to Denver. Down at Pueblo, General William Jackson Palmer was pushing his three-foot Denver and Rio Grande up the canyon of the Arkansas River, blasting and chipping his way through what had been considered impassable barriers.

It was only the beginning. Before it was over, the railroad builders of Colorado were to make the state the recognized narrow-gauge capital of the world. No mountain gold camp, however inaccessible, was beyond the genius of such intrepid builders as little Otto Mears. By a score of trestles and switchbacks, the two-foot-gauge Gilpin Gold Tramway brought ore down from Central City to the mills and smelters that lined North Clear Creek at Blackhawk. As for Otto Mears, he had his Denver and Rio Grande Southwestern within four miles of Ouray when he realized he had twenty-four additional mountain miles to go before he reached the camp. He was out of money, but somehow he got there.

Colorado soon had more railroads than any other Western state. As new discoveries were made and a camp had established its worth, the first thing it wanted was a railroad. Shortly after the great silver strike at Leadville was creating millionaires overnight, it had three trains daily to and from Denver; when Cripple Creek began to dazzle the world with its gold, the railroads were there to serve it.

Although accidents, often resulting in fatalities, occurred with distressing frequency, the steam cars pushed the stage lines out of business, and as they disappeared, so did the road agents, their peculiar field of banditry gone. Very few graduated into the ranks of the bank and train robbers, the so-called outlaws on horseback, who were to terrorize the plains for half a century.

What is generally recognized as the last holdup to occur in South Park took place at Ute Crossing (sometimes referred to as the Eleven Mile Canyon robbery), down the South Platte below Alma. The robbery was committed by two masked bandits, identity unknown, who mortally wounded the driver and made off with an estimated $3,000 in gold bullion. Converging posses from Park and Summit counties tracked the road agents to their hideout at the waterlogged and long abandoned Dexter mine. In a shoot-out both robbers were killed, but no trace of their loot was found.

The matter had been largely forgotten when it came to the attention of that remarkable soldier of fortune, Captain Gilly Gillioso, thirty years later. Favorably known among mining men all over the Southwest and Mexico as an excellent engineer as well as adventurer, Captain Gilly decided to go after the lost treasure. He secured title to the property by the simple means of paying the back taxes, and went to work. In the course of a year he succeeded in draining the mine and at the bottom of the shaft he found an iron chest containing the buried loot.

Gilly never disclosed even to his intimate friends, including this writer, how much he took out of the Dexter mine. It must have been a sizable amount. But money never remained with him long, for he was alternately rich and broke.[3]

XVI

The Border Bandits

FOLLOWING the conclusion of the War Between the States there appeared a desperate breed of young men, hardened by war, reckless, expert riders all, who robbed banks and trains and terrorized the prairie states for half a century. A few possessed the rudiments of education, but for the most part they were illiterate. Without exception they were brave, fearless young men, unsurpassed when in the saddle. Not only were they veterans of the war just concluded, in which they had fought on the side of the Confederacy, but veterans of the bloody border wars between Missouri and Kansas.

They were ruthless in their banditry, never hesitating to kill when they found themselves in a tight corner, but their apologists gilded them with a patina of romance, excusing their lawlessness on the ground that they were only cowboys who somehow had gone wrong.

Although largely untrue, that hoary myth still persists in some quarters. Actually, among the early gangs of long riders there were none who could claim to have been working cowboys before they drifted into outlawry. In fact, few had any record of previous employment at anything other than working at odd jobs or piecing together a living with a patch of corn and a few hogs on an acre or two of bottom land. In 1890, twenty-five years later, when Bill

148

Doolin put together the last of the great gangs of prairie bandits, a number of his cowboy cronies followed him into outlawry.

But by then it was getting late; the United States marshals and their deputies were closing in on the various groups of horseback desperadoes who had been running free for almost a quarter of a century.

In calling the roster of the various outlaw gangs who largely confined their activities to robbing banks and the steam cars, the proper place to begin is with the James-Younger Gang. They were the first, the longest-lived, and the most ruthless. Few, if any, much worthier men have had the attention lavished on them that historians, feature writers, the screen and television have given Frank and Jesse James and their companions in outlawry, Coleman Younger and his brothers Jim, Bob, and John—not to mention Belle Starr, the so-called "outlaw queen" who was born Myra Belle Shirley and named her daughter Pearl Younger because the child's father was handsome Cole Younger.

Over the years the mass of material dealing with the outlaw activities of the James-Younger Gang has been so carefully sifted and resifted that the fiction and dubious folklore regarding them can be brushed aside. However, the hardy myth that there was a blood strain of outlawry in the James and Younger families that was passed on to the Dalton boys, who came a bit later, still exists. This is nonsense. First of all, the Jameses and the Youngers were not related by blood; the Youngers and the Daltons were only second cousins by marriage. The parents of the Younger boys, Colonel Henry Washington Younger and his wife Sheba, were persons of some consequence in Jackson County, Missouri. The Colonel was considered to be a wealthy man, and he was twice elected to the state assembly and held other public offices.

Louis Dalton and his wife (the former Adeline Younger), living on their farm north of Coffeyville, Kansas, were highly esteemed by their neighbors. They had a family of thirteen children: nine boys (eight of whom reached maturity) and four girls.

Four of the boys became tarred with the brush of outlawry; the others lived and died respected citizens.

The father of Frank and Jesse was the Reverend Robert James, a Tennessee back-country preacher-farmer. He joined the gold rush to California in 1849, contracted a fatal illness, and died at Marysville in 1851. Zerelda James did not remain a widow for long. Her second husband was a man named Simms, whom she divorced a few months later for nonsupport. A third marriage to Dr. Reuben Samuel, a Kentuckian, followed. A year later Dr. Samuel and his new family removed to Missouri and settled on a farm in Jackson County, where, in addition to farming, he resumed the practice of medicine.

It is as Zerelda Samuel that the mother of the James boys is known to history. She was an excellent mother and in many ways a remarkable woman. To suggest that the criminal tendencies her sons were later to display had been transmitted to them by their mother is too absurd to be taken seriously. Certainly it was the lawlessness that surrounded them as they grew to manhood that bent them in that direction. The bitter confrontation between pro-slavery and non-slavery factions; the almost nightly raiding across the Missouri-Kansas line; the frequent assassinations; men called to their door and shot down as they stood exposed to the lamplight; William Clarke Quantrill and his pro-slavery guerrillas inflaming his followers with the cry of an eye for an eye and a tooth for a tooth—how could any young man remain immune to the unleashed passions swirling about him?

Cole Younger's father was robbed and murdered by Kansas Redlegs, the Younger family home burned to the ground. Then followed the Civil War, and Union troops were sent into Missouri to ride herd on the rebellious population. Numerous clashes occurred between Union troops and Rebel guerrillas, the advantage going first to one side and then to the other. Still smarting over his failure to be granted a commission in the Army of the Confederacy, Quantrill decided to force the issue by doing something spectacular. His lieutenants, Fletch Taylor, Frank James, and several others were aghast when he told them they were going on a raid seventy miles inside the Kansas line to sack the town of Lawrence.

Quantrill's command numbered as many as 450 men, still young but tough, seasoned and inured to danger. Eighteen-year-old Jim Younger was there. Jesse, just turned seventeen, was ordered home, being considered too young for what was ahead.

For two days the guerrilla camp was busy. Food was being procured and horses were shod. Quantrill expected a battle at Lawrence; he knew the town was defended by a company of volunteer troops. Hoping to take them by surprise, he led the way westward as evening fell.

Avoiding the main roads, the raiders were within a few miles of Lawrence on the second morning. After pulling up for an hour to rest their horses, they continued their advance and were in sight of the town at daybreak. Raising the Rebel yell, they charged into Lawrence.[1] All was panic. Without attempting to make a stand, the volunteer defenders fled. Some of them did not stop running until they reached Paola, thirty miles to the south.

Within four hours, Lawrence was in ashes. Women and children had not been molested, but the bodies of 142 dead men (a conservative figure) littered the streets. Burdened with loot, the raiders turned back the way they had come, their casualties amounting to one man killed. Between looting and property destroyed by fire, the overall loss was estimated at $2 million.

Retaliation, brutal and devastating, came two days later with the issuing of the infamous Order No. 11 by General Thomas Ewing, who commanded all Union forces on the Missouri border. It called for the removal of all persons from Bates, Cass, Jackson, and part of Vernon counties. People living within the proscribed area were given fifteen days in which to remove themselves and such goods as they could carry with them. All buildings—homes and barns—were to be burned. All hay or grain in the field or under shelter would be confiscated or destroyed.

Where were they to find shelter? The best that was promised the stunned victims was that they could report to the nearest commanding officer, and if they could satisfy him of their loyalty to the United States they would be given temporary shelter in one of the garrisoned towns. To those whose sympathies were with the Confederacy, no helping hand was offered. With what belongings they could pack into a wagon, they took to the road, boys and girls, driving a few head of cattle, bringing up the rear.

It was not until after the end of the war that the ejected Missourians began returning to what had received the name "the Burnt District." They found a scene of vast desolation, with only the chimneys rising like gaunt skeletons from the ashes of their former homes. "Jennison's Monuments" they called them, for Charles Jennison, the captain of the Kansas Redlegs, who had directed most of the burning. He didn't take orders from General Ewing, who spent the rest of his life trying to live down the ignominy he richly deserved, but from that madman, United States Senator Jim Lane of Kansas, the archenemy of all Missourians.

Jim Lane was the author of Order No. 11. He threatened General Ewing with dismissal from his command if he failed to issue it. Lane had been in Lawrence on the morning of the attack and had escaped through a cornfield in his nightshirt when the first shots sounded. Aflame with vengeance and determined to erase the damage to his prestige, he struck back with Order No. 11.

Both Lane and Quantrill were egomaniacs. For the latter, the Lawrence massacre marked the beginning of his downhill slide into obscurity. Disowned by the Confederacy and no longer able to find sanctuary in Missouri, he crossed into Kentucky with a handful of followers, where he was gunned down. As for fiery, semi-irrational Jim Lane, he reached the end of his trail one day in Washington, D. C., by blowing out his brains. But the legacy of hatred and violence the two men left behind did not disappear when the long and costly War Between the States finally ground to a close. For years the soil of Missouri had been fertilized with animosities and political strife, preparing it for the quarter of a century of open, organized outlawry that was to follow.

Let's turn to Clay County (across the Missouri River from

today's Kansas City) in midwinter of 1866. It was not in the Burnt District, but some homes and barns had been destroyed. They had been replaced by new buildings as the inhabitants who had returned busied themselves mending the broken threads of their lives. Jesse and Frank James were back and living with Dr. Samuel and his family. They were not working; just marking time, it appears. They were not pinched for money. They often rode over to Liberty, the county seat, and bought drinks for their friends of guerrilla days, among them Cole and Jim Younger, Clell Miller, Charlie Pitts and Payne Jones. They usually ended these get-togethers by hoorahing the town—racing down the main street while firing their guns into the air and screaming the Rebel yell. They bothered no one, and no one bothered them.

Some accounts have it that it was not the innocent fun it appeared to be; that what they were doing was practicing for the serious business of holding up the Clay County Savings and Loan Company Bank. Some people noticed that it was always Jesse James who was in the forefront of the pack. They were all young men, but he was the youngest, with an unmistakable air of leadership about him. His brother Frank was taller but colorless. His long, bony face was usually expressionless. But between Frank and smiling, laughing Cole Younger, the brothers' most dependable ally, there was an unvoiced bond of loyalty and understanding from which Jesse was excluded.

In the beginning it was of little importance that Cole and Jesse did not always see eye to eye. As the years passed, however, and the gang sank deeper and deeper into outlawry, their clashing wills began to erupt into open hostility. They reached a bitter showdown in the aftermath of the debacle at Northfield in September, 1876.

February 13, not 14, 1866, as some writers have it, was a cold, raw morning with a skift of snow on the ground and the overcast skies threatening more to come. The shopkeepers of Liberty, Missouri, were sweeping out their stores and getting the fires going in their cast-iron stoves. At the bank, Greenup Bird, the cashier, and his son, the assistant cashier, had completed their preparations for the day's business and unlocked the doors. On the street, a few late students hurried by on their way to classes at William Jewell College, when suddenly a band of young desperadoes raced into Liberty, brandishing their pistols and cowing the town with their shooting.

They had done this before, but they were not there for fun that morning. Pulling up with a flourish in front of the bank, four hurried inside, herded Greenup and his son into the open vault, scooped up gold and silver coin, greenbacks and bonds from the shelves, and dumped them into a grain sack. Pausing only long enough to lock the Greenups in the vault, they rushed to their horses, and flung themselves into the saddle; in a matter of seconds the robber band was dashing out of town. Young George Wymore, a student at the little college, scurrying to safety, was gunned down without reason as he ran across the street.

The wanton slaying of young Wymore was tragic enough, but what was more stunning was the realization that the bank had been robbed—*the bank!* Banks had been known to fail, officials embezzling funds entrusted to their care. But banks had never been robbed, at least not until then. Jesse had planned it, and it set a pattern for a successful bank robbery.

A posse was organized to track down the bandits, but it was late in getting started. Since there was no question about the identity of the desperadoes, nor that they would put up a fight if overtaken, the possemen were not disgruntled when snow began to fall that afternoon, blotting out any trail they might have followed.

According to Cashier Greenup, the bandits made off with about $15,000 in gold coin, some silver and greenbacks, and $45,000 in bonds. The bonds, not being negotiable, were of no value to them and were thrown away. The gold coin also presented a problem. There was so little gold in circulation that they dared not use it for fear of drawing suspicion to themselves.

Cole Younger came up with a way out of the dilemma. During the war, while campaigning in Louisiana, he had become acquainted with a Texan who had told him about a money dealer in San Antonio by the name of Gonzales who handled "hot" money at a discount. Even for men at home in the saddle, it was a long ride to San Antonio. But four of them, the Jameses and Cole Younger and his brother Jim, set out for Texas. They found Gonzales a hard man to do business with, and for their $15,000 in gold the best he offered them was $9,000 in currency. After some haggling, they accepted it.

On their way north, they stopped at the village of Sycene, a few miles from Dallas, still a small frontier town itself, to visit John Shirley and his family, old friends from Missouri.

In the summer of 1863, when Jennison and his Kansas Redlegs had been ravishing the border county of Jasper, Shirley, a prosperous and widely known innkeeper of Carthage, the county seat, and a rabid Southern partisan, had packed some household goods in two wagons. With his wife and his daughter Myra Belle he had headed for Texas. He drove one team himself and Myra Belle, although she was barely sixteen, the other. They had picked up the Texas Road, the old cattle trail between Red River and Joplin, and got through without difficulty.

On reaching Sycene, where Preston Shirley, the elder of the two Shirley sons, had been located for some time, John Shirley bought a farm, built a commodious house, and resumed his old occupation of innkeeper. Bud Shirley, the younger of the family's two sons, had been killed the past June at Sarcoxie, Missouri, in a clash with Federal Irregulars, while riding with General Jo Shelby's Confederate command. He was Myra Belle's younger brother and had exercised far more control over her than her parents did, which has prompted the speculation that if he had lived, the wild streak in her might have been curbed.

The four bandits were returning to Missouri to divide the money they had collected in San Antonio—divided ten ways, it amounted to less than a thousand dollars a man. They tarried in Sycene for about ten days, long enough for Belle (she was beginning to drop the Myra from her name) to fall madly in love with

Cole Younger. How that brief but torrid affair went, no one knows. But certain it is that eight months after his departure, she gave birth to a baby girl, the future Pearl Younger, a beautiful child, who was to reach womanhood as wild and reckless as her mother.[2]

A month after the members of the gang had received their share of the money, they were broke again. This presented no serious problem; all they had to do to replenish their funds was to crack another bank. They discussed the matter with Jesse. He put them off for a week, not because he was averse to the idea but to impress on them that he was the leader.

On October 30, 1866, following the same tactics they had employed at Liberty, they charged into Lexington, Missouri, fourteen strong, guns popping as they raced down the main street and hauled up with a slithering stop at the Alexander Mitchell and Company bank. Into the grain sack went $2,000 in silver and paper currency. Twenty minutes later they were back in the saddle and heading out of town. It was a neat job, performed with precision. It appeared to have been accomplished so easily that five members of the gang, Jim White, Bill Chiles, Bud McDaniels, Sam Pope and Jack Edmundsom, all former Quantrill guerrillas, decided to stick up a bank on their own, thereby avoiding having to divide the proceeds so many ways.

After canvassing the situation, they decided to make a run at the private bank of retired Judge William McLain in Savannah, Missouri. On the morning of March 2, 1867, they rode into Savannah, their faces masked by bandannas, and without resorting to the hoorahing that had been used at Liberty and Lexington, pulled up quietly in front of the bank. Three of them got down from the saddle quickly, the other two holding the horses, and hurried inside. Judge McLain was behind the counter. When he looked up from a ledger and saw the three masked men, he seized a pistol and opened fire. One of the bandits, believed to have been Bud McDaniels, shot him in the chest. But although seriously wounded, the Judge continued shooting. Sounds of commotion on the street warned the bandits that they had lost the play. Running out to their horses, they fled empty-handed.

The Savannah fiasco convinced those members of the gang who had entertained the idea they could get along without Jesse's leadership that they were mistaken. He knew their loyalty to him was questionable, dictated only by the circumstances that all were known to be outside the law. Over the years, no fewer than twenty-six men are known to have ridden with the James-Younger Gang. Of that number less than ten were his devoted followers.

No doubt having in mind that he would show Bud McDaniels and the other Savannah bumblers how a bank should be robbed, he led the way into Richmond, Missouri, on May 23, at the head of fourteen men, his brother Frank, and Cole, Jim, and Bob Younger among them. Screeching the Rebel yell and with their guns roaring, they sent people scurrying to cover. Pulling up in a swirl of dust at the Hughes and Mason Bank, six of them hurried inside. Nine thousand dollars in gold, silver, and paper currency was stuffed into the ever-present grain sack that was part of their trade.

But it had taken them too long. The town had had time to re-cover its wits. From behind trees and the second-floor windows of the buildings across the street from the bank, citizens, armed with rifles and shotguns, led by Mayor Shaw, began firing at the bandits. The latter, experts with the pistol, returned the fire, their bullets splintering windowsills and shattering glass. Mayor Shaw was killed. Several minutes later, the heavy grain sack tied to a saddlehorn, the marauders dashed up the street. As they were passing the jail, jailer Griffin and his son, a fifteen-year-old boy, fired at them from the jailhouse steps. A blast from a bandit gun killed the boy, and as his father ran to the lad's side, he was shot dead.

The bank robberies at Liberty and Lexington had not aroused any great wave of public indignation. The Richmond robbery, which had snuffed out the lives of Mayor Shaw, jailer Griffin, and his young son, was a different story. Not only in Richmond but all over stunned Ray County and adjoining Clay and Lafayette counties the cry was raised that the outlaw gang had to be run down and eliminated.

Some of the Richmond bank robbers had been recognized. Warrants were issued for Jim and John White, Payne Jones, Dick Burns, Ike Flannery, Andy McGuire, and Allen Parmer. The warrants were meaningless; what the posses that took out to serve them meant to do was string up the wanted men as soon as they got their hands on them.

Payne Jones was located at a farmhouse near Independence where he was hiding. It was after dark when the posse closed in. Leaping from a window, he fired both barrels of his shotgun, killing a posseman named Wilson and fatally wounding the little girl who had guided the posse to his hideout. In the black, rainy night, he escaped into the woods. Dick Burns was found sleeping in a farmhouse within two miles of Richmond. He was taken outside and strung up on a convenient elm. Andy McGuire was caught near Warrensburg several days later and hanged. Tom Little, for whom no warrant had been issued, shared the same fate a day or two later, the presumption being that he deserved hanging. The other "wanted" men were not apprehended. Eventually most of them were sent to prison for other crimes.

The gang leaders decided that it was a good time to get out of Missouri for a spell. Frank James went to Arkansas; Jesse and Cole to California, where they spent a few weeks before settling down in the hospitable little town of Santa Barbara. There is no evidence to support the story told by the romanticists that when they returned to Missouri in the spring of 1868, it was by way of Dallas, Texas, because Belle was there. Nor do we have any evidence of where and under what circumstances Cole and Jesse became convinced that the Long & Norton Bank, at Russellville, Kentucky, was bulging at the seams with money.

Cole could claim some knowledge of that country, having been with Quantrill on his last raid. It was thinly populated hill country, sloping up to the Tennessee line. Jesse knew nothing about it, but he had returned home determined to make a big strike and he was convinced that Russellville was worth investigating. He conferred with George Shepherd, a seasoned member of the gang and a Quantrill diehard who had been with the now dead leader up to the very end. He nodded yes when Jesse had finished: Russellville wouldn't be any problem.

Cole, Shepherd, and Jesse met Frank James at New Madrid four days later and were ferried across the Mississippi at Dorena, unrecognized and without arousing suspicion. They spent the night in the woods twenty miles west of Russellville and jogged into town the following morning, May 20, 1868, timing themselves so that they pulled up in front of the Long & Norton Bank a minute or two after Cashier Nimrod Jones flung open the doors for the day's business.

Cole and Jesse slipped from the saddle and hurried inside. As the cashier approached the counter to wait on these early customers, he was startled to see Cole reach for his gun. Spinning on his heels, he bolted for a side door. Jesse snapped a shot at him that creased his scalp and knocked him to the floor. He was up in a flash and ran down the street, crying a warning and dodging behind trees and lampposts to escape the bullets that Frank James and Shepherd fired at him.

In the bank, Cole and Jesse cowed a clerk into opening the vault. Fourteen thousand dollars in coin went into the grain sack. By now Russellville was alive to what was happening. Storekeepers and clerks seized their guns, pistols, rifles, shotguns, and sought points of vantage from which they could blast away at the desperadoes. Frank James and George Shepherd, veterans of a score of gun battles, held off the Russellville men until Cole and Jesse hurried out of the bank with the bulging grain sack. Swinging their horses around in the direction from which they had entered the town, they raced away.

"Some forty citizens, mounted on such animals as they could collect from buggies, wagons and hitching posts, started in hot pursuit," wrote J. W. Buell in *The Border Outlaws*, the first biographer of the James-Younger Gang. "All the advantage, except in point of numbers, was with the robbers. They rode splendid horses, and were daring and accomplished highwaymen. Five miles from Russellville their trail was lost in the woods."

Although they were soon home free, the Russellville robbery was directly responsible for their historic confrontation with the Pinkertons. Responding to the demands of its member banks for protection, the American Bankers Association engaged the Pinkerton National Detective Agency, the foremost organization of its kind in the United States, to track down the outlaws and bring them to what, for want of a more accurate term, was known as "justice."

The Pinkerton Agency had been founded by Allan Pinkerton, who had distinguished himself as a top secret-service officer during the War Between the States. It was now directed by his son Robert, and had achieved an awesome reputation for its dogged and wily pursuit of criminals. They have been credited with breaking up the Reno Gang, back in Indiana, America's first train robbers. This is debatable, for on the evening of November 8, 1868, a vigilante mob entered the New Albany jail and hanged three of the Reno brothers and their companion Jack Anderson from the rafters.

However, when the Pinkertons bent to their task of running down the James-Younger Gang, they quickly discovered that they were dealing with a craftier, sterner breed of men than the country bumpkins of Indiana.

That the Pinkertons pursued their task in Missouri with their usual tenacity cannot be questioned. But as Wellman says forthrightly in his excellent *A Dynasty of Western Outlaws*, "The stubborn fact emerges . . . that the Pinkertons [in Missouri] unfortunately, were more active than effective."

It was the turning away of former friends and Southern sympathizers, who could no longer condone the activities of the James-Younger Gang, that led to its downfall. "Professional thief catchers had nothing to do with it." [3]

XVII

"They Went Thataway"

SHORTLY AFTER the robbery of the Long and Norton Bank there arrived in Russellville a Pinkerton detective by the name of A. B. (Yankee) Bligh. He spent a week there, interviewing a score of persons who claimed they had been eyewitnesses of what had occurred at the bank on the morning in question. As usual in such circumstances, their descriptions of the bandits were confusing and contradictory. But a man named Owens, who had been shot in the leg during the fracas, insisted that he had recognized one of the robbers. He didn't know the man's name, but claimed he had seen him before in Fort Smith on several occasions.

Convinced that he had struck pay dirt, Bligh got a good description of the unnamed outlaw from Owens. With nothing more to be learned in Russellville, he headed west, hoping to pick up the trail of the wanted men. The bits of information he gathered convinced him that they were making for the Mississippi and were intent on getting out of Kentucky as quickly as possible. A week later he discovered where they had crossed the river and long since gained the safety of Missouri.

By horse and buggy, posing as a lightning-rod salesman, Bligh made his way across that state, making very few sales but gathering some valuable bits of information. He was convinced by now that the four or five bank robberies that had occurred in that region

161

were local jobs and that the perpetrators were very likely former Confederate guerrillas.

In making the rounds of Jackson County, he stopped at the home of the widow of Dick Maddox. Maddox, a noted Quantrill lieutenant, had been killed a year back in a saloon brawl with a mixed-blood Cherokee at Fort Smith. Six months later, George Shepherd had moved in with the buxom widow without benefit of clergy and without the lifting of too many eyebrows. Tall, rugged, in his early thirties, he was a stout man when he found himself in a fix, as he had demonstrated at Russellville.

He was home on the afternoon when Bligh stopped by. The Pinkerton man was struck at once by how closely Shepherd fitted the description Owens had given him of one of the bandits. Subsequently, Detective Bligh learned that Shepherd was spending more money than a man with no visible means of support should be spending. That clinched the matter in his mind. Satisfied that he had tracked down one of the Russellville four, he descended on the house with a warrant and a posse of deputies.

Shepherd refused to give himself up. A battle to smoke him out lasted most of the night. Running out of ammunition, he leaped from a window at dawn. A slug in the leg stopped him. Before there was any talk of extradition, he was whisked out of Missouri and returned to Russellville. Largely on the strength of Owens' testimony he was convicted and given an indefinite sentence of two to five years in the Kentucky penitentiary. The court offered him leniency if he would name his associates in the robbery. He refused, saying he didn't know who they were.

It was a victory for the Pinkertons, the only one they were to achieve. It must have impressed Jesse, for he and the leading members of the gang got out of Missouri and were not heard from again for eighteen months. As they began to drift back, they discovered the truth of the old axiom that the law as well as the public soon forgets.

It would be interesting to know where and how they had spent that year and a half of seeming inactivity. But of the many writers who have applied themselves to telling the story of the James-Younger Gang, not one has shed any light on the long period of their disappearance, other than that Jim and young John Younger were living in Dallas, Texas: Jim being employed as a Dallas County deputy sheriff and John working in a general store.

On December 7, 1869, Jesse James, his brother Frank, and Cole Younger served notice that they were back by riding into the little Daviess County town of Gallatin and robbing the Daviess County Savings Bank. They rode in quietly, and this is the way it went: Frank gathered up the reins and remained on guard outside; Jesse and Cole walked into the bank. Captain John W. Sheets, a former Union officer, was at the counter taking a deposit from a young farmer named McDowell. When he was finished with Mc-Dowell, Sheets turned to wait on the men who had just come into the bank. Stalling, to give the farmer time to leave, which he did not do, Jesse presented the cashier with a hundred-dollar bill and asked him to change it.

Sheets examined the bill carefully, and after making sure it was not counterfeit, walked to the safe. It took only half a minute. Some commentators say that Jesse and Cole exchanged some whispered comment and followed it with an identifying nod in Sheets' direction.

Still stalling for time, Jesse carefully counted the bills of low denomination the cashier placed on the counter. Looking up, Sheets was startled to find Cole's pistol covering him. Simultaneously Jesse drew his gun on the frightened farmer. Cole got around the counter and rifled the safe and cash box. Only a disappointing $700 went into the grain sack. Ready to leave, Jesse whirled on Sheets and shot him dead, the slug tearing a wicked hole through the man's head.

The shot was heard up and down the street and recognized as gunfire. Storekeepers seized their weapons and ran out of their shops, endangering their fellow citizens as well as the bandit holding the horses in front of the bank with their wild shooting. The high-spirited animals were becoming skittish, and it was all Frank could do to hold them.

Cole was the first man out of the bank. He tied the grain sack to his saddle horn and vaulted into the saddle. When Jesse was getting up his horse whirled and he was thrown to the ground, his foot caught in the stirrup. He shook himself free after being dragged a short distance and regained his feet. His brother swept in alongside him and Jesse nimbly vaulted up behind Frank. A moment more and they were away in a swirl of dust. Just beyond town they relieved a farmer named Smoot of the fine horse he was riding.

A few miles south of Gallatin they encountered the Reverend Helm, plodding toward town in his buggy. The country preacher was known to have harbored strong Rebel tendencies during the late war. Jesse pulled up and spoke to him. He is alleged to have said, "Reverend, I've just killed S. P. Cox, if I haven't mistaken the man."

This may be fiction. While it is true that the Rebel guerrillas believed to a man that Lieutenant S. P. Cox had led the contingent of Union troops that captured and beheaded Bloody Bill Anderson, foremost of Quantrill's raiders, no evidence has ever been turned up that Cox was hiding his identity under the alias of John W. Sheets. Although the war had long been over, it is altogether unlikely that Cox, aware of the vendetta that had been sworn against him, would have settled in a region which was still alive with Southern sympathizers. Some sources, determined to make a hero of Jesse at all costs, have endorsed the Cox-Sheets story. Indeed, they may have invented it to put a better face on what was wanton, inexcusable murder.

On December 16, 1869, nine days after the Gallatin bank robbery, the Kansas City *Times* published the following bulletin:

"The horse, held by the sheriff of Daviess County [the horse that had thrown one of the bank robbers and which had been rounded up] has been fully identified as the property of a young man named James, whose mother and stepfather live about four miles from Centreville, Clay County, near the Cameron branch of the Hannibal & St. Joe Railroad."

Presumably Jesse and his brother read the item and realized that they were in trouble. It materialized the following day, when Deputy Sheriff Tomlinson, armed with warrants and accompanied by his grown son and two Gallatin men, rode up to the Samuel place. Frank and Jesse, already mounted, burst out of the barn and fled. Tomlinson, who had a better horse than his companions, pursued the fleeing pair. A few shots were exchanged to no effect before the lawman gave up the chase.

Almost four years had passed since that frosty morning when Jesse had led his band of reckless young desperadoes into Liberty and sacked the Clay County Savings and Loan Association. There wasn't much doubt then or later as to their identity. But there were no arrests. Naturally their kinfolk had nothing to say. Among the general public, men who had been strong for the Lost Cause made excuses for the supposed culprits, simply because they had once worn Confederate gray. But now the evidence against them could no longer be denied.

Jesse must have realized that the security the gang had enjoyed in Clay and the neighboring counties was gone. But he made no attempt to find a safer sanctuary somewhere else. Instead, he appears to have been satisfied that with bold and careful planning he could still keep ahead of the law. He and Frank continued to visit Dr. Samuel, their mother, and the two Samuel children, young Archie, aged eight, and his sister Fannie, just turned five. There was a fifth member of the household, old Susse, a former slave, who had been brought out from Kentucky by the doctor and Zerelda.

Jesse waited months for the furor following the robbing of the Gallatin bank and the killing of Cashier Sheets to die down before making another strike. When he did, it was across the Missouri line into Iowa and the little county seat town of Corydon. When he, his brother Frank, Cole, Bob, and Jim Younger, and Clell Miller set out on the 125-mile ride to Corydon, it can be taken for granted that they knew what their destination was and what they would find when they got there. Put in today's vernacular, the bank they meant to hoist had been carefully "cased," very likely by Cole Younger and one of his brothers. Having timed themselves to ride into town on the day a big political rally was being held at the fairgrounds, they rode into Corydon at noon on June 3, and found it deserted.

On walking into the Ocobock Brothers Bank, they saw they had only the cashier to deal with. They tied him up and looted the bank of $45,000, the richest haul they had ever made.

On their way out of town, Paul Wellman says, they pulled up in passing the fairgrounds, and Jesse, interrupting the Honorable Henry Clay Dean, the thundering, arm-waving speaker of the day, informed him that there appeared to be something wrong down at the bank; in fact, that it had just been robbed. Before the shocked crowd regained its wits, the bandits roared out of Corydon with a whoop and a holler.

The best reason for doubting the foregoing is that it reveals a streak of humor in Jesse, something he never displayed before or after, for he was a notoriously humorless man.

Several weeks after the Corydon robbery, Clell Miller was arrested on suspicion, but he could not be identified and was released. Plentifully supplied with money, the gang scattered for a few months. Arkansas was a comparatively safe retreat; Indian Territory even safer. What was known to men on the dodge as "Tom Starr country," a wild, mountainous region of rushing streams and limestone caves, without roads, provided an almost perfect refuge. No one entered it without being followed and their presence being reported to the six-foot-five Cherokee clan leader. If the visitors were unfriendly to him, they seldom left the area alive.

Ever since its forced removal from its homeland in Georgia and Carolina to Indian Territory (Oklahoma), the Cherokee Nation had been split by a feud that had taken the lives of several hundred men. "Old" Tom Starr, as he was always referred to, was closely allied with the "Treaty" faction and its leaders, Major John Ridge, Stand Watie, and Elias Boudinot, and in open revolt against the rule of Chief John Ross.[1] During the late war, he had fought for the Confederacy and had become acquainted with such guerrilla fighters as Frank James (possibly Jesse) and Cole Younger. Now, as old friends, he welcomed them to his stronghold. He had four sons, big, reckless men who recognized no law but Old Tom's. One of his "boys" was Sam Starr. Mark him well, for he was to figure prominently in the annals of Indian Territory outlawry.

For some inexplicable reason, Fort Smith had been excluded from the roster of rough, tough cow towns such as Abilene, Ellsworth, and Dodge City. And yet in the days before the Texas trail drivers shifted from the old Texas Trail to the newer Chisholm Trail, much farther west, it was a preordained stopover for thousands of young Texans returning home from the northern markets. Writers have expounded at great length on Judge Isaac Parker, the Hanging Judge, and his Fort Smith court, but they have had very little to say about the town itself, with its deadfalls, gambling joints, saloons, and wide-open prostitution. When a body had to be disposed of in a hurry, it was a simple matter to roll it into the Arkansas River and leave it for the current to carry away.

The James brothers and Cole Younger dropped out of sight following the Corydon robbery. Riding south through the Ozarks, they were among friends. When they struck the old Osage Trace and crossed the Neosho, they were in familiar country. Several days later they put their feet under Old Tom Starr's table and relaxed. They put in most of the summer there. Whenever they felt the need to break the monotony of their placid existence, they had only to make the seventy-five-mile ride to Fort Smith and take on some excitement.

Cole had informed his brothers Jim and John, down in Dallas, where they could reach him if necessary. Early in September came word that John was in trouble. In a bit of barroom horseplay he had attempted to shoot the pipe out of a man's mouth and seriously wounded him. The law was after him at once, and the following noon, in a shoot-out at nearby Sycene, he killed Deputy Sheriff Nichols. Although painfully wounded himself, accompanied by his brother Jim, he escaped from Texas into Indian Territory and reached Robbers' Cave, a well-known owlhoot hideout in the San Boise Mountains, north of Wilburton, where he stayed while recovering from buckshot surgery.

Cole left for the San Boise hideout at once. Some say that Jesse accompanied him, which he may well have done, just to break the months of inaction, if for no better reason. In any event, John Younger was brought to Old Sam Starr's bailiwick to recuperate. Later, when the Territory was resplendent in its gorgeous autumn raiment, Jesse and Cole journeyed to Texas once more. Some accounts say that for Cole, Belle Shirley and baby Pearl were the attraction, which is not true; Jesse and he were back in Texas because they had some business to transact with Señor Gonzales, the money dealer. As for Belle, her man of the hour was Jim Reed, a handsome, second-rate bandit, originally from Rich Hill, Missouri, a few miles from her childhood home at Carthage.

When Jesse and Cole got out of Texas and rode north several weeks later, Jim and John were with them. Bob Younger came down from Missouri during the winter to rendezvous with them at Old Tom's place. It was the first time in almost two years that the four brothers had been together.

Of the old feudist's sons, only Sam Starr lived with his father; the others came at different intervals, remained a few days, and quietly slipped away. But Jesse and his associates saw Sam every day. He was a big man, as tall as his father, copper-skinned and handsome by Indian standards. As much for sport as for gain, he was a horse thief. His name was destined to become closely associated with Cole Younger's. But of the chain of circumstances that were to bring it about, there was as yet no hint.

The Pinkerton Agency had opened a branch office in Kansas City, and its efforts to track down the James-Younger Gang were being directed from there. They had found several mountain caves that the bandits had used as temporary hideouts. But they had not turned up any outlaws, made no arrests. The best they could say for themselves was that months had passed without a bank being robbed. But that state of affairs was not to continue much longer. On April 29, 1872, the Columbia Savings Bank of Columbia, Kentucky, was held up and Cashier R. A. C. Martin killed when he refused to hand over the keys to the safe.

The actual robbery can be easily explained, but no James-Younger chronicler has ventured to explain what Jesse and Frank James, Cole and Jim Younger, and Clell Miller, men of some experience in such matters, were doing that deep in western Kentucky, a hundred and some miles east of Russellville. Had they crossed the Mississippi for no other purpose than to crack a likely-looking bank? Or was this a nonbusiness trip that was to take them through the Cumberlands to visit relatives in Tennessee?

Presumably they were not pressed for money. They were daring, brave men, but they were not fools. Columbia was then a pleasant little town of not more than a thousand inhabitants. There is no reason to believe that they had ever seen or heard of it before they rode down its main street, saw the red brick bank on the corner, and decided that it could be knocked off without risk. After passing through Columbia they circled around the town, acquainting themselves with the roads leading out of Columbia. The one to the south led into the hills and the Tennessee line, some forty miles away.

The bank stood at street level; there were no steps to climb, which was always an important consideration. Through the window, Cashier Martin saw the five strangers pull up their horses in front of the bank and must have sensed their business at once, for he turned from the counter and slammed shut the doors of the safe. Cole and his brother Jim gathered up the reins of the five horses and remained outside; Jesse, Frank, and Clell Miller walked in.

Martin's suspicions were realized as the three strangers leveled their guns at him. Jesse pushed through the wicket and reached the safe. Finding it locked, he whirled on the cashier and demanded the keys. When Martin refused, he was shot dead. After a fruitless search for the keys, the cash till was rifled—yielding only a humiliating two hundred dollars, and the bandits hurried out to their horses and got away before the town was aware of what had happened.

There was no pursuit. But measured in dollars, bank robbery had hit an all-time low. It may explain why the James-Younger Gang turned their talents in a new direction on September 26 of that year with the much disputed so-called Fairgrounds Robbery. Some writers of note say it never happened. But Buell, who was there, covering the fair for the Kansas City *Journal*, in his account of the robbery established a series of facts that his detractors have not been able to refute.

The Kansas City Fair had been in progress for several days, long enough for anyone who was interested to discover how the daily receipts, amounting to five to ten thousand dollars, were being handled. By arrangement with the First National Bank of Kansas City, the Fair Association was able to send the money into town for deposit after regular banking hours. A few minutes after 4 P.M. on September 26, a messenger (not a boy, as the scoffers have it) stepped out of the Fairgrounds office carrying a tin box in which reposed the day's receipts in paper currency. The amount of silver taken in at the gate would have been too heavy to be carried to the bank by messenger. Then, too, silver would be required for the following day's business.

In his account of the robbery, Buell says nothing about the tin box being heavy. At the time there was no reason why he should; a score of people saw the messenger carrying it. But now, a century later, it is the pivotal point on which his detractors base their case against him.

According to Buell, the robbery was committed by three men, one of whom had leaped down from the saddle. As the messenger carrying the tin box was hurrying to his rig for the short ride into town, the bandit snatched it and handed it to one of his mounted companions. "When all three were ready to make their get-away, they fired a few shots into the air to cow the gathering crowd, and fled," relates Buell. "A young girl was knocked down by one of their horses. It was at first thought that she had been shot, but that was not the case."

Wellman identifies the desperadoes as Jesse James, Frank James, and Bob Younger. It was the sort of bizarre adventure in which Jesse gloried. As for the Pinkertons, they were dismayed to discover that the outlaw gang they had been trying to run to earth for three years was alive and well and committing a bold robbery under their very noses.

In the long list of robberies committed by the James-Younger Gang the principals were nearly always the same—Frank, Jesse, the Younger brothers, and Clell Miller, George Shepherd, and one or two others. But they were abetted by almost a score of lesser lights who were at their beck and call. Some were "kissing cousins" of the Youngers; some were not. Without exception they were back-country illiterates of limited intelligence. Sometimes the trust Jesse reposed in them was misplaced and they failed him. Several paid for their mistakes with their lives; others, given the choice between long imprisonment and telling what they knew, refused to turn traitor. That they received a "cut" of the proceeds of a robbery in which they had played a minor role is unquestionable, nor can it be doubted that when they needed to make a "touch" they knew to whom to turn.

Perhaps no one in the United States had a livelier interest in the marauding of the James-Younger Gang than Richard K. Fox, the millionaire New York publisher of the sensational pink-paper *National Police Gazette*, which was to be found in every barber shop in the country. Its writers and artists lavished their unremitting attention on the exploits of the robber gang, real or imagined.

Other publications, hardly less lurid, treated their readers to similar tales. What effect this publicity had on Jesse is unknown. Perhaps, in today's vernacular, he didn't read his own press notices. But very likely he did, for bank robbery appears to have palled on him and he was casting about for something new to do; something more sensational. The unlikely tale persists that some member of the gang, on being released from the Missouri State Penitentiary, where he had become acquainted with John Reno, the Indiana train robber, convinced Jesse that an express car could be looted as easily as a bank and would pay better.

This ignores the fact that robbing the steam cars was no longer that new: counting the Verdi robbery, at least half a dozen trains had been stopped. It could hardly have required any prodding to turn Jesse's thoughts in that direction.

On May 23, 1873, they were back at their old trade, crossing the state to the district known locally as Swampeast and stuck up the Ste. Genevieve Savings Association. Ste. Genevieve was a sleepy little town, hard by the Mississippi River, fifty-odd miles south of St. Louis. Settled by the French, more French than English was still spoken there. That only five men—Cole and Bob Younger, Clell Miller, Bill Chadwell, and Jesse—took part in the robbery is proof enough that the gang regarded it as a routine matter. They separated outside of town, two men riding in from one direction and three from another and timing themselves so that they met at the bank. Cole, Jesse, and Clell Miller went inside.

Cole had the grain sack. Into it went $4,000. They had no trouble, not a shot being fired. "As the five were mounting to leave, Cole's horse broke away. It was embarrassing, for the grain sack with the $4,000 was tied to the saddle horn. A Frenchman jogging into town obligingly caught the animal and turned it over to Cole. The bandits then jogged out of town. Ste. Genevieve was not yet aware that its bank had been robbed." [2]

Shortly after their return to their home bailiwick, Jesse was tipped off (by some unidentified source) that the Chicago and Rock Island Railroad was transporting large shipments of gold coin from California to the East. Stopping a through express and making a big strike appealed to his love of the spectacular. When he broached the subject to the others, Cole and Clell Miller refused to listen. He could not have been unaware of their growing animosity. The pot boiled over when his brother Frank took sides with them —the three men he needed most. "We were heartily sick of his high-handed manner and the airs he had been giving himself," Cole Younger wrote many years later. [3]

XVIII

Robbery on the Rails

No ONE has pretended to know how the breach was healed. However, the confrontation was serious enough to threaten Jesse's leadership and the breaking up of the gang. It wasn't in Jesse's nature to eat humble pie, but in this instance he must have backed away and changed his tone if not his tune. Somehow, he won them over and on a hot mid-July Sunday evening Jesse and seven others left Clay County and headed north for Adair, Iowa, a station on the Chicago and Rock Island Railroad, some sixty miles east of Council Bluffs. With him were his brother Frank, Cole, Jim, and Bob Younger, Clell Miller, Bill Chadwell, and Charlie Pitts.

It was after dark when they reached the vicinity of Adair on the evening of July 21, 1873. They were in unfamiliar country, a good 130 miles from home. Presumably they knew when the train would be coming through; it would not stop at the tiny settlement of Adair. With several hours to wait, they broke into a shed in which track workers kept their tools. Securing a spike bar and sledgehammer, they rode a short distance east of town to a hidden curve. After prying off a fishplate, they removed the spikes from a rail and fastened a rope around it so that it could be pulled out of alignment. Concealing themselves in the high brush at the side of the right-of-way, they settled down to what must have seemed endless waiting. Actually, it was no later than midnight when they

173

caught sight of the big headlight of the eastbound express knifing through the night.

As the locomotive took the curve, the startled fireman screamed a warning to Engineer John Rafferty as he saw the loosened steel rail being pulled out of position. Rafferty threw his engine into reverse. But there wasn't time; the locomotive keeled over on its side, crushing Rafferty, the escaping steam scalding him to death. The fireman was seriously injured but was able to crawl out of the cab.

Cole, Jesse, and Clell Miller got into the express car and rifled the safe. It yielded less than $3,000. Chadwell and Jim Younger collected a bit more from the passengers when they went through the coaches with their greedy grain sack.[1]

There were no arrests; but the Pinkertons questioned the passengers and on the information they gathered charged the Rock Island robbery and the killing of Engineer Rafferty to the James-Younger Gang. If Jesse wanted to see his name in the newspapers, he more than got his wish; from coast to coast the headlines reviled him as a merciless fiend who, without any thought for the lives of the crew and passengers, had wrecked a train so that he might rob it. Someone wrote a teary ballad entitled "Dan Rafferty, the Brave Engineer," which became immensely popular, the forerunner of such classics of the rails as "Casey Jones," "In the Baggage Coach Ahead" and "The Wreck of Old 97." [2]

It is worth noting that of the eight men who took part in the Adair train robbery, five were subsequently to die violent deaths. Bob Younger, who never fully recovered from the wounds he received in 1876 in the Northfield robbery, died in prison. Only Cole Younger and Frank James were to die in bed of natural causes.

The railroads now joined the banks in a united effort to track down the bandits. Although the Pinkertons brought in additional men and redoubled their efforts, Jesse and his followers slipped out of Missouri and took up temporary residence with old Tom Starr again. On January 15, 1874, in what was certainly an offbeat job, they held up the Hot Springs–Little Rock stage at Malvern, Arkansas, looting the passengers of several hundred dollars. Their real destination on this foray was the village of Gads Hill, Missouri, on the St. Louis, Iron Mountain and Southern Railroad, which allegedly was transporting sizable amounts of money to the Mound City. Again they were acting on information Jesse had received from one of his numerous spies.

They reached the vicinity of the village of Gads Hill in the early evening of January 31, 1874, and closed in on the railroad station shortly after dark, where they found a half dozen young rustics waiting to see the express go through. They herded them into the tiny waiting room and tied up the agent. When the train appeared out of the darkness, it was flagged. The engineer and fireman were invited to step down from the cab, and they obliged when they saw half a dozen guns trained on them. Jesse and Cole climbed through the door of the express car and ordered the messenger to open the safe.

Meanwhile, as the rest of the train crew was held at bay, Clell Miller and Charlie Pitts went through the coaches taking up a collection. Everything had gone so smoothly that the holdup had not taken more than a quarter of an hour. As the bandits were about to ride away, Jesse spoke to the conductor. "When you see the reporters, tell 'em you were talking to Jesse James."

It was a workmanlike job. Jesse was proud of it. Regrettably, however, there was less than $3,000 in the grain sack. "But getting into the saddle, they fired a few shots into the air just for the hell of it," says Stewart Holbrook, "and lit out for the Missouri-Arkansas line."

Under pressure from their employers, the railroads and the bankers, the Pinkerton Agency sent its best men into Missouri in an all-out effort to run the James-Younger band to earth, trusting that they might succeed where other able men had failed.

It was an almost suicidal assignment. Their greatest danger lay in being unmasked as Pinkertons. Gathering information was almost impossible, for in addition to the network of spies Jesse had established were other hundreds who, fearing for their own safety, refused to speak.

Somehow, detectives Louis J. Lull and James Wright learned that the Younger bandits sometimes gathered in the vicinity of Monegaw Springs, in St. Clair County, a sparsely populated, heavily-wooded country, cut up by small rushing streams and hidden valleys. Knowing they were putting their lives on the line, they made their way into St. Clair County, accompanied by E. B. Daniels, a former peace officer in adjoining Benton County. Posing as stock buyers looking for cattle and horses, an old dodge used by the outlaws themselves at times, gave them an excuse for stopping at the small roadside farms along the way.

Of course they could never be sure whether the backwoodsman with whom they were speaking was a friend or enemy of the Youngers; but they knew well enough from the answers they got that word that strangers were in the country had gone winging up and down the valleys.

On the afternoon of March 16, they pulled up at the home of a farmer named Snuffer, a friend, if not a distant relative, of the Youngers. They were watched as they dismounted and walked to the door. Snuffer himself opened it in response to their rapping. Instead of giving them the usual hill-country invitation to "come in and sit," he looked them over and asked their business. Lull made some talk about buying cattle or a good horse. Snuffer shook his head; he had no livestock for sale. Lull then asked if the farmer could direct them to the Widow Simms's place. It was a safe name to use, a dozen families of Simmses lived in that part of St. Clair County.

"Jest keep to this trail; 'bout five miles will bring you to her place."

The detectives thanked Snuffer for the information, not knowing that Jim and John Younger were concealed in the unfinished attic, overhearing every word. Getting into the saddle, the officers rode on.

Young John Younger hurried down the ladder from the attic, his brother Jim only a step behind him. Both were convinced that the "cattle buyers" were Pinkertons. They ran to the barn, saddled their horses, and took off after the strangers.

The three detectives had not gone more than half a mile when they heard the hard pounding of horses' hooves behind them. Wright, realizing what it meant, put spurs to his horse and fled; in a moment, Lull and Daniels found themselves confronted by the Younger brothers, Jim armed with a pair of pistols, John with a shotgun.

On command, Daniels tossed his revolver into the dust; Lull threw down a brace of pistols. Under his shirt, he had a third weapon. A few remarks, freighted with death, were exchanged. Desperate, Lull snatched out his hidden pistol and fired a shot that killed John Younger. The latter, as he was tumbling to the ground, pressed the trigger of his shotgun. Lull fell, mortally stricken as the load of buckshot ripped into his chest.

Jim Younger, seeing his brother lying dead in the road, wild with grief and rage, killed Daniels. Picking up his dead brother, he carried the body back to Snuffer's farm and buried it in the apple orchard.

Some time later two men in a wagon happened on the scene of the slayings. Detective Lull was still alive. He was taken to the nearby village of Roscoe, where he succumbed a few weeks later.

That day, March 16, 1874, was to be marked by another slaying. Several days earlier, Pinkerton operative John W. Whicher, a brave and determined man, had arrived in Liberty, in faraway Clay County, the stronghold of the James-Younger Gang. He had come for the purpose of watching the comings and goings at the Samuel place, outside the village of Kearney (formerly named Centreville). Dressed as an itinerant laborer, it was his intention to find work at some nearby farm.

He left Liberty on the morning of the sixteenth and walked all the way to Kearney, arriving there in the early evening. He was then only four miles from the Samuel farm. To avoid having to answer questions, he went on. What he didn't know was that he had been spied on all the way. It may have been as late as ten o'clock when a steely-eyed man, with a cocked revolver aimed at him, stepped out from a pile of dead brush and ordered him to stop. It was Jesse himself. He was joined a moment later by Frank James, Clell Miller, and a gang hanger-on by the name of Jim Latche.

Whicher must have realized that his fate was sealed as he told his faltering story of being a penniless itinerant looking for work. Jesse asked him to show his hands. They were not the hands of a farmhand. That was enough. They killed him and carted the body across the county line and dumped it in Jackson County, the Younger home bailiwick—a scurvy trick to cast suspicion on them, which Cole never forgave.

In sharp contrast to the recurring robberies and killings, a long interlude of peace and quiet seemed to settle on the James brothers. Not without reason, for both of them married in 1874. Somehow, one pictures them as old men by then. But they were not: Frank was thirty and Jesse only twenty-seven. Frank eloped with Annie Ralston, his long-time sweetheart: Jesse married his cousin, Zerelda Mimms, something he had wanted to do for eight years. She had nursed him back to health in her parents' home at Rullo when he had been seriously wounded in trying to surrender to Union soldiers at the close of the war. With the bravado that was part of him, he rode alone into Kansas City, wearing his finest outfit, and married Zerelda before a minister.

Both girls had the respect of all who knew them. The manner in which they remained loyal to their husbands in the years that followed is proof enough that they deserved it. When Frank and Jesse were "on the dodge," as they often were, Annie and Zerelda followed them whenever possible, living in rough cabins, even caves, shut off from society and in constant fear for their safety.[3]

The Pinkertons had not relaxed their pursuit of the James-Younger Gang. Robert Pinkerton had come out from Chicago and taken charge of the Kansas City office. He was searching among his operatives for one brave and rash enough to volunteer to go into

Clay County and remain there if he could, gathering information and transmitting it to him by telegraph—in code. He found the man he wanted in Jack Ladd.

Ladd had better luck than Whicher. Wearing rough clothes and having some experience in handling horses and cattle, he got a job with Dan Askew, whose farm was no more than a mile from the Samuels' place. He talked the farmer's lingo and worked so hard that he was not suspected of being other than what he seemed to be. He managed to keep a close eye on the Samuel house, and when he noticed some unusual activity there, he concluded that it could only mean that Jesse and Frank were visiting their mother and the Samuel family. How he managed to get a wire off to his boss without coming under instant suspicion has never been disclosed.

Robert Pinkerton lost no time getting into action. He asked the Hannibal and St. Joe Railroad to ready a special train of two boxcars for the horses that would be needed and a coach for the posse he was organizing. The special pulled out of Kansas City at eight o'clock the same evening, January 5, 1875. Of the train crew, only Conductor William Westphal knew its destination. His orders were to stop at a crossroad two miles south of Kearney, permit the possemen and their horses to disembark, and then steam on to Lathrop, a junction point on the main line of the railroad. This secrecy was imposed to prevent the news getting out that an armed posse had invaded Clay County.

Without incident the Pinkerton party reached the Samuel house around 10 P.M. and quickly had it surrounded. It was a bitter-cold night, the silence broken only by the horses champing on their bits. The house was in darkness save for the faint glow from a fireplace, indicating that the family was asleep.

What followed has always been told one way by the Pinkertons and quite differently by others. All stories agree, however, that a living-room window was opened and that a device of some sort tossed into the house. The Pinkertons insisted that it was only a round iron oil pot equipped with a burning wick, such as were used as warning lights at construction sites after dark. A shocked and outraged public charged that it was a deadly grenade, a leftover from the Civil War.

Whatever it was, it exploded. Of the five people in the house only old Susse escaped death or injury. Mrs. Samuel's right arm was torn off at the elbow. Little Archie Samuel was disemboweled and died before daylight. His little sister Fannie was severely burned. Dr. Samuel received numerous cuts and burns.

The bitter irony of the tragedy was that Frank and Jesse were several hundred miles away. Detective Jack Ladd, whose blunder was responsible for what had happened, got out of Missouri immediately. If one thing was certain, it was that Frank and Jesse would not let the mutilating of their mother and the killing of their half-brother go unavenged. On April 12, three months later, Jesse rode up to the home of Dan Askew, the farmer who had employed Ladd and was an innocent victim of the circumstances, and shot him dead without waiting for an explanation.

"That blast in the Samuel home ended the usefulness of the Pinkertons," says Wellman. If he means "in Missouri," it is too obviously true to be doubted. They had not only lost face but had dried up the rivulets of information they had been at such pains to keep flowing.

Jesse and his brother had slipped away with their wives and were not seen again in Missouri for nine months. As previously noted, they had relatives in and around Nashville, Tennessee. It was there that they spent most of 1875, Jesse using the alias of J. B. Howard, and Frank, not so fanciful, became plain Frank Woods—not Frank Woodson, as some accounts have it. Although the law had many grudges against them, there is nothing in the accumulated evidence to indicate that they had to live a watchful, secluded life during their stay in Tennessee. They attended church regularly and on several occasions Jesse was invited to deliver the sermon.

The Huntington, West Virginia, National Bank was held up on September 1, 1875. Huntington was no great distance from Nashville for such long riders as Frank and Jesse. Becoming restless with their inactivity, it is possible that they visited the town, figured that the bank would be an easy touch, and relayed word to the gang. There is no evidence that they participated in the robbery, which netted the bandits very little and cost them a man, later identified as Art McCoy, who, if ever a member of the James-Younger band, was never recognized as such.

But late that year the James brothers, the Youngers, Clell Miller, and others served notice that they were back on the job. On the evening of December 13, at the tiny village of Muncie, Kansas, a few miles west of Kansas City, they held up the Kansas Pacific Railroad's eastbound night express from Denver, using much the same tactics they had employed in their train robbery at Gads Hill. Muncie, of course, was not a scheduled stop for the fast express (forty miles an hour), but they flagged it down, after herding the little crowd, which was on hand to see it pass, into the tiny depot. The express car was cut off and the engineer ordered to proceed down the track a hundred yards. While some of the gang went through the coaches with the grain sack, the rest went to work on the express car.

Frank Webster, the express messenger, on being given his choice of opening the door or being blown to high heaven, ran the door back and was promptly slugged unconscious for his cooperation.

This time they hit the jackpot, gathering in $60,000, the richest haul they ever made.

A few days later Bud McDaniels, a long-time member of the gang, was picked up on a drunk and disorderly charge by the Kansas City Police. He had over a thousand dollars on him, for which he could not account. Subjected to intense grilling, he confessed taking part in the Muncie robbery. He was brought to trial in Topeka and sentenced to ten years in Leavenworth. He escaped his guards as he was being taken to the penitentiary. A posse of prison guards and sheriff's deputies tracked him down and blasted him into eternity. The rest of the gang had already found a safe refuge in Arkansas, the Indian Territory, or Texas.

During their absence from Missouri, several stage holdups were attributed to them. Considering how flush they were, such minor incidents must have been undertaken for the sport of it, or because thievery had become their way of life.

By early summer they were back in their old stamping ground. On July 7, 1876, they stopped the Missouri Pacific's *Kansas City–St. Louis Flyer* at Otterville, a few miles east of Sedalia. At a spot around a curve that the engineer of the oncoming train would not be able to see until he was almost upon it, they piled wooden ties on the track. The surrounding wooded, thinly populated country, with which they were well acquainted, couldn't have been more favorable for a safe getaway.

This was a daylight robbery, but they heard the train approaching before it came into view. On rounding the curve, the engineer saw the ties piled high on the track. He slapped on the air and the train ground to a stop, brakes screeching. He and the rest of the crew offered no resistance as the bandits lined them up beside the cars. Cole, Jesse, Clell Miller, and Charlie Pitts climbed into the express car. The messenger tossed the keys to Jesse and backed away, hands raised. But the safe, bound from Denver to Chicago, was supposedly a "through" safe, which could not be opened until it had reached its destination.

But the robbers were not to be stopped. Swinging the pick and ax with which most express cars were provided for emergency use in case of a wreck, they hacked a hole through the top of the safe and, reaching through the opening, sprang the time lock.

This is a familiar incident, presented by many writers. It is wholly untrue; the time lock would have been encased in the thick steel door and could not have been manipulated from within the safe.

In any event, the desperadoes took away from the Otterville robbery no more than an estimated $8,000, which further refutes the nonsense that the *St. Louis Flyer* was carrying a rich shipment of money in a "through" safe.

Several weeks later, Hobbs Kerry, as the result of some loose talking, was arrested by the St. Louis police—not the Pinkertons—

and under grilling confessed that he had taken part in the Otterville robbery. He was tried, convicted, and sentenced to four years at hard labor in the Missouri penitentiary. Although he had been a recognized member of the James-Younger Gang, he had never been regarded as overly bright, and for that reason had been relegated to a minor role in its affairs.

Of far greater importance to Jesse than losing Hobbs Kerry—had he known it—was the increasing influence Bill Chadwell, new to the gang, was gaining with him. As the future was to prove, he should have run from him as from the black plague.

Bill Chadwell—born William Stiles—a horse thief and all-around minor desperado, was a refugee from Minnesota, where he was wanted for various crimes. A small, swarthy-faced man, with a mouthful of prominent teeth, he was a persuasive talker. His argument was that the gang was wasting its time making small touches in Missouri, when it just as easily could make a real killing up north in Minnesota, where the country banks were bulging with money and bank robbery was practically unknown.

How could they miss with—according to him—only a bunch of foreigners, Swedes, Norwegians, bohunks, to deal with?

Not only Jesse, but Frank, the Youngers, Clell, and other gang stalwarts began to listen and catch fire. They didn't know it, but what they were heading for was disaster.

XIX

High Noon at Northfield

IN HIS little paperback, *The Story of Cole Younger, by Himself*, published more than a quarter of a century later, Cole Younger holds Jesse personally responsible for promoting and organizing the misadventure in Minnesota. The evidence is indisputable, however, that Cole abetted Jesse's planning, even acceding to the latter's request that he write his brother Jim, who was ranching out in San Luis Obispo County, California, and through with outlawry, urging him to come back for one "last" ride.

Cole's letter brought Jim hurrying back to the old haunts in Missouri, and early in August, Jesse named the seven men who were to accompany him on the long jaunt north to Minnesota: his brother Frank, Cole, Bob and Jim Younger, Clell Miller, Charlie Pitts, and Bill Chadwell.

Although they were horseback outlaws, never so sure of themselves as when in the saddle, they broke with tradition when they left Missouri, traveling by train and in pairs to avoid suspicion. Two days later they rendezvoused safely in St. Paul, some of them putting up at the Merchants' Hotel and the others at the adjacent European Hotel.

The first order of business was to equip themselves with good horses and riding gear, meanwhile gathering what information they could about the roads and the towns in the southern part of the state. It was pleasant country, at its best at that time of the year, the dirt roads smoothed out in tawny dust. The dust didn't bother them for they had equipped themselves with long white linen dusters, the accepted garb for men moving about the country— farm buyers, land speculators, lightning rod salesmen and seed men. For the James-Younger Gang, the long linen coats served not only to protect them from the dust but to conceal the weapons they were wearing. To avoid suspicion, they abstained from riding through the country with a Winchester showing in a saddle boot.

In the evening, back in St. Paul, Jesse and the others exchanged what information they had gathered in the course of the day. By the end of the week, based on what they had learned, there wasn't any doubt about it: the First National Bank of Mankato promised the richest pickings. Mankato, halfway across the state at the big bend of the Minnesota River, was a thriving town. To the west there were only a few small villages between it and the South Dakota line, promising easy escape in that direction.

Shortly after dawn on September 3, 1876, the gang made camp in a stand of timber a mile and a half east of Mankato. Shortly after noon Jesse and Charlie Pitts jogged into town to size up the bank and acquaint themselves with the streets and adjacent buildings. When they turned a corner into the main thoroughfare, they were taken aback by the sight of several hundred townsfolk gathered on the sidewalk facing the bank, watching a crew of men putting a new ornamental metal cornice in place on the roof of the bank building, a job that obviously would not be finished until late the following day, with a crowd of onlookers hanging on to the end.

Jesse and Pitts exchanged an understanding glance; the Mankato First National Bank would have to be forgotten. That was the discouraging word they carried back to the outlaw camp. It caused some dismay, but Bill Chadwell was ready with a suggestion: Why not have a go at Northfield, fifty miles to the east? Northfield, with a population of four thousand, was smaller than Mankato, but it was in the heart of the most prosperous farming area in the state. Its First National Bank was the richest bank in Rice County. In addition to its other resources, the town had the large payroll of the Ames and Company flouring mill.

As they listened to Chadwell, the disappointment over Mankato disappeared and they struck out that evening for Northfield. They rode most of the night, laid over the following day, and the next evening made camp on the Cannon River, several miles south of the town.

In the brief time they had been in Minnesota they had observed enough to convince them they were not dealing with the "bunch of ignorant Swedes, too dumb to get out of their own way" that Chadwell had dismissed so contemptuously. Minnesota was deer country, and among the late-comers from Europe, as well as the natives, there were few men who did not know how to use a rifle.

On September 6, riding in pairs and posing as farm buyers, the gang spread out over the country to the west of Northfield, acquainting themselves with the roads, rivers and bridges, and settling on the best escape route. Satisfied with what they had learned, they bivouacked again on the Cannon River, and the following morning Cole Younger and Clell Miller rode into Northfield for a close look at the bank and the business district. The latter centered on Bridge Square, so named because of the iron bridge that spanned the Cannon River, which, flowing from west to east, cut Northfield in two.

The day was hot for September, the sun riding high in a cloudless sky. On the bluffs overlooking Northfield, the modest buildings of little Carleton College could be observed among the young maples that were just beginning to don their autumnal dress. Down below, Bridge Square drowsed in quiet contentment.

The Scriver Block, a two-story brick and stone building on the southwest corner, dominated the square. Scriver's general store and the establishment of Lee and Hitchcock, furniture dealers, occupied the lower floor. The First National Bank was located at the rear end of the building, a few feet from the corner. There were offices on the second floor that were reached by an outside iron stairway.

Across the street from the bank entrance, Wheeler & Blackman conducted a drugstore, and next to it was a small hotel, the Dampier House. The bank had a back door which opened on an alley that gave access to Bridge Square. The Scriver Block formed one side of the alley; on the other were Northfield's two hardware stores. All were to play a part in what followed.[1]

Cole and Clell, wearing their dusters, smoking big cigars and looking like prosperous land buyers, took a leisurely turn around the square before leaving. The information they carried back to Jesse and the others was so favorable that the final touches were put on their plans in a few minutes. After they had finished at the bank, they would stop at the Winona & St. Peter railroad station and cut the telegraph wire to slow up pursuit.

Jesse named the three "inside" men who were to enter the bank: he, his brother Frank, and Charlie Pitts. They were to jog into town at once, leave their horses at the hitchrack in front of the Scriver Block, have lunch, and be waiting at the corner when the rest of the gang came roaring into town, guns blazing and screeching the old Rebel yell. Bob Younger, Clell, and Chadwell were to come in from the south; Cole and Jim Younger from the west. The five of them were to move up to the outskirts of town and wait there until the clock in the belfry of the Lutheran church struck one. That was to be the signal for the wild dash into town, the two groups timing themselves so they would reach Bridge Square within a minute or two of each other.

It was a few minutes to twelve when Jesse, Frank, and Charlie Pitts walked their horses across the Division Street bridge and tethered them in front of the Scriver Block. When they asked a passer-by where they could find a good place to eat, they were directed to Jefft's Restaurant, a few doors up the street. They unbuttoned their dusters as they sat down but did not remove them.

The proprietor himself waited on them, little suspecting that he was serving three of the most notorious outlaws in America. They were heading west, Jesse told him, to look at some farms out Mankato way.

When they finished paying their check, Jefft treated them to cigars. "They sure were a jolly bunch," he testified later.

The strangers strolled back down the street, and having a few minutes to wait, sat down on a packing case in front of Manning's hardware store. The church bell struck the hour presently. The three bandits walked leisurely to their horses and, to have something to do, pretended to examine the riding gear. Then, suddenly, it happened: Bob Younger, Bill Chadwell, and Clell Miller roared into town, yelling like savages, their guns blazing. As they thundered across the bridge, Cole and Jim Younger swept in from the west, their .45's barking.

The startled citizenry dashed for cover. For a moment or two it looked as though Northfield had been thoroughly cowed. Jesse, Charlie Pitts, and Frank James hurried into the bank. Out in the middle of the street, Cole dismounted, a pistol in each hand.

Nicholas Gustavson, a boy of seventeen who had recently arrived from Sweden and who knew no English, started to run across the street. Cole yelled at him to get back inside one of the stores. When the boy, not understanding the command, failed to stop, Cole killed him. Meanwhile, Bob and Jim Younger and Clell Miller were shooting right and left to keep the street clear.

From a second-floor window of his father's drugstore, Henry Wheeler, a college student home on vacation, saw young Gustavson killed. He said later that he had no doubt that the bank was being robbed; he had done a lot of hunting and wanted to get into the battle, but his rifle was at home, blocks away. "I remembered that an Army rifle and a sack of cartridges was kept behind the desk at the Dampier House," he was quoted as saying in an interview that appeared in a St. Paul newspaper. "I figured if I could get my hands on it I could run upstairs to one of the front rooms of the hotel and start shooting from the window. When I stepped out of the drugstore, a bullet whizzed by so close it drove me back. I made it the next time. I snatched up the rifle and cartridges behind the desk and raced upstairs.

"Across the street, a man on horseback saw me and snapped

a shot at me. He was using a pistol. I took dead aim on him and he tumbled out of the saddle and lay still. I knew I had killed him."

It was Clell Miller, veteran of a score of raids and robberies, who lay huddled in the dust.

By now there was shooting from a dozen directions. Manning and Allen, the proprietors of the two hardware stores, had been handing out loaded rifles to whoever wanted to use them. Manning himself got into the action. Stepping around the corner of his building, in full sight of the bandits, he put a bullet into Cole Younger's right shoulder. Cole started to charge him but turned back when a second slug tore his hat from his head. From a window in the Scriver Block, a man was blasting away with a shotgun, his shells loaded with No. 6 shot, too light to do much damage at thirty yards. But the pellets stung. They bloodied Bill Chadwell's face and half blinded him as he weaved about. Manning dropped him with a bullet through the heart. Two of the Youngers were also struck.

Bob Younger's horse was struck. Bob leaped clear and as the animal fell ran to the foot of the iron stairway that led up to the second floor of the Scriver Block. He found little cover there; from across the way, young Wheeler could see him. His aim was good and he shattered Bob's right elbow.

Seeing how things were going, Cole ran into the bank and yelled, "Come on! They're killing us!"

When they walked into the First National, Jesse, Frank, and Charlie Pitts had found three men facing them: Joseph Heywood, the cashier, Frank Wilcox, and A. E. Bunker, tellers. The outer door of the vault stood open. Jesse stepped through the swinging gate in the counter and confronted Heywood with his pistol, ordering the cashier to open the inner door. This Heywood refused to do. Jesse drove him back and stepped into the open vault. Heywood reached for the door to lock him in. Pitts knocked the cashier's hand away and felled him with the barrel of his pistol.

Bunker made a break for the back door at that moment. The door was latched but he hit it hard enough to go crashing through.

Pitts fired at him and missed. Jim Younger had ridden around the corner of the bank and was in the alley. He snapped a shot at Bunker that struck the teller and drove him to his knees. But he recovered his balance and disappeared through the side entrance of Manning's store. Wilcox, the other teller, stood facing the wall, hands raised, and was not harmed.

Many accounts of the battle have it that while the inner door of the vault was closed, it was not locked. Had Jesse given it a tug, it would have swung open. His failure to do so can best be explained by his realization that the swelling thunder of gunfire without was making it more important to get out of town alive than looting the bank. When Cole sounded his desperate call, Jesse hesitated only long enough to loot the counter tills before backing toward the door with his brother and Pitts. When he saw Heywood reach under the counter for a gun, he put a bullet into his brain, killing him instantly.

Jesse knew they had run into trouble, but he had not realized how serious it was. Clell and Chadwell were lying dead in the street. Cole had been struck half a dozen times; his face was smeared with blood. Jim Younger's jaw had been shot away and both shoulders pierced by bullets. Bob, under the iron stairs, was trying to work his pistol with his left hand, his right arm hanging uselessly at his side.

As they were mounting their horses, a bullet tore through Frank's right leg between the knee and thigh.

The story that Bob Younger thought they were about to leave him behind when they made their dash from town has been told so often that most people accept it today.[2] "Don't desert me boys, I'm shot!" he is supposed to have cried as he ran out from the stairs. He had no horse, of course. The same sources say that Cole got Bob up behind him and raced after the others.

This story first appeared in the *National Police Gazette*, in which so many myths were given birth. It must have been written by an Easterner. Bob Younger, with his right arm hanging helplessly at his side, could not have clung to Cole if he had got up behind. We can be sure that he got up in front of his brother for the mad dash from Northfield.

In their haste, they did not stop to cut the telegraph wire as they had planned, and which they should have done at all costs, for when the Northfield operator began putting news of the raid on the wire, he did not leave his key until the entire state had been aroused. By nightfall hundreds of men had taken up the trail of the fugitives. Posses were everywhere the following day, and in the confusion they often found themselves hunting one another.

Rewards totaling several thousand dollars were posted for the capture of the bandits. Miraculously, however, the fleeing men eluded pursuit, which becomes the more remarkable considering the condition they were in. They had relieved a farmer of his horse and saddle for Bob. But of the six, only Charlie Pitts was not injured.

The fugitives were moving in a southwesterly direction, proceeding mostly by night. Their condition was steadily worsening, Jim Younger growing weaker every day and slowing them up. That he must die unless he was soon given medical attention seemed certain. The only food they had was what could be purloined from a farmer's truck patch or henhouse.

They had been dodging pursuit for a week when the heavens opened and rain fell in torrents, day after day, turning dirt roads into quagmires. Swamps and sloughs became treacherous morasses in which both horses and men mired and had to turn back. The surrounding forests, wet, dripping, became dark and gloomy caverns, clogged with underbrush, with trails washed out. Hundreds of wet and weary possemen gave up the search and returned home, discouraged and bedraggled. New men took their place and the great manhunt continued. Several times they stumbled upon one of the camps where the outlaws had bivouacked and found bloody rags they had left behind after caring for the wounded.

A few miles west and south of the little town of Medalia, Jesse brought matters to a head by declaring that they would have to do something about Jim Younger, who could no longer sit in a saddle without being supported. "The best thing to do is put him out of his misery so the rest of us can get going."

Cole recalled that moment many years later. "I said, if you shoot him I'll kill you." Frank also spoke up, saying, "We're not going to kill Jim, or anyone else. What we can do is split up."

The Youngers stuck together and Charlie Pitts elected to stick with them; stony-faced Frank and Jesse struck off by themselves.

Nothing further was heard of the James brothers until a Nobles County farmer, eighty miles to the west, reported that at gun point they had exchanged their worn-out mounts for two of his best horses. Although they were unacquainted with the country through which they were fleeing, it was now obvious that they were bent on getting out of Minnesota and heading for South Dakota. That was confirmed when a Dr. Mosher, of Sioux Falls, driving back to town in his buggy after visiting a patient, was stopped by two men who forced him to dress their wounds, after which he was made to exchange clothes with one of them (Jesse, no doubt) to make identification more difficult. After that, nothing. As the months, then the years passed, it became the widely accepted opinion—without any corroborating evidence being offered—that Frank and Jesse had made their way to Mexico or to one of the banana republics of Central America, where they had been joined by their wives. One can only add—perhaps.

The Younger brothers and Charlie Pitts were still mired in Hanska Slough when Frank and Jesse got out of Minnesota. Their horses had played out, and they were trying to proceed on foot. Jim was barely able to walk; Cole, leaning on a staff he had fashioned for himself, stumbled along; Bob was in terrible shape. Only Charlie Pitts, unhurt, had any fight left in him. They were so desperate for food that in broad daylight Charlie made his way to a farmhouse and bought eggs, bread, and a slab of bacon. He was followed when he returned to camp. An hour later the rendezvous was located by Sheriff Jim Glispin of Watonwan County and a posse of a hundred men.

They surrounded the patch of dense timber and brush and

began firing. The fire was answered, but again it was an unequal confrontation, pistols against rifles. The sheriff and half a dozen possemen, risking their lives to catch a glimpse of the fugitives, moved in. Glispin and Charlie Pitts got a flash of each other at the same moment. Both fired and Charlie went down, dead as he sank to the ground. The others tried to fall back, only to run into gunfire from that direction. Cole and Jim were struck again and went down. Only Bob was left standing. Clutching his .45 in his left hand, he continued firing until it was empty. There was no going on.

"Hold your fire!" he cried. "We give up!"

"Throw your gun away!" Glispin called back.

Bob obeyed, and in a few minutes he and his brothers were prisoners. The great manhunt was over. It was September 21, an even two weeks from the day the James-Younger Gang had held Northfield at bay for a few minutes.

The wounded prisoners were taken by wagon to Medalia, and after doctors had done what was immediately possible, they were moved by train to Faribault, the Rice County seat. News of the capture of the bandits rocked the state. As the prisoners began to mend, they were questioned about the two who had got away, but the Youngers refused to identify them, insisting that they had known them only as Howard and Woods, newcomers to the gang. Of course, those were only the aliases Jesse and Frank had used in Tennessee.

Weeks passed before they were well enough to be brought to trial to answer four indictments: the murder of cashier Joseph L. Heywood; the murder of Nicholas Gustavson; assault with a deadly weapon on A. E. Bunker, bank teller; and robbery of the First National Bank. They had no defense and were in grave jeopardy of being sentenced to hang. But under Minnesota law, a man charged with murder could not be hanged if he pleaded guilty. The Youngers decided to so plead. When the verdict was read, they listened with bowed heads: they were to be confined in the state penitentiary at Stillwater for the rest of their natural lives.

XX

The Wages of Outlawry

ON THE evening of October 7, 1879, three years and a month after
the shoot-out at Northfield and the subsequent escape of Frank
and Jesse James, a Chicago and Alton express was flagged down
and robbed twenty-two miles east of Kansas City, the railroad
company stating that $35,000 had been taken from the express car.
This was the "Glendale train robbery" made famous in the popular
ballad.

The details of the holdup were singularly reminiscent of those
employed so successfully by the old James-Younger Gang. It unleashed a flood of speculation; was it possible, men asked, that Frank
and Jesse were back, after their long disappearance. Not only were
they back, Jesse had put together a new gang. It did not compare
with the old. In it were second-raters, men with whom he would
have disdained to ride in former days. But times had changed, and
they were the best he could muster.

It is likely, as so many writers have speculated, that Frank and
Jesse had been living a life of ease in Mexico or one of the "banana
republics" in the years they had been away from Missouri and had
returned because their funds were running low. It is not of record
that they ever confirmed or denied such tales. Perhaps Cole
Younger shed some light on the subject when he said: "We never
got the huge sums the papers said. When we made a strike the

money had to be cut up ten ways. After a few months we were broke again."

The low caliber of the men with whom he had surrounded himself must have been a blow to Jesse's pride. In addition to his brother Frank, only two—Dick Liddil and Bill Ryan—had been recognized members of the original James-Younger Gang. Of the other six, Tucker Basham, an inexperienced farm boy, and Ed Miller, Clell's younger brother, were embarking on outlawry for the first time; Clarence and Wood Hite and the Ford brothers, Bob and Charley, were no better than two-bit thugs.

The first break in the Glendale holdup came when Tucker Basham, who had been doing some foolish talking, was picked up by the Kansas City police and could not explain how he came into possession of the big bankroll he had on his person. William H. Wallace, the recently elected prosecuting attorney of Jackson County, gave him a grilling that resulted in a full confession. He did not make it public, confident that he now had the ammunition to run the new James gang to earth. It began to pay off with the arrest in Nashville, Tennessee, of Bill Ryan, who was hustled back to Jackson County and placed on trial for his part in the Glendale robbery.

Tucker Basham remained behind bars, which was the safest place he could have found, for he had turned informer and as a consequence, his home had been burned down. Wallace's life was threatened but he was not to be cowed; he knew that public opinion in Jackson County was changing, that men who had condoned outlawry in the past were beginning to regard it in a different light.

That things had changed was made crystal clear to Jesse when Ryan was sentenced to twenty-five years in the Missouri penitentiary and Tucker Basham sent up for five years, he having turned state's evidence. It was incredible. In the old days no member of the James-Younger Gang could have been found guilty in Jackson County.

On July 10, 1881, Jesse led his followers across the state line and cracked the bank at Riverton, Iowa. As they expected, they got very little. But it was more or less just a practice run for what he had in mind.

On the night of July 15, three men, Frank, Jesse, and Dick Liddil, boarded a Rock Island train bound for Davenport and Chicago at Cameron, forty miles north of Kansas City and took seats in the smoker. William Westphal was the conductor. They scrutinized him carefully as he collected their tickets and nodded to one another as he passed. There was no doubt about it: he was the man Jesse and Frank wanted. This was to be more than just a holdup. They had been waiting four years to square accounts with Westphal, the conductor of the special that in 1875 had brought the Pinkertons to Kearney and the bombing of their parents' home.

The train stopped at Gallatin that evening and took on several passengers. As it pulled away from the depot, two men darted out of the shadows and swung aboard between the baggage car and tender. Climbing over the coal, they confronted the fireman and engineer with drawn revolvers. On approaching Winston, they ordered the engineer to stop the train. Conductor Westphal had re-entered the smoker to collect the tickets of the passengers who had got aboard at Gallatin. As he came up the aisle, Frank James leaped to his feet and fired at him and missed. Jesse's aim was deadly accurate.

Westphal was mortally wounded but he managed to reach the rear door. Plunging through it, he rolled down the steps and died on the station platform. In the smoker the terrified passengers cowered in their seats. One of them, Frank McMillan, a mason by trade, leaped to his feet and bolted for the door. He was killed before he reached it.

Killing Westphal was a matter of long-delayed vengeance, of course, but he was blameless if ever a man was. But not in Jesse's eyes.

After the double killing, the gang proceeded to rob the train. They didn't get much, estimates placing the take at between $8,000 and $9,000.

Rumors began flying that Governor Thomas T. Crittenden

was contemplating offering a reward of $10,000 for the capture of Frank and Jesse. When it got back to Jesse that Ed Miller had done some foolish talking about how easy it would be for one of the gang to collect it, he killed Miller with less compunction than he would have shown a mad dog. He was no longer the peerless leader, sure of the loyalty of his men. His brother Frank and Dick Liddil were the only ones left on whom he could count. Soon, Liddil was to play him false.

Another Chicago and Alton train was stopped at Blue Cut, Missouri, on September 7, the same year. If you disregard several stage holdups in which Jesse may or may not have had a hand (the evidence is slight), the Blue Cut robbery was his last.

In the days that followed, several incidents occurred that must have troubled Jesse. Dick Liddil had had a girl in Kansas City for some time, but he tired of her and transferred his affections to Martha Bolton, the young and buxom widowed sister of Bob and Charley Ford. It got him into trouble with Wood Hite, who felt he had prior rights to Martha. Hite went gunning for his rival and Liddil killed him.

Liddil must have regretted his impetuosity almost at once. He had not only violated the gang code but there was Clarence Hite, the dead man's brother, to be faced. Looking for a way out of his difficulties, Liddil sent Martha to Jefferson City to see the governor and find out what would happen to him if he gave himself up. Crittenden assured her that Liddil would be given clemency if he supplied information leading to the capture and conviction of other members of the gang.

When Liddil got the news, he lost no time surrendering himself to Prosecuting Attorney Wallace. The full confession the prosecutor got from him convinced Wallace that at last he had enough ammunition to bring Frank and Jesse to trial and convict them of armed robbery and murder.

On the strength of Liddil's confession, Clarence Hite, Wood Hite's brother, was taken into custody at his home in Richmond, Missouri, was convicted for his part in the Winston robbery, and sent to the Missouri penitentiary for the customary twenty-five years.[1]

Frank was now the only man Jesse had left. Of the gang he had recruited after Northfield, four were in prison: Bill Ryan, Tucker Basham, Dick Liddil, and Clarence Hite. Two were dead: Ed Miller and Wood Hite. The Ford brothers, Bob and Charley, rated no better than hangers-on. To tip the odds even more against Jesse, the State of Missouri had posted a reward of $10,000 for his capture dead or alive.

To repeat a question I posed many years ago: Why didn't Jesse get out of Missouri—or even out of the United States? There was still time. No one will ever know the answer. Using the alias of J. B. Howard, he settled in one of the better sections of St. Joseph with his wife and two children. He must have made a good impression on his neighbors, for they never suspected that the bearded gentleman living in the little white cottage was the most notorious outlaw in America. Many later recalled seeing him walking downtown with his son, holding the boy by the hand.

Governor Crittenden was in Kansas City early in January, stopping at the St. James Hotel. No one claims to know how it was arranged, but Bob Ford had a secret visit with him and made him a proposition: If the $10,000 reward on Jesse would be for taking him dead or alive, Ford and his brother would go after him, provided that Missouri would forgive the several grudges it had against them.

For the rest of his life Crittenden strenuously denied that he had made a deal with Bob Ford. But it was plain enough that he had conferred with him and certainly must have agreed to something. In a statement made under oath at the coroner's inquest, Ford testified that

> Governor Crittenden asked me if I thought I could catch Jesse James, and I answered yes. . . . The governor therefore agreed to pay $10,000 apiece for the production of Jesse and Frank James, either one or the other, whether dead or alive.

Shortly after breakfast, on the morning of April 3, 1882, a single shot was heard in the modest home in St. Joseph, in which Jesse was living. The neighbors ran in and found the bearded man lying dead on the floor. There is only Bob Ford's sworn statement for what had happened:

> Jesse and I had a talk yesterday about robbing the bank at Platte City, and which Charley and I both agreed to assist. . . . Between eight and nine o'clock this morning while the three of us were in a room in Jesse's house, Jesse pulled off his coat and also his pistols, two of which he constantly wore, then got up onto a chair for the purpose of brushing dust off a picture.
>
> While Jesse was thus engaged, Charley winked at me, so I knew he meant for me to shoot. So as quickly as possible, I drew my pistol and aiming at Jesse's head, which was no more than four feet from the muzzle of my weapon, I fired, and Jesse tumbled headlong from the chair on which he was standing and fell on his face.

A wave of revulsion at the cowardly manner in which the assassination had been accomplished swept over Missouri. On the street and in the newspapers, his crimes temporarily forgotten, Jesse became "our Jesse." Into instant and everlasting popularity sprang the ballad about the "Robbery of the Glendale Train" and its refrain:

> *The dirty little coward,*
> *Who shot Mr. Howard,*
> *Has laid poor Jesse in his grave.*

His mother buried Jesse in the yard of the Samuel place. The stone which marked the grave was inscribed:

> Jesse W. James
> Died April 3, 1882
> Aged 34 years, 6 months, 28 days.
> Murdered by a traitor and a coward whose
> name is not worthy to appear here.

Bob Ford got out of Missouri with his share of the reward. But no matter where he went, he could not run away from the stigma attached to his name. Some years later he was conducting a tent saloon in the booming mining camp of Crede, Colorado, when a desperado named Kelly walked in and caught him behind the bar. Pointing his gun at Ford, he is alleged to have said, "This one is for Jesse." Pulling the trigger, he put a slug through Ford's throat, the bullet striking the latter's collar button and driving it through his neck.

Charley Ford, in ill health and bogged down by the opprobrium attached to his name, committed suicide with a pistol in a clump of underbrush near his home in Richmond, Missouri, scene of one of the early raids of the James-Younger Gang.

Early in June, some eight weeks after the treacherous killing of Jesse, two women were ushered into Prosecutor Wallace's office in the Jackson County courthouse at Independence. The younger of the two was Annie James, the wife of Frank James. The one-armed woman who accompanied her was Zerelda Samuel, mother of the James boys. They were there to tell him that Frank was anxious to give himself up if he could surrender to Wallace personally.

"He is living in a perfect torment," Annie told him. "Afraid every minute that someone will kill him to claim the reward. If he surrenders to you will the reward be withdrawn?"

Wallace assured her that it would. He had to say no, however, when she asked if Frank could be released on bail, for there was an old but still "live" indictment against him in connection with the killing of John Whicher, the Pinkerton detective, and although there was little chance that a conviction could be obtained, a murder indictment was not bailable.

"Frank will be treated fairly," he told his visitors, "but he will have to take his chances with the law."

Several days later Wallace received a telegram from Governor Crittenden, informing him that Frank James had surrendered to him personally and was being sent under guard to Independence. "I realized that bringing Frank James to trial would have the wildest political repercussions," Wallace wrote much later. "Daviess County had a much better case against him for the killing of Frank McMillan, the stone mason, on the night of the Winston train robbery when Jesse killed Conductor Westphal. I therefore induced William D. Hamilton, the prosecutor of Daviess County, to bring Frank James to trial on the McMillan indictment."

When Frank James arrived in Independence, he was taken to Gallatin and lodged in the Daviess County jail. There he remained during the pre-trial wrangling. It was as near as he ever came to spending a day in prison.

No trial in the history of Missouri attracted such a throng as descended on Gallatin. Tempers ran high when young Hamilton announced that he was stepping out of the case and that Prosecuting Attorney William H. Wallace of Jackson County would conduct the prosecution for the state. The demonstrations within the courtroom, as well as without, told Wallace that he was battling something more potent than evidence. Despite his best legal maneuvering, he was convinced that he had a packed jury and that a conviction was impossible. He threatened to withdraw but was persuaded to continue, only after stating publicly: "We will simply try Frank James before the world. The verdict of the jury that has been selected is already written." [2]

As Wallace had predicted, Frank James was acquitted. General Jo Shelby and other graying veterans of the War Between the States hailed it as a great victory for the South, overlooking the fact that John F. Phillips, who had won Frank James his freedom, was an ex-Union officer.

A free man again, Frank and his wife moved in with his mother and half-sister on the old Samuel place, where they were joined a bit later by Jesse's widow and children. They lived frugally, not from choice but necessity, until Frank took the job of special policeman at the Tivoli Variety Theatre in St. Louis, where he became a bigger attraction than the comedians and dancing girls. During the fair season, he was employed as assistant starter or starter at the various Missouri and Arkansas race tracks.

Cole Younger and his brothers had been behind the walls at Stillwater for six years when Cole, who worked as a nurse in the prison hospital, was taken to the warden's office and informed that Bob Ford had assassinated Jesse. He offered no comment, for he felt that he could not recognize their old, close association without damaging his own case. But the news must have shaken him, his old friend, turned enemy, cut down in that fashion.

Newspapers were filled with pictures and accounts of the James-Younger Gang. In the *Kansas City Star*, a Missourian named Warren C. Bronaugh recognized in a picture of Cole the man who had saved his life in Civil War days, in the battle of Lone Jack. Although nearing fifty and in modest circumstances, Bronaugh felt that he must go to Stillwater and talk with Cole.

The incident on the Lone Jack road had slipped Cole's mind, but as he talked with Bronaugh through the steel mesh in the visitors' gallery, he recalled it. Before the interview was over—the first of several hundred that were to follow—Warren Carter Bronaugh had found his mission in life. No matter how long it took, no matter what it cost him, he was not going to stop until he had won pardons for the Younger brothers. It was to take him twenty-one years and impoverish him and his family.

Warren Bronaugh, perfectly sane, became a fanatic overnight, a man with a one-track mind from whom other men tried to escape if they saw him coming in time. He absorbed rebuffs like a duck sheds water. He wrote thousands of letters, interviewed hundreds of political leaders, clergymen, and educators, solicited funds to keep his campaign going, and conferred time after time with the Board of Pardons.

Cole and his brothers knew that Bronaugh was working to gain their release. At first, he raised their hopes, but after seven years of waiting had dragged by without anything happening, their faith in him began to fade.

In February, 1889, a reporter for a St. Paul paper, hoping for a story, brought Cole word that Belle Starr had met a violent death. All Cole had to say was, "I used to know the lady, but it has been a long time since I have seen her." Not a word about Pearl Younger, then in her early twenties, whom he had never seen or acknowledged.

Bob Younger had never fully recovered from the bullet wounds he had received in the Northfield shootout and had been assigned to the prison library where the work was light. In September he contracted pneumonia and died six days later. Retta Younger, the boys' sister, came up from Missouri and took the body back to Lee's Summit where it was interred in the family plot.

Due largely to the campaign Bronaugh was waging as vigorously as ever, the Board of Pardons granted the Youngers a conditional pardon in 1901. Under its terms they were not only forbidden to leave the state but were not "to exhibit themselves in any dime museum, circus, theatre or opera house or any other place where a charge was made for admission." Furthermore, they were to observe the law, abstain from using intoxicating liquors and make a monthly report to the warden of the state prison "on their whereabouts and how occupied."

In its beneficence—believe it or not—the state had provided jobs for them, selling, of all things, gravestones. For their labor they were to be paid sixty dollars a month, plus commissions.

Bronaugh was there to greet them as they came out. After twenty-five years behind the walls, they were too stunned to have much to say; the world had changed and they would have to adjust themselves to it. They made the little inexpensive Reardon Hotel in St. Paul their headquarters and began canvassing the town and its environs for families that might be interested in purchasing a gravestone. It soon appeared that very few were.

Jim Younger then tried his hand at selling real estate. Nothing came of it and to add to his difficulties, some accounts say, he fell in love with a young widow who rejected him. However it was, on Sunday, October 19, in a fit of depression, he put a pistol to his head and killed himself. Retta came up again from Missouri and took him home. Jim Younger lies in the little cemetery beside his brothers John and Bob at Lee's Summit.[2]

Cole was the only one of the boys left and he was no longer a boy; he was fifty-nine, fat, nearly bald, and no longer the handsome, dashing guerrilla fighter and bandit leader he had been. Strangely, but understandably, he had made many friends since being released from Stillwater. He had not only observed the stipulations of the Board of Pardons with meticulous care, he had found comfort in old-time religion. It all helped Bronaugh to win a full pardon for him in 1903. The indomitable Bronaugh was present to see him receive it and later to accompany him back to Missouri.

Cole made his home with his niece Nora Hall in the house he had given her. He was satisfied to sit in a rocking chair on the front porch and chat with neighbors and old friends. Several weeks after his return, he had a visitor. It was Frank James. He had made the long drive over from the Samuel place not only to see his old friend but to talk business with him. The Wild West show was riding the crest of its popularity. A dozen such outfits, topped by the Buffalo Bill Wild West Show, were on the road. Frank had been in touch with a wealthy Chicago brewer who had agreed to finance a Cole Younger–Frank James Wild West show, starring themselves and featuring the necessary cowboys and Indians. The proposed venture appealed to Cole and the following spring, under the guidance of Edward Arlington, a professional circus man, the Cole Younger–Frank James Show began exhibiting throughout Missouri, Kansas and the South.

It was a small show but profitable. After several seasons, however, Frank's health failed and the outfit disbanded. Cole joined the Lew Nichols Carnival Company as a star attraction. He stayed with it until the rigors of circus life, the constant moving on from town to town, began to wear him down and he retired to Lee's Summit to spend his remaining years. In the meantime Frank James who had bought a small farm down in Arkansas, only to discover that he was physically unable to work it, was living once more at the old Samuel homestead, thinner and bonier than ever. There, on February 18, 1915, he died.

Cole was so desperately ill that he was not permitted to attend his old companion's funeral. But he hung on for another year and a week before he died in his sleep on February 21, 1916. He was seventy-two—the last of the famous outlaws of his era.

XXI

The Notorious Daltons

PRIOR TO October 5, 1892, when they attempted to do what even the far more accomplished James-Younger Gang had never done, rob two banks at one stroke, the Dalton Gang, successful horse thieves and train robbers, were largely unknown beyond the borders of Oklahoma Territory.

The place they chose for their tragic melodramatics was the prosperous little farming town of Coffeyville, Kansas, just north of the Oklahoma–Kansas line. Few people had ever heard of it until that morning, but within hours, or as quickly as the telegraph wires could send the news winging over the country, newspapers from coast to coast were screaming "Coffeyville" and acquainting the public with the ghastly details of the gun battle that had left the town square littered with dead and dying men. It was, as Eye-Witness, the author of that sensational volume *The Dalton Brothers*, reported, "the bloodiest fifteen minutes in the history of American outlawry."

Five strong, the bandits had ridden into Coffeyville shortly after nine o'clock that morning. Fifteen minutes later four were dead and the fifth so shot up that it was thought he could survive only by a miracle. On the other side, the town marshal and three citizens had been killed and an additional dozen wounded.

More fiction masquerading as fact has been written about the "ferocious" Dalton brothers—Bob, Grat, Emmett and Bill, the last named being the eldest of the four—than has been devoted to the James brothers and the Youngers. The reason for this seems fairly obvious. The James boys and the Youngers were authentic desperadoes who left a record that could be checked: the Daltons were hardly more than amateurs about whom little was known. If they were to be palmed off on a gullible public as desperate outlaws, a background of criminal violence had to be—and was—invented for them. Its principal architect was the anonymous writer who signed himself "Eye-Witness" and has never been otherwise identified. Very likely he was a local newspaperman who found himself sitting on top of a sensational story and made the most of it.

He has Bob, Grat and Emmett Dalton fleeing from Indian Territory to escape the net the U.S. deputy marshals were weaving about them for their horse-stealing activities, and he has them bobbing up in California in time to fasten on them the robbery of the Southern Pacific Railroad's Atlantic Express at the way station of Alila (now Earlimart), a few miles south of Tulare on February 6, 1891. Actually, the Atlantic Express was stopped at Alila that evening, the express safe looted, and George Radliff, the fireman, shot and killed. There is nothing in the Tulare County records, however, linking the Daltons with the robbery.

Apparently the only thread in the writer's mind connecting them with the Alila robbery was that Eye-Witness had somehow learned that Bill Dalton, the eldest of the four brothers, was ranching somewhere in the San Joaquin Valley (Merced County) and that the other boys were living with him.

Eye-Witness says that Bill and Grat Dalton were tried for complicity in the Alila robbery, that Bill was acquitted and Grat sentenced to twenty years in the California penitentiary. Apparently the anonymous historian must have realized that he was going to need Grat for he effects a miraculous escape for him, having him leap from the moving train that is carrying him to prison as it crosses the bridge that spans the San Joaquin River. Of course his brothers were waiting on the bank below with a spare horse.

This is all fiction, dished up in the best *National Police Gazette* style. What are the facts? A good place to begin is with Frank Dalton, the second-eldest of the numerous Dalton boys. He broke away from home in 1888 and found employment as a deputy marshal with Judge Parker's court at Fort Smith, Arkansas. He was killed by Cherokee horse thieves. The next son to break away from home was Bill, who left Kansas for the gold fields of Montana. He did not remain there long before going on to California, where, in the spring of 1890, he was ranching in the San Joaquin Valley, married, and getting into politics, which is only another way of saying that he had aligned himself with the Tulare County farmers and ranchers in their battle with the hated "Octopus," the Southern Pacific Railroad Company. There was no surer way to invite harassment than to oppose the Southern Pacific.

Bill Dalton and his wife got out of California in the summer of 1891. Undoubtedly his reason for leaving was that he was finding it increasingly difficult to make a living.

When that part of the original Indian Territory known as Old Oklahoma was opened to white settlement on April 22, 1889, Louis Dalton and his sons still remaining at home—Ben, Charles, Henry, and Littleton—left the farm north of Coffeyville and took up free land near the present town of Dover, ten miles north of Kingfisher. Their sisters and mother accompanied them. Grat (Grattan), Bob, and young Emmett had found employment as deputy marshals out of the Fort Smith court. Their principal duty was the capture of horse thieves, mostly Indians. It was dangerous work, as their brother Frank had found, but it paid better than farm laboring.

Roaming over the Territory as deputy marshals provided them with an excellent knowledge of various hideouts where stolen horses could be held until it was safe to run them across the line for sale in Kansas. In the Cherokee Strip—more or less the northern tier of counties of present Oklahoma—white men were ranging thousands of cattle and horses under leasing arrangements with the

Cherokee Nation. To cut out a bunch of fifteen to twenty head of horses and drive them forty miles or so to a secret hiding place, where they could be held until the hue and cry over their disappearance had subsided, was a comparatively simple matter, for it often happened that the animals had been gone for a week or more before the owner became aware of their disappearance. When the government established a federal court at Guthrie, the Fort Smith court lost a great slice of its former jurisdiction and the Dalton brothers lost their jobs. Instead of applying to the Guthrie court for reinstatement as deputy marshals, they turned to stealing horses for a living, a profession at which they were successful for a time.

While serving their hitches as deputies for the Fort Smith court, they had discovered a limestone cave on the old Berryhill farm, just above where the Cimarron flows into the Arkansas River. In after years it was known locally as the "Dalton Cave." With its overhanging shelf of rock, it was an admirable hideout. Not far away Tom Mann, for whom the present town of Mannford was named, conducted a rope ferry. But he was astute enough not to see or know anything it wasn't safe to know. The legend endures that Tom Bartee, a Creek half-blood who did odd jobs for Mann, kept the Daltons supplied with food and such bits of information as came his way.

Grat was the oldest of the three Daltons, but Bob was the fiery, tempestuous leader. Returning to the Territory from Kansas after disposing of the cavy of horses they had driven across the line, it was their custom to stop over for a day or two with their parents and the rest of the family. It must have made quite a houseful for, in addition to their brothers and sisters, their cousin Minnie Johnson was living with the family, as she had been for the past five years. She was the daughter of Mrs. Dalton's deceased sister and at nineteen was a very attractive young woman. She was the magnet that drew Bob home on his periodic visits. He was in love with Minnie and planned to marry her, a prospect to which she was not averse. But something happened; handsome young

Charlie Montgomery, wanted for bootlegging whiskey to the Indians, came along and Minnie transferred her affections to him and they ran off together.

The Daltons were well-acquainted with the young men, very much like themselves, who worked range and busted broncs for Oscar Halsell's sprawling H X Bar ranch north of Guthrie. The former always found a welcome when they rode over from the Dalton farm to spend a night at a H X Bar line camp. It is not difficult to understand how that range camaraderie led some of Halsell's cowboys to follow Bob Dalton into outlawry, with its promise of excitement and quick, easy money.

Early in May, 1891, the gang rendezvoused for the first time at the hide-out near Mannford. Present were the three Daltons— Bob, the leader, dominating, aggressive, Grat (Grattan), and young Emmett. From the H X Bar were rawboned, six-foot-three Bill Doolin, shrewd, intelligent and a born leader; unsmiling, black-browed Bill Powers, a cowboy roughneck; and laughing, reckless Dick Broadwell, little more than a boy in years. There was a seventh man, Black-faced Charley Bryant, the shiftless brother of Daisy Bryant, a young widow, in whom Bob Dalton had a proprietary interest.

On May 9, their plans completed for their first strike, the gang left the Dalton Cave and headed northwest on the long ride to Wharton (now Perry) to hold up the Santa Fe's northbound Guthrie-Wichita Express. Making sure that their horses would be fresh for a fast getaway after the robbery, they dawdled along the way. But they were in plenty of time; the Guthrie-Wichita Express was not scheduled to pass Wharton until 10:15 P.M., where it would stop only on signal.

A few minutes before it was due, two armed men, the lower part of their faces masked behind bandannas, stepped into the depot. Taking the agent-operator by surprise, they ordered him to set the lights against the express. After he had done their bidding, they tied his hands and lashed him into his chair.

It was a clear night, and the express was pounding along at

forty miles an hour when the alert engineer saw the signals set against him. He responded with a toot of the whistle and cut the throttle. As the panting locomotive clanked to a stop, a masked bandit darted out of the shadows and scurried up the engine's iron steps. The surprised engineer and fireman backed off, hands raised.

The express messenger ran back the door of his car a foot or two and peered out to find out the reason for this unexpected stop. A moment later two of the masked train robbers had him covered. One of them climbed into the car and the other followed. Given his choice of opening the safe or being killed, the messenger opened the safe. One of the bandits tossed him a folded grain sack and ordered him to fill it. There was very little in the safe. The railroad company later placed the figure at less than $1,500.

Several coaches back, the conductor had got down and was running forward along the path beside the tracks to discover what was wrong. A blast of gunfire from the brush turned him back. Retreating several yards, he looked around and saw a flash of fire from the open door of the express car. One of two bandits who was about to leap out had seen that the station agent had freed himself and was bending over his telegraph key, frantically calling for help. Whipping up his rifle, the desperado sent a slug crashing through the operator's window, killing him where he sat.

A few minutes later the gang got away with its meager pickings without a further shot being fired. Being thoroughly acquainted with the country through which they had to pass, they very likely could have made it back to the hideout without incident if they had resisted the temptation to make off with a bunch of horses they found grazing unattended in the meadows at the head of Beaver Creek northwest of Orlando the following morning. The ease with which they could be rounded up and driven along was too great a temptation to be resisted. But it took time. When they reached Skellton Creek at midday, without any sign of pursuit materializing, they deemed it safe to drive the horses into the dense scrub brush and hold them there till evening.

But the theft of the animals had been discovered, and a posse of ranchmen and cowboys was hard on the trail of the thieves. The outlaw gang was taking its ease in the blackjack scrub and paying little attention to the contraband horses when the posse charged into them. It did not occur to the possemen, knowing nothing about the robbery at Wharton, that they had anything more serious than a bunch of horse thieves to deal with; as for Bob Dalton and his men, they had to believe that the news from Wharton had caught up with them.

After a sharp exchange of gunfire, in which a rancher named Bill Starmer was killed, the bandits made a run for it, taking the stolen horses with them. After getting back to their hideout in the cave near Mannford and dividing the proceeds of the Wharton job, Doolin, Powers, and Broadwell went back to work on the H X Bar. Presumably the Daltons ran the stolen horses into Kansas and sold them. Dropping out of sight, they were not seen again for months. Black-faced Charley Bryant, in the meantime, had returned to his old haunts in and around Hennessey, where his sister Daisy, Bob Dalton's acknowledged mistress, was living comfortably in the pleasant little cottage he had provided for her.

In the meantime, the Wharton affair was having some repercussions. The Santa Fe Railroad had offered a reward of a thousand dollars for information leading to the arrest and conviction of the man who had killed its Wharton agent. Descriptions of the robbers, given by the train crew, were sent out. The express messenger had seen the fatal shot fired by a man with a black powder burn on his left cheek just below the eye. Several men so marked were picked up, but they had no difficulty proving themselves innocent. Deputy marshal Ed Short, who made his headquarters in Hennessey, must have pinched himself when he finally realized that Black-faced Charley Bryant fitted the description of the wanted man. Even more to the point, Bryant, through his sister Daisy, was connected with Bob Dalton.[1]

Marshal Ed Short, a bulldog of a man, deserves to be rated with such immortals as Bill Tilghman, Heck Thomas and Chris Madsen, who broke up the reign of outlawry in Oklahoma. He went looking for Bryant, and found him in bed on the second floor of the ramshackle Rhodes Hotel in the heart of town, recovering from a recent illness. When Mrs. Thorne, the wife of the proprietor, took Bryant's noonday dinner up the stairs to him, Short was only a step behind her. Before Bryant could reach for his revolver on the chair beside his bed, the marshal had him covered. After Mrs. Thorne had left the room and Bryant had got his clothes on, Short handcuffed him. Evidently fearing that an attempt might be made to take his prisoner away from him, he decided to get him out of Hennessey as quickly as possible. The Rock Island train north to Wichita was due in a few minutes. He decided to take it and to double back from Wichita to Guthrie that evening on the Santa Fe's night express.

Marching Bryant to the depot without incident, he got into the baggage car with his prisoner. It was Sunday, August 23, 1891, and the train, being a "local," stopped every few miles to discharge and take on passengers. At Waukomis, a few miles south of Enid, Short told the baggageman that he was going to get out on the platform to "stretch his legs a bit," and handing him his revolver, told him to keep his eye on the prisoner.

From where he sat, Bryant could see the marshal on the platform, cradling his rifle, and though Bryant's hands were manacled, he leaped for the revolver, now lying on the desk. Clutching the gun in both hands, he backed the baggageman into a corner and leaped to the depot platform. Short was standing only ten feet away, and Bryant began firing at him as rapidly as he could squeeze the trigger.

The first shot would have been fatal, but stricken though he was, Short brought up his rifle and fired twice, felling Bryant, before he himself tumbled to the platform. Black-faced Charley Bryant was dead, and as Conductor Jim Collins bent down over the dying marshal, Ed Short breathed his last.

Although there was very little evidence implicating the Daltons in the Wharton robbery, they were tried by the public following the killing of Charley Bryant, and found guilty by association. The

hunt for them began, but as previously noted, they were not to
be found. Folklorists and grass-roots historians have never offered
a satisfactory explanation. One guess, more valid than most, had
them down in the wilds of lawless Greer County, on Red River.
Meanwhile, country banks were being robbed with monotonous
frequency. When the holdups were committed by "parties unknown," suspicion fell on the Daltons, which may have been justified. Still, no evidence was ever presented against them. Knowing
their aversion to hard work, it is to be doubted that they had put
their outlawry behind them and were leading honest lives. Certainly when they surfaced again and stuck up another Santa Fe
train, it was with an expertise that could have been acquired only
from practice.

On June 1, 1892, the Dalton Gang held up the Santa Fe's southbound Texas Fast Express at Red Rock station, only twelve miles
north of Wharton. It was due to pass Red Rock at 9:40 in the
evening, with Guthrie its next scheduled stop. It never got past
Red Rock this night. A few minutes before it was due, an exact
repetition of the Wharton holdup took place. Two masked men
walked into the tiny depot and with drawn six-guns ordered the
agent to set the signals against the express. He had no choice but
to do as ordered. The telegraph wire was then cut, isolating Red
Rock.

When the engineer saw the lights set against him, he cut the
throttle, and with brakes grinding the train rolled up to the depot
and stopped.

Red Rock was a shipping point for cattle, which accounted
for its existence. Aside from the depot, shipping pens and two
stores, the rest of the tiny hamlet could have been covered with a
horse blanket.

With the exception of Black-faced Charley Bryant, Bob had
with him the same men who had sided him at Wharton, twelve
months back. He was the boss, and it wasn't necessary for him to
issue any orders; this job had been carefully rehearsed, and each
man knew what was expected of him. Bill Powers and Dick Broad-

well leaped up the steps into the cab of the fretting iron horse and backed the engineer and fireman up against the tender with their menacing Winchesters. Bob and Emmett Dalton started through the coaches, relieving the passengers of their money and valuables. Meantime, Grat Dalton and Bill Doolin had pushed in through the rear door of the express car and caught the express company's messenger and a shotgun guard playing checkers. The surprised pair raised their hands on command and were disarmed. The express company's messenger yielded up the keys to the safe. Doolin stuffed $3,000 into the grain sack. The Santa Fe and Wells, Fargo placed the loss at half that figure; but minimizing their losses was always railroad and Wells, Fargo policy, pursued in the hope that it would discourage further holdups.

The Red Rock robbery had not taken more than twenty minutes. Not a shot had been fired. Twenty-four hours later the gang was safely back in its old hideout in the limestone cave west of Mannford.

Bob Dalton, anxious to see what the newspapers were saying about him, had his curiosity satisfied when Tom Bartee, the Creek half-blood, who was again keeping the gang supplied with food, handed him a copy of the Wichita *Eagle*, then several days old. There it was! His name in headlines: "The Dalton Gang." It was the first time he had seen the words in print. The Pullman conductor had recognized him as he and Emmett went through the car at Red Rock and identified him to the authorities. Like Jesse James, Bob welcomed notoriety. Perhaps it was now that the ambition to do something more spectacular than anything Jesse had ever done began yeasting in Bob Dalton.

On July 14, 1892, only six weeks later, the Dalton Gang made the headlines again. This time it was at the hamlet of Adair, on the Cherokee Division of the Missouri, Kansas & Texas Railroad, in the Cherokee Nation, roughly sixty-five miles east of Mannford. Leaving the Dalton Cave at nightfall, they were across the Verdigris River by daylight. Several hours' riding brought them to Pryor Creek, three miles south of Adair, the following evening. Number

2, the northbound M. K. & T. (Katy) express, was not due to stop at Adair until 9:45 P.M.

With time to spare, Bob Dalton and his bandit crew rode up to the depot, where they found no loungers, just the agent. He offered no resistance and was tied up and deposited in a corner of his tiny office.

There were only a few dollars in the cash drawer. If that was a disappointment, it was short-lived, for tonight Number 2 had $17,000 in currency in the express-car safe, an unusually rich shipment for the Katy to be forwarding. The bandits could have stopped Number 2 on almost any other night and got very little. Was it just by chance that they struck the jackpot? Of course it was said later that they had been tipped off. That has been said of other train robberies but never substantiated. If the Daltons had been tipped off that there would be $17,000 in the express car that evening, why weren't they also informed that Captain J. J. Kinney of the Indian police and ten of his men would be aboard to see the shipment safely through from Muskogee to Vinita?

When the express ground to a stop, Bill Powers and Dick Broadwell swung up into the cab and cowed the engine crew. Conductor George Scales and a colored porter ran up the depot platform from the rear to see what was wrong. Several warning shots from the group gathered at the door of the express car turned them back. George Williams, the express messenger, had refused a demand to open the car door. He changed his mind when he was warned that, unless he opened the door, the car would be blown up.

It was a hot July night. Back in the smoker, Captain Kinney and his guards had the windows open. One of them, Joe LaFlore, thrust his head out to see what was happening. He ducked back in a hurry when a spatter of bullets splintered the window frame above his head. Kinney ordered his men to crouch down on the floor and start firing their rifles from that safe but disadvantageous position. Several of the Cherokees, more courageous than the others, scrambled out of the smoker and from underneath and between the cars began firing. None of the bandits was struck, and when they were finished, they fired a mocking blast and galloped off.

Adair had been thoroughly aroused by now. A small group of citizens had gathered in the drugstore across the open square in back of the depot, among them Dr. W. L. Goff and Dr. Youngblood. Slugs from the high-powered rifles with which Captain Kinney's police were armed had crashed through the drugstore windows. Dr. Goff was struck and went down mortally wounded. Youngblood was seriously wounded. Since the bandits were firing in the opposite direction from the stores, there was no question about who was responsible for the killing of Dr. Goff.

For the Dalton Gang, Adair was its most lucrative robbery, carried out with workmanlike precision. Next time, Bob promised himself, they would pull off something spectacular. Less than two months later, they were on their way to Coffeyville.

XXII

Morning at Coffeyville

IN HIS book *When the Daltons Rode*, written in collaboration with Jack Jungmeyer, and published in 1929, Emmett Dalton says: "When Bob first broached the idea of knocking off the two Coffeyville banks in a double-play, Dick Broadwell was the only one who was for it. Dick would have been for anything that Bob suggested. But Grat then fell in line and I agreed with them. Bill Powers was won over. Bill Doolin was the last to agree to go through with it. Coffeyville was our home town. We'd grown up there and were acquainted with the layout of the streets and the banks and how to make a quick run at them. Making the raid was all we talked about for weeks."

According to Emmett they left the Dalton Cave on October 2, camped the first night north of Tulsa, and continued north through the Osage Nation. On October 3, they lay out in the timbered hills at the head of Hickory Creek. During the night they moved on to the Davis farm in the Onion Creek bottoms. They were then not more than three and a half miles southwest of Coffeyville.

Eye-Witness says that the outlaw camp was awake early on the morning of October fifth and that "they paused to shave themselves, not that they wanted to appear at their best when they rode into Coffeyville but because the false beards with which they had

218

equipped themselves would adhere better to a smooth cheek than to several days of stubble."

"That's hogwash," Emmett told me when I became acquainted with him in 1928. "We wore no disguise when we rode into Coffeyville. If we could have put our hands on false whiskers, we would have been ashamed to wear them."

Eye-Witness says that "they did not put on the false beards until after they had tethered their horses in the alley behind Slosson's drugstore and Kloehr's livery barn, a hundred yards from the plaza." Fifteen minutes later four of the bandits were dead. The bodies were propped up against Kloehr's fence and photographed almost as the smoke of battle had drifted away. The only hair visible on their faces is Grat Dalton's closely cropped moustache and the luxuriant fringe covering Bill Powers' upper lip; Bob Dalton and Dick Broadwell are clean-shaven.

In the years that have passed since the original paperback, *The Dalton Brothers and Their Astounding Career of Crime,* was first published a few weeks after the Coffeyville raid, at least a hundred writers have applied themselves to re-telling the Dalton story. Although they have mostly derided the anonymous author's account of what preceded the Coffeyville raid as melodramatic trash, they have only the highest praise for him when he turns from fiction writer to reporter and pens a graphic account of the events to which he was a witness. I must do the same.

It could not have been much later than eight-thirty in the morning when Bob Dalton and his men left the bivouac on the Onion Creek bottoms and headed for Coffeyville. It was a brisk, sunlit morning. When they were within a mile and a half of town, a man named Hollingsworth and his wife passed them, driving west. The couple later testified that they noticed the men particularly because all six were armed. Ten minutes later the Seldomridge brothers, also driving west, pulled over to the side of the road to permit a group of six armed men to pass. They counted the horsemen and were positive there were six. But when the mounted group turned into Maple Street, on the southern outskirts of town, and were noticed by a number of citizens, all were positive that only five men passed them.

They were correct; Bill Doolin's horse had gone lame and he had turned back to put his rope on a good-looking sorrel gelding he had noticed grazing in a pasture beside the road. He exchanged mounts and was racing back to catch up with Bob and the others when he encountered an excited horseman near the old cheese factory on the outskirts of town who shouted that the Dalton Gang was shooting up Coffeyville and robbing the Condon and the First National banks. Allegedly—and the story has been repeated a thousand times—Doolin told him, "My horse is faster than yours. I'll turn back and spread the warning that the bandits may be heading this way." [1]

Whether or not this was the exact verbal exchange, it is close enough to account for the fact that Doolin did not participate in the Coffeyville raid. He got out of Kansas as fast as he could.

Leaving their horses in the alley, Grat, Powers, and Broadwell, followed closely by Bob and Emmett, walked briskly up to Walnut Street and the plaza, less than a hundred yards. Ahead of them, a few feet to the right, stood the Condon Bank, privately owned, and opposite it, on the far side of the plaza, the First National Bank. Walnut Street was the heart of the town's business district, the mouth of the alley being flanked on both sides by a score or more of shops, stores, and business offices.

The Daltons were on familiar ground in Coffeyville. Many times in the past, when the family was living on the farm north of town, they had driven in on errands or just to enjoy the excitement of the place.

Coffeyville had changed very little in the past several years. That was also true of the three Dalton brothers. Alex McKenna, standing on the steps of his dry-goods and grocery store at the mouth of the alley, glanced at them casually as they passed, and then, thinking he recognized Bob Dalton, took a second look. Watching, he saw three of the five men walk into the Condon Bank. After a momentary hesitation, the other two proceeded across narrow Union Street and disappeared through the doors of the First National. His suspicions definitely aroused, he moved to the corner of the store steps, from where, through the bank's plate-glass windows, he saw Charles Ball, the cashier, and Charles Carpenter, one of the owners, standing at the counter, their hands raised and a rifle pointed at their heads. McKenna ran back into the store, crying a warning to his clerks and customers that the banks were being robbed. Few men had a weapon they could lay their hands on in a hurry. But the town's three hardware dealers began handing out rifles and ammunition to whoever wanted them. It was Northfield all over again.

In the vault of the Condon Bank there was $18,000. As at Northfield, the vault door was closed but not locked. There were several thousand dollars in silver in the cash drawers at the counter. Grat Dalton disdained it as being too heavy to carry. He ordered Cashier Ball to open the vault. Ball, using his wits, told him the time lock was set for 9:45 A.M. and the vault could not be opened until then. Grat glanced at the clock. It was 9:42. "All right!" he snapped. "We'll wait." The delay was to prove fatal. Several customers came into the bank. They were made to stretch out on the floor as the seconds ticked away.

Across the street in the First National, Bob and Emmett were having better luck. Tom Ayers, the cashier, and W. H. Shepherd, the teller, were at the counter, transacting some business with a customer named Brewster. The bandits quickly covered the three men. Emmett then darted into the back room, where young Bert Ayers, the cashier's son, was working on the books. Young Ayers offered no resistance and was marched back into the counting room, hands raised. Bob tossed the inevitable grain sack to Cashier Ayers and watched him stuff $20,240 into it. Their work finished, Bob and his brother marched the four captives to the door, intending to use them as a screen for their dash across the street. At the door they ran into a blaze of gunfire from the south side of the plaza. It drove them back. Realizing that attempting to cross Union Street would be suicidal, they freed the four men and ran back through the bank to the alley in the rear, the two Ayers, Brewster, and Shepherd meanwhile darting into Isham Brothers' hardware store next door to arm themselves.

Young Lucius Baldwin, who clerked in Isham Brothers', had snatched up a pistol and run through the store to the alley, hoping to shoot the fleeing bandits from the rear. When the two Daltons came out of the bank and found Baldwin confronting them, Bob flung up his rifle and killed him. Running up the alley to Eighth Street, a matter of fifty yards, they turned west to cross the north side of the plaza. Once across it, a side alley would bring them to their horses.

From in front of the old Eldridge House, they had an open view of the plaza. From several directions a score of men were firing a stream of lead into the Condon Bank. Bob realized that his brother Grat, Powers, and Broadwell were trapped inside and stood little chance of escaping alive.

Standing on the sidewalk in front of Brown's shoe store, several hundred feet away, Charlie Brown, the elderly proprietor, and George Cubine, a shoemaker, had their attention fixed on the entrance of the First National, evidently believing that the bandits were still in the bank. Cubine was armed with a six-gun; Brown was unarmed. Infuriated by the way things were going, Bob Dalton whipped up his rifle and put a bullet through Cubine's heart. As Brown bent down to succor his fallen friend, Bob killed him.

There was a display of farm tools, hardwood butter tubs and the like, on the porch of Isham Brothers' hardware store. Tom Ayers, the First National cashier, had armed himself with a rifle and moved out on the porch. Crouching there partly concealed, also believing that the bandits were still in the bank, he was surprised when he saw Bob and Emmett Dalton run across the north side of the plaza. When they stopped in front of the hotel and Bob dropped both Cubine and Brown, Ayers threw caution to the wind and leaped up to fire at the bandits. Bob caught the movement on Isham Brothers' porch and snapped a shot that dropped Ayers, blood streaming from the side of his head.[2]

The three members of the gang pinned down in the Condon Bank were as surprised as Ayers had been to see Bob and Emmett running up Eighth Street, obviously bent on reaching their horses by a roundabout route. It convinced Grat, Powers, and Broadwell that they had to grab the money in sight and make a break to get across Walnut Street.

Somehow they got across the bullet-ridden street. When Charlie Gump, a laborer, ran out of Slosson's drugstore and fired a shot at them, Powers blasted the pistol out of the man's hand. A bullet fired from the second floor of the Condon Bank struck Broadwell but failed to stop him. Once he and the others were in the alley, they were out of the line of gunfire from Walnut Street and the south end of the square. Directly across the way, the men who had run out from Isham Brothers' store had a clear shot at them. They began blasting away at once, but their marksmanship was so poor that it accomplished nothing.

Running up the alley at the rear of the building facing the square, Bob and Emmett Dalton, the latter carrying the money bag, met Grat, Powers, and Broadwell where the two alleys intersected. They were not more than sixty feet from their tethered horses. Bob and Emmett were unscathed up to that moment; the other three were wounded and bleeding but very much alive.

Up the alley a hundred yards to the east, a man delivering kerosene to his customers had left his wagon partially blocking the way. Otherwise, escape from town was open. The moment had arrived for John Kloehr, the liveryman, often referred to as "the hero of the Coffeyville fight," to take charge. Shooting down fleeing bandits from behind a board fence may have been something less than heroic; but Kloehr was courageous and an excellent shot.

He had been in the fight on the plaza, firing into the Condon Bank from the steps of Boswells' general store. When he saw the three bandits, Grat Dalton, Powers, and Broadwell, dash from the bank and disappear into the alley, he ran through the store and reached his barn and wagon yard on the alley in the rear. He was in time to see City Marshal Connelley leap out into the alley and start running toward Maple Street, obviously believing the bandits were ahead of him. They were behind him. Grat Dalton flung his rifle to his shoulder and killed Connelley with a single shot.

Kloehr's rifle cracked and the slug tore into Bob Dalton's bowels. Clutching the fence to keep from going down, Bob saw the liveryman and snapped a desperate shot at him. It went wide, and Kloehr killed him with a second shot. Bill Powers, ready to leap into the saddle, hesitated long enough to kill the oilman's horse to clear the way. A moment later Kloehr reached him with a bullet that tumbled him into the dust. Grat caught a glimpse of the liveryman and brought up his Winchester despite his shattered right shoulder. He was too slow; Kloehr snapped a shot at him that tore a gaping hole in Grat's throat. Of the bandit gang, only Broadwell and Emmett Dalton were left alive. A slug had shattered Emmett's right shoulder; Broadwell was in worse shape. But they still could ride. Down the alley they flashed in a desperate attempt to escape from the hail of lead the citizens gathered in front of Isham Brothers' store were pouring into the alley, the screaming of the dying and of the injured horses that rose above the roaring of the guns.

Emmett and Broadwell reached the Maple Street corner. And then the incredible happened: Broadwell went on; Emmett Dalton turned back. In his book *When the Daltons Rode,* published many years later, he says: "When Broadwell and I reached the corner, I glanced back and realized for the first time that Bob and Grat were not with us. So I turned back to help them."

They were beyond help. He tried to put Bob on a horse, but his shattered shoulder made that impossible. He was struck again and again as he struggled to lift his brother. Finally a blast of buckshot from the gun of Carey Seaman, a barber, stretched him out unconscious.[3]

Broadwell was bleeding profusely from the several wounds he had received. Clutching his saddle horn with both hands, he turned the corner and disappeared from view. He got as far as the creamery on the Independence road, north of town. He had his bridle rein clutched in his hand, holding on to his horse, when they found him dead in the tall grass at the side of the road.

Emmett Dalton was taken to the Farmer's Home, a small inn on Eighth Street. He was not expected to survive his terrible wounds. With Coffeyville seething with excitement, there was talk of lynching him. Tom Callahan, the sheriff of Montgomery County, had arrived. He posted guards at the Farmer's Home and put an end to any talk of lynching his prisoner. However, he waited four days before he was convinced that it was safe to take Emmett to Independence and lodge him in the county jail, where he could be given adequate medical attention.

Months passed before the youngest of the Dalton brothers was physically able to be brought to trial. He was found guilty of armed robbery and sentenced to twenty-five years in the Kansas State Prison at Lansing. After he had served fourteen years, President Theodore Roosevelt granted him a full pardon.

The Coffeyville disaster marked the end of the Dalton Gang, but the town had not heard the last of the Daltons. Bill Dalton, late of California, had moved in with the family on the farm north of Kingfisher. On the sworn statement by Emmett that his brother Bob had had $900 on his person when they rode into Coffeyville on the morning of October 5, 1892, he demanded, acting as agent for his mother, that the town return the money. This was not taken seriously at first, but when a careful accounting was made of the money recovered, it was found to be $900 in excess of the sum lost.

If the $900 was ever turned over to the Dalton family, no evidence of it appears in town records.

XXIII

"They Done Wrong"

ON THE only occasion that Bill Doolin was brought in to be lodged in the Guthrie jail, a crowd was on hand to see him put away. A young woman caught his eye and smiled. "You don't look so fierce, Mr. Doolin," she said. "I believe I could have captured you myself." Bill nodded and laughed. "Madam, I'm sure you could."

The most famous of all Oklahoma outlaws, he was cool, nerveless, and intelligent. The son of a poor Arkansas farmer, possessing only the rudiments of an education, he had a code of his own and the instincts of a gentleman and the respect of marshals who hunted him down. They included such notables as Bill Tilghman, Chris Madsen, the remarkable Dane, and Heck Thomas.

Following the debacle at Coffeyville, Doolin hid out at a remote line camp on Oscar Halsell's H X Bar ranch, where he was among friends. The wiping out of the Daltons did not put any check on Oklahoma and Indian Territory outlawry. The Cook Gang, the Rufus Buck (all Indian) Gang, Cherokee Bill and his followers, the Henry Starr Band, and several other outfits were robbing banks, country stores, and post offices. A score of marshals working out of Guthrie were in the field, trying to track down the renegades. Over at Fort Smith, Judge Isaac Parker had a hundred deputies in the field and was keeping George Maledon, his hangman, busy dropping the guilty into eternity.

226

The United States District Court at Fort Smith had jurisdiction over the eighteen western counties of Arkansas, and for years over all of Indian Territory before the western half was sheared off to form Oklahoma Territory. Although it was designated a district court, it had the status of a circuit court. Judge Isaac Parker was its presiding officer, with life tenure, and from his decisions there was (for many years) no appeal. In his time, he sentenced eighty-eight men to death; seventy-nine were actually hanged.

It was routine with the judge to put in a full day's work six days a week, taking the bench at eight every morning and remaining until five-thirty in the evening, with only an hour's break for dinner at noon. He was a deeply religious man and prided himself on being fair and just in the sentences he imposed. When the jury had found a man guilty, whether it was for stealing horses, peddling whiskey to the Indians, or murder, he was long-winded in pronouncing sentence. If the crime was murder, he would glare down at the offender like an avenging angel and excoriate him. When young Clarence Goldsby, the infamous Cherokee Bill, born of a Negro father and a mixed-blood Cherokee mother, and guilty of seven or eight wanton murders, stood before Parker for the second time, the judge lashed out in trembling fury.

At such moments, Judge Parker was at his crusading best, under a full head of steam, self-righteous, intemperate. His critics, who denounced his methods, say that "he accomplished very little for all of his trying . . . that when he finally stepped down from the bench, conditions in Indian Territory were no better than when he took over." They might have said with greater honesty that conditions were no worse, a just tribute that Judge Parker richly deserved.

In the approximately twenty years that Isaac Parker presided over the Fort Smith court, he tried no fewer than several thousand cases. Of those who were found innocent, there is no record; but among the guilty appears the name of practically every prominent male and female in the history of Indian Territory–Oklahoma outlawry, including Belle Starr. Belle faced Judge Parker on two occasions; the first time as a witness in the robbery of old Watt Grayson, a Creek tribal official, and his wife; the second time as a defendant charged with horse stealing, along with Sam Starr, her "husband" of the moment. They were found guilty, Belle being sentenced to serve a year in the House of Detention at Detroit and Sam being confined for a similar period in the Michigan State Prison at Jackson.

It is time to do a little catching up with Belle. She was no longer the young thing she had been when she fell in love with Cole Younger. Now in her early thirties, rather thin, with a somewhat boyish face, she possessed a fire and vigor that made her attractive to men. Her daughter, Pearl Younger, was twelve, or thereabouts, a beautiful child. There was a third member of the family, Belle's son, little Eddie Reed. The boy's father was Jim Reed, a handsome, worthless, second-rate desperado. Not more than a year after Belle had seen the last of Cole Younger, she "married" Reed in a mock ceremony and went to live with him on his small farm near Sycene. He was a Missourian from Rich Hill, not far from Belle's old home. With two other men of his caliber he had taken part in the torture and robbery of old Watt Grayson and his wife. Flush with his share of the proceeds, he was cutting quite a figure in the saloons of Dallas, and he supplied Belle with money for gambling, fine clothes, and a fine horse. But those gay weeks ended when he got word that his brother Scott Reed had been killed in the outgrowth of a family feud. It was a summons home, and he left for the north at once, taking Belle with him.

How he became acquainted with old Tom Starr and gained his friendship is not known. But however it was, Reed and Belle broke up their journey through the Nations by stopping over with old Tom. Before she and Reed continued their journey, Belle became well acquainted with Sam Starr, old Tom's strapping big son. She undoubtedly was attracted to him, for all through her life she showed a decided preference for big men.

On reaching Rich Hill, Reed proceeded with the business that had brought him north. Two of the Shannon brothers, with whom the Reeds were feuding, were shot down from ambush. Suspicion soon fastened on Jim Reed, and he hurriedly got out of Missouri with Belle and went to Los Angeles, where Belle gave birth to their son. They were back in Texas a year later, where Reed was killed by a deputy United States marshal following a mail and stagecoach robbery.

Belle Shirley became Belle Starr on June 5, 1880, when she and Sam appeared before Abe Woodall, district judge for the Canadian District, Cherokee Nation, and were married. She bore the name for the rest of her life. Rascoe and Wellman sneer at this marriage, but it was legal and was so recognized by the Cherokee Tribal Council when on Sam's death his headright of sixty acres in a bend of the Canadian River, sixty miles west of Fort Smith, was awarded to her.[1]

Back when Belle and Starr established their home there, a tiny cabin was the only building on the place. Several years later, after he had succeeded in getting himself killed at an Indian "stomp" dance at Whitefield, some miles down the river, Belle rebuilt the old cabin and erected two new ones. She named the place Younger's Bend. It was in wild, semimountainous, sparsely settled country that could be entered by only one winding dirt road. There she lived, with her two children, for seven years. It soon became the rendezvous for Indian horse thieves and lesser outlaws—undoubtedly as she had planned.

Belle Starr has been established in history as "The Bandit Queen" or "The Queen of Outlaws." In a left-handed way she probably deserves that distinction. She consorted with outlaws, shared her bed with many, and, with her superior intelligence, must have planned and undoubtedly advised them on how to proceed with their forays. She must have shared in the proceeds of their robberies, for she was always well supplied with money with which to rush to their defense when the law caught up with them.

Such errands took her to Fort Smith, where she became a familiar figure, riding her prancing black mare Venus. She was an expert horsewoman, and although far from pretty, she was a striking figure, always riding sidesaddle, holding it to be unladylike to ride astride. In all of the many photographs of her she is seen wearing a gray velvet riding habit, with a full bodice and tight sleeves, and on her head a broad gray felt hat, set at a rakish angle, an ostrich plume trailing out behind.

In a senseless argument over some land she owned that a neighbor, Edgar Watson, was using, Belle angrily informed him that she knew his secret. That Mrs. Watson had told her that he was wanted in Florida for murder.[2] To stop that tale before it got any further, he decided to bushwhack her at the first opportunity.

Belle had been off on an overnight visit with her friend Mrs. Richard Nail, on San Bois Creek, and it was not until the middle of the afternoon of Saturday, February 2, 1889, that Watson saw her coming. Crouching in a fence corner, he brought up his shotgun and fired both barrels into her. Milo Hoyt, who lived on the south side of the Canadian, heard the shots and a minute later saw a horse that he recognized as Belle's mare Venus dash up the road and cross the river. Fearing something was wrong, he ran back up the road.

He didn't have to go far. Belle was quite dead when he reached her.

Because of the similarity of their names, it has often been said, erroneously, that Henry Starr, the last of the horseback outlaws, and Belle Starr were related by marriage. Henry Starr was at some pains to deny it on several occasions. "My people and the Tom Starr clan were not related," he told Marshal Bill Tilghman. "I saw Belle Starr several times at Fort Smith but I was never acquainted with her. She was twenty-eight when I was born."

As for Bill Doolin, he was not yet thirty when he missed the Coffeyville fiasco. Belle, had she still been alive, would have been forty-four. It is unlikely that she ever heard of Bill Doolin. But he was only at the beginning of his career as a bandit leader as he hid out on the H X Bar and began putting his own gang together. He picked his men carefully, and they were to more than justify his judgment of them. In three years, according to the figures compiled by United States Marshal Evett D. Nix, they garnered $165,-000 from their train and bank robberies. He recruited three men from the H X Bar crew and four others from among the drifters who were not on the ranch payroll but, on a temporary basis, were eating Oscar Halsell's grub. All seven were or had been working cowboys. All were young, wild, strangers to fear. An eighth man was a bit older. He was Bill Dalton.

Undoubtedly the stigma his brothers had put on the Dalton name had closed so many doors to Bill that outlawry was about all that he had left to him. It has been said that Doolin took him into the fold with some reluctance, fearing that Bill might try to take over leadership of the gang. But he does not appear to have entertained such ambitions; to the end, he was Doolin's faithful follower.

The Doolin Gang's first rendezvous was the old Dalton Cave near Mannford. Accompanied by Ol or Oliver (alias Crescent Sam) Yountis, George (Bitter Creek) Newcomb, and Bill Dalton, he led the way to the old hideout. There they waited for the others to join them. But the days passed without bringing them. It got to be the middle of November. Determined to make a strike before snow fell to make tracking easy, he set out with the men he had and crossed the Kansas line to Spearville, a small town on the Santa Fe, a dozen miles east of Dodge City. There they cracked the bank and made off with $18,000. It was a surprisingly easy touch. They divided the money equally among themselves and made tracks for Oklahoma, keeping ahead of Chalk Beeson, the sheriff of Ford County, and a hastily organized posse.

Once they were in the Strip, the bandits separated, Doolin and Bitter Creek Newcomb heading for the Dalton Cave, Bill Dalton striking south for the Dalton farm at Dover, and Ol Yountis making tracks for his sister's home outside Orlando, a decision prompted by the fact that Beeson and his posse, not stopping when they reached the Kansas line, were pounding hard on their trail. It seems that the irrepressible Chalk, part owner of the Long Branch Saloon (the real one) as well as sheriff of Ford County, had the eccentric notion that when he was chasing outlaws, his jurisdiction ended when he caught up with them, not at a state or county line.

Doolin, Dalton, and Bitter Creek got away safely, but the horse Ol Yountis was riding went lame. He drove the animal until it could go not farther. He was still a dozen miles from his sister's home when he started walking, packing his saddle. Meeting a stranger on horseback, he killed him, exchanged saddles, and dashed away. The posse found the murdered man and the foundered horse. After wasting some precious minutes, it drove into Orlando, where Sheriff Beeson got in touch with the United States marshal's office and asked for help. Deputy marshals Madsen, Houston, and Thomas reached Orlando that evening.

Yountis had been in trouble with the law on several previous occasions. Madsen reasoned that he was the man they wanted. By daylight, they had his sister's house surrounded, and when he stepped out and headed for the barn, carrying a feed bag, Heck Thomas ordered him to throw up his hands. Yountis reached into the bag with his right hand and it came out clutching a .45. He fired instantly, the slug missing its target by inches. From behind the stone wall at which he was standing, the marshal flung his rifle to his shoulder and pressed the trigger. The shot would have been fatal if it had not struck the sheaf of bills in Yountis' breast pocket. The impact sent him staggering backward, however, and before he could fire again, Madsen and Houston blasted the life out of him.

To be killed like this by officers of the law was a hazard that faced every man who rode the outlaw trail. The record does not show that it was ever a lasting deterrent; a few drew back temporarily but, having had a taste of outlawry, they soon returned to it, trapped by the lure of making a big stake.

By the middle of December the late arrivals Doolin was expecting had joined him at the Dalton Cave. He had found a safer and more comfortable retreat in the wild brakes of the Cimarron, twenty miles to the west. South of the river, in the Sac and Fox country, a safe distance away, there was a wide place in the road with several stores and a few houses named Cushing, destined to explode one day into the first of Oklahoma's "oil capitals." In the other direction was the safe, quiet little town of Ingalls with its population of a hundred, where supplies could be had as well as a little fun. The Doolin Gang moved to the new hideout and settled down to wait out the winter.

Including Bill Doolin, the gang now numbered ten. They conducted themselves circumspectly, usually no more than two or three appearing in town at a time. Ingalls had two saloons. Ransom and Murray's Trilby Saloon was favored by the Doolin Gang. But they didn't indulge in any hell-raising or drunken frolicking. Widow Mary Pierce installed several brushwood courtesans in her two-story "hotel" for their pleasure. It was all very orderly. Zoe Tilghman, widow of the famous marshal, who was born and raised on a farm near Ingalls, relates in her book *Outlaw Days* how the long riders were "welcomed at the local dances and church box parties."

Ingalls and the Doolin Gang have become inseparable in fact and fiction. The story of the battle of Ingalls has been told many times. This writer had his turn at it, basing his account on the diary of Dr. J. H. Pickering, one of Ingalls' three physicians, fragments of which appeared in the Oklahoma Historical Society's *Chronicles of Oklahoma* in 1958. Pickering was present during the battle and in his professional capacity took part in it as a noncombatant. His is the only eyewitness account we have.

Street battles between outlaws and marshals usually tend to be forgotten after a few years. Not so with the Ingalls' fight; the warm, friendly relations that had existed between the bandits and the good people of the little town kept the memory of it green and provided the soil in which germinated the seemingly indestructible myth of the Rose of the Cimarron. This was the beautiful young woman who purportedly slid down a rope of bed sheets from an upper-floor window of Mary Pierce's "hotel" and braved the terrors of the bullet-ridden street to carry a rifle and a bag of ammunition to her beleaguered outlaw sweetheart, Bitter Creek Newcomb, and helped him to escape.

It took time—twenty years—for Richard Graves, the promoter of the Rose of the Cimarron legend and author of *Oklahoma Outlaws—A Graphic History*, to identify the mysterious Rose as Rose Dunn, the fifteen-year-old stepdaughter of Dr. Call. "The old-timers of Ingalls knew better; on the day of the battle young Rose was not even in town, being off visiting her brother Bee Dunn at his ranch two miles east of Ingalls." [3]

When Bill Dalton rejoined the gang in its new lair in the Cimarron brakes in February, it was at full strength. In addition to the two Bills, Doolin and Dalton, George (Bitter Creek) Newcomb, a big, handsome, smiling man, was there; and so were George Waightman, alias Red Buck, a homicidal killer; Clifton Grimes, alias Dynamite Dick; Charlie Pierce; Jack Blake, alias Tulsa Jack; Little Dick West, so wild a man that he could not sleep under a roof; Roy Daugherty, alias Arkansas Tom, the youngest of the lot; and Little Bill Raidler, a scowling, educated introvert.

Late in May, 1893, Doolin and his men rode west for two hundred miles, more or less following the Cimarron River. Passing to the north of old Camp Supply, they turned north and crossed the Kansas line. Three days later they reached their objective, the main line of the Santa Fe Railroad at Cimarron Crossing, where the Santa Fe Trail crossed the Arkansas River, and where the town of Cimarron, Kansas, had taken root. There, only some twenty-five miles west of Dodge City, on the night of May 26, they held up an eastbound express and made off with $13,000 without any difficulty.

It was another big haul. But they were a long way from home, giving the law plenty of time in which to cut them off. By telegraph, county sheriffs and the United States marshal's office in Guthrie were alerted. Within a few hours several hundred were in the field, trying to cut the trail of the fleeing bandits. In Guthrie, Evett Dumas Nix, the recently appointed United States marshal for Oklahoma, put the matter up to Chris Madsen. It was the reliable Dane's opinion that the outlaws would pass somewhere north of Camp Supply in their dash to cover. Nix dispatched Madsen to Camp Supply at once and ordered him to take charge.

Madsen was correct in surmising the course the Doolins were taking. He was too late to cut them off, but only by a few minutes. He and his handful of men exchanged shots with the outlaws, in which a bullet struck Doolin in the right foot, a minor injury. Keeping only Arkansas Tom with him, he ordered the others to ride on.

At a friendly cow camp in the Strip, the bullet was removed from Doolin's foot, Arkansas Tom remaining with him until the wound mended. Soon thereafter the gang was together again in the hideout in the Cimarron brakes. But not for long. After cutting up the Cimarron Crossing melon, they scattered for a few weeks. Doolin returned to his old home near Siloam Springs, in western Arkansas. Bill Dalton, richer than he had ever been, bought a house and a few acres of land in southern Oklahoma near Ardmore and lived there quietly with his wife.

Via the outlaw grapevine, Doolin called the gang together again at the old stronghold on the Cimarron, early in July. He knew, as everyone else did, that the Cherokee Strip was to be thrown open to settlement on September 16. Signs were already abundant that it was going to be the greatest land rush in history. The vanguard of the thousands of men and women who would be rushing in from the north was already arriving at Caldwell, Hunnewell, and the other Kansas border towns for the wild dash across the line. From the south, other thousands would be streaming in, all in a mad race for free land. Chaos would follow. The Strip would be settled by the six-gun, not by Marshal Nix and his deputies.

"All we have to do is wait a few weeks and we'll have things our own way," Doolin prophesied.

It was one of the few miscalculations he ever made.

XXIV

The Law Catches Up

On July 1, 1893, in addition to his other duties, Marshal Nix [1] was instructed from Washington to recruit a force of a thousand men to patrol the southern line of the Cherokee Strip and assist the military in preventing "Sooners" from rushing in to stake claims before the official bugle blew at twelve noon on September 16. Several times that many would have been too few. Nix, busily hiring guards, was temporarily unable to devote himself to his resolve to rid the Territory of its organized bands of outlaws. He therefore welcomed Deputy Marshal Orrington (Red) Lucas' offer to take to the brush for several weeks with a companion to try to locate the hideout of the Doolin Gang.

Red Lucas was certainly aware of the dangerous nature of the mission he was undertaking. If he and his companion, Doc Roberts, came under suspicion, they were not likely to get out of the wilds of Payne County alive. But Lucas was of an ingenious turn of mind, and he believed that by pretending to be a team of engineers locating the route for a proposed railroad, and making no attempt at secrecy, they would be able to proceed without too much difficulty. They traveled in a light wagon, apparently unarmed, stopping at frequent intervals to squint through the surveyor's transit with which they had provided themselves.

Without mishap they rolled into Ingalls late one afternoon. The

236

townsfolk were delighted when they learned the nature of the visitors' business and that Ingalls could look forward to having a railroad in the near future. That evening in the Trilby Saloon, they stood up to the bar and exchanged courtesies with several unsuspicious members of the Doolin Gang.

Lucas and Roberts, in a cool display of nerve, withstood the urge to get away from Ingalls as quickly as possible with the information they had gathered, and spent the following day "working" southwest of town, doing a lot of measuring and sighting. To the little group of citizens who had turned out to watch them, the two "engineers" could not agree on where their railroad should cross Black Creek. They invited suggestions from the onlookers, which led to some interesting conversation, out of which Lucas and his partner were able to put together a complete dossier on the comings and goings of the Doolin Gang. Some of them, they gathered, could usually be found at Bee Dunn's ranch or at his cousin's place, ten miles east of Ingalls.

The word "ranch" was used so loosely that it applied to any place on which a man had a cabin or dugout. The Dunn cousins had progressed beyond that. Although the law had no grudges against them, both were suspected of throwing the wide loop, and that rustling accounted for their prosperity. That they, as well as many others, were well paid for the services they rendered the outlaws with whom they associated must be taken for granted; without such "tick birds," who lived on outlaws, no gang could have survived for long.

When Lucas and Roberts left Ingalls, they headed west for Stillwater, from where they got in touch with Marshal Nix by wire. The latter began putting together a posse of deputy marshals at once. John Hixon was put in command and Frank Canton, Charlie Colcord, Jim Masterson (Bat's brother), Dick Speed, Tom Houston, and Lafe Shadley were assigned to him.

They set out from Guthrie in two covered wagons, some accounts say three, pretending to be "boomers" looking for land, a plow and coop of chickens tied on the end-gates. The country was used to seeing such parties of movers. The real ones were always burdened with children. For obvious reasons Hixon's party had to dispense with that touch. On September 1, they reached the vicinity of Ingalls at ten o'clock in the morning. Circling around to the east, they drove in from the north. They were lucky enough to catch six members of the gang in town. Four had their horses stabled in Light's Livery Barn. Hixon was never able to explain why he didn't make the barn his original point of attack. Instead, the marshals left the wagons and proceeded up the main street.

A young man identified as Jerry Simmonds in some accounts and called Walker in others (Dr. Pickering, who treated him, names him Walker) dashed across the street and was shot down by one of the deputies in the belief that he was carrying a warning to the gang. Walker died that evening about six o'clock.

A minute after the first shot, the street was wracked by gunfire. Of the six bandits caught in Ingalls that morning, five—Doolin, Bill Dalton, Dynamite Dick, Tulsa Jack, and Bitter Creek Newcomb—were standing at the bar in Ransom and Murray's saloon. The sixth, Arkansas Tom, was sick in bed in a room on the second floor of Mary Pierce's place.

The marshals, working their way up the street and taking advantage of whatever cover they could find, concentrated their fire on the Trilby Saloon. In justification of the act, Hixon later testified, "We knew they were in there."

Bitter Creek's horse was tethered in back of the building. He got to it and made a dash across the main street. Deputy Marshal Dick Speed snapped a shot at him that knocked the magazine off Newcomb's rifle. A second shot struck him in the leg, but he turned the corner into a side street and got away to the southwest.

From his window, Arkansas Tom saw Jim Masterson peering around a tree. He drilled a shot at him that cut the bark off the tree within inches of Masterson's head. The latter promptly leaped into the ditch at the side of the road, where he tumbled over Marshal Hixon, who had also sought cover there. The two of them then began firing over the lip of the ditch at the hotel window, but to no purpose. As Deputy Houston tried to zigzag across the street, a bullet from Arkansas Tom's rifle struck him in the stomach and sent him sprawling. Hixon and Masterson dragged him out of the line of fire, but Houston was mortally wounded.

By now the windows of the Trilby Saloon had been shattered and a rain of bullets was ripping through the saloon's thin walls. Doolin, Dalton, Dynamite Dick, and Tulsa Jack realized that to remain where they were meant death or capture. They decided to risk everything on the hundred-to-one chance that they could get across the street alive and reach their horses. Doolin and Dalton burst out first. Darting right, then left, they got halfway across when both were struck, Dalton in the shoulder and Doolin receiving a slug across the back of his neck that cut a nerve. A few seconds more and they turned the corner and reached the barn. Their wounds were not serious, but Doolin's gave him a nervous affliction that persecuted him for the rest of his life.

Tulsa Jack and Dynamite Dick reached the barn a few moments later, neither having received a scratch. The tempo of the shooting swelled again as the four men began firing from the wide entrance of the barn. Doolin, half crazed with pain, saw Deputy Marshal Dick Speed drop down behind the town pump and watering trough at the corner, from where he could fire into the barn. Doolin pumped a shot at him and missed, but leaning against the door to steady himself, he took careful aim and fired again. Speed tumbled over, dead.

The bandits were mounted by now. Doolin and Dynamite Dick dashed out the rear door; Dalton and Tulsa Jack plunged through the front entrance. Deputy Lafe Shadley got Dalton in his rifle sights and fired. The bullet missed Dalton but struck his horse in the jaw. The animal became unmanageable. Dalton kept his seat on the bucking animal for a hundred yards or more, when Tulsa Jack turned back and Dalton got up behind him. Together they made their escape. The fight was over. Hixon and several deputies ran to where Shadley lay at the corner of Dr. Call's fence. Whether it was Dalton or Arkansas Tom who shot him, no one knows for certain.

Even when he realized that he was the only member of the gang left in Ingalls, Arkansas Tom refused to surrender, expecting that Doolin and the others would return and try to effect his escape. But several hours passed without any sign of them, and shortly after two o'clock Tom surrendered.[2] He was taken to Stillwater that afternoon, as were Marshals Houston and Shadley, where the stricken men died two days later.

The final score was three deputy marshals and two civilians killed and three of the outlaws wounded. The gang ran no farther than the hideout on the Cimarron. A doctor was brought up from Cushing to attend the injured. As soon as they were in shape to ride again, Doolin and Bitter Creek crossed the line into Arkansas and hid out in the wild brakes on the Illinois River. Eventually they risked going to Hot Springs in the hope that the baths would restore them to health. They were safe enough, for public attention was fixed on the riotous conditions produced by the opening of the Cherokee Strip on September 16.

Typical of the chaos that reigned everywhere was the tiny hamlet of Wharton, where the Daltons had robbed their first train. Renamed Perry, it had become a brawling town of eight thousand frenzied men and women by nightfall, with late special trains bringing in additional thousands, and arguments being settled by the six-gun. Marshal Nix and his augmented force of deputies were temporarily overwhelmed, as Doolin had foreseen they would be. By the end of the year, conditions had become sufficiently stabilized to permit Nix to resume his hunt for the Doolin Gang. They had killed three of his deputies, and he meant to have them for it.

In the meantime, Bill Doolin had slipped back into the blackjack hills of Payne County and was courting Edith Ellsworth, the daughter of a minister living near Lawson P.O. They were married in the early summer of 1894. A few weeks later he called the gang together again, the rendezvous occurring north of Siloam

Springs, in Benton County, Arkansas. Bill Dalton was not among those who responded. In fact, there is no evidence that, after Ingalls, he ever rode with the Doolins again. But the other regulars were there. When they were ready to ride, Doolin led them across the state line to Southwest City, Missouri. They rode into the little town with guns blazing in Wild West fashion and robbed the Seaborn Bank of $14,000. As they were roaring out of town, J. C. Seaborn and his younger brother ran into the street and fired at them. One of the bandits, never identified, turned in the saddle and killed the elder Seaborn.[3]

Instead of returning directly to the rendezvous, the gang swept west across the Arkansas state line into Pawnee and relieved the bank there of an additional $10,000.

The Doolin Gang did not strike again until noon, May 4, 1895, when they held up a Rock Island train at Dover, far across the Territory, in the vicinity where the Dalton family had lived for years. From the express car and the passengers they collected several thousand dollars, the smallest haul they ever made. Marshal Chris Madsen, thirty-five miles away, got news of the robbery by wire a few minutes after it happened. The railroad company put a locomotive and boxcar at his service. Into the car Madsen loaded men and horses and steamed north at full speed.

Confident that pursuit could not be quickly organized, the gang pulled up in a wooded valley ten miles east of Dover to blow their horses and divide the loot. They were taking their ease when the posse poured over a ridge to the west and surprised them. They rushed to their horses, but before they could mount, Red Buck's horse was killed. A moment later, Tulsa Jack's horse went down. Doolin and the others had dropped back among the cedars. Red Buck and Tulsa Jack ran to join them. Only Red Buck made it. Madsen, fearless as usual, charged into the cedars, but his posse-men lost their enthusiasm as bullets began humming past their ears. Red Buck got up behind Bitter Creek, and off the bandits fled.

With the inactivity that winter always imposed only a few weeks away, Doolin led his men into the northwestern corner of the Territory, a region which, because of its long distances, he had avoided ever since the Cimarron Crossing robbery. Woodward, the county seat, a prosperous town on the Santa Fe, was their destination. The *California Limited,* eastbound, made a regularly scheduled midnight stop at Woodward to take on water and coal, and it was on the *Limited* that their attention was focused. When the locomotive pulled up at the water tower, they intended to board it, take charge of the engine crew, get into the express car, gather up what they could, and get away in a hurry without bothering to go through the coaches and Pullmans with the old grain sack.

Doolin had only five men with him—Bitter Creek Newcomb, Little Bill Raidler, Dynamite Dick, Little Dick West, and Charlie Pierce. But, if only five, they were five of the best in their line. Shortly after dark, Doolin sent Bitter Creek, Raidler, and Pierce into town to pick up what information they could about the express shipments that were going through.

They made the rounds of the saloons and learned by chance that a shipment of money for the Woodward National had reached town on the evening train and was being held overnight in the express company's office. On learning where the agent lived, they went to his home, kidnapped him, brought him to the office, and compelled him to open up. It was the easiest touch the gang had ever made and netted some $6,000. They were long gone before any pursuit could be organized.

In the weeks following the Woodward robbery, the Doolin Gang scattered again and remained inactive for months. Doolin had named the place where they were to rendezvous the following summer. The place was Bee Dunn's ranch near Ingalls, with which all were familiar. Unquestionably this was by prearrangement with Dunn.

Doolin's wife and infant son were living on the small farm he had bought near Burden, Kansas. He joined them, and using the alias of William J. Barry, spent the long months of inactivity on the Burden farm.

It was apparent by now that Marshal Nix and his little army

of deputies were putting down the rash of outlawry that followed the opening of the Strip. A score and more of small-time bandits had been eliminated or packed off to prison. Henry Starr, no small-time outlaw he, was behind bars. But there could be no real victory for law and order until the Doolin Gang was smashed. Nix issued his famous edict: "Bring them in dead or alive."

Bill Dalton was the first to pay the maximum penalty for his outlawry. He had been living quietly for weeks with his wife on his farm near Ardmore, when the express agent there called Deputy Marshal Loss Hart's attention to a shipment that had been received prepaid and marked to be held until called for. Hart agreed with the agent that it undoubtedly was a shipment of liquor. Under federal law it was a criminal offense to bring alcoholic beverages into the Chickasaw Nation. When Mrs. Dalton called for the case, Hart learned her identity and where she and Bill were living. He swore in a posse and went to the farm at once. When Dalton, who was aware of the indictment against him, saw the house surrounded by half a dozen men, he buckled on his gun and jumped from a second-floor window. Loss Hart caught him on the wing, and Dalton was dead when he hit the ground.

Not more than a week later, Chris Madsen met up with two Texas Rangers who were on the trail of two men that were wanted for robbery and murder. The description they gave Madsen of the fleeing pair satisfied him that one of the two was Red Buck Waightman, who had been kicked out of the Doolin Gang for the wanton killing of an old man. So Madsen threw in with the Rangers. In northern Comanche County they closed in on the men they were hunting. One of the pair was killed; the other, though wounded, escaped. He was Red Buck.

Near Arapaho, in Custer County, Madsen caught up with him and killed him as he stepped out of the dugout in which he was hiding.

That same September, Marshals Tilghman and Thomas were making their headquarters in Stillwater, twelve miles west of Ingalls. They had a visitor, Will Dunn, by their standards a treacherous, unsavory character who would do anything for money. No one knows what Will Dunn received for secretly switching sides and turning traitor and informer on his cousin Bee Dunn.

Several days later he was back in Stillwater and reported to Tilghman that his cousin had confided in him that Bitter Creek, Bill Raidler, Dynamite Dick, and Charlie Pierce had been at his place earlier in the week, expecting to find Doolin there. Before leaving they had informed Bee that they would be back a night or two later. The two marshals swore in several possemen and, accompanied by Will Dunn, left for Bee's ranch at once, arriving there at daylight. Bee denied having seen anything of the Doolins, but he wilted when his cousin told him he had changed sides and was now riding with the law.

Bee Dunn, on being given the choice of cooperating with the officers or arrest for consorting with known outlaws, chose the former. He made room in his barn for their horses. Normally anyone using the road could be observed from either of the two front-room windows for several minutes before he passed; but a recent hailstorm had broken the glass on the east side of the room and it had been boarded up. To overcome that handicap, a shallow pit was dug out in the yard and roofed over with poles and sod. Tilghman and Heck Thomas, in company with Will Dunn and a posseman, took turns lying out in the pit, watchful and alert.

For two days and nights, no one rode into the trap that had been prepared for them. On the third night, bright with moonlight, the watchers caught the drumming of hooves approaching from the east. Several minutes later, two horsemen pounded up to the darkened house and were tethering their broncs when Thomas ordered them to throw up their hands. For a shocked second the two men, Bitter Creek and Charlie Pierce, froze in their tracks. In the next breath their pistols were spitting fire, an orange flash from the makeshift pit telling them where the enemy lay hidden.

What followed was inevitable. Outmanned, outgunned—.45's versus Winchesters—it was no contest. Bitter Creek went down first; Charlie Pierce charged the pit and was riddled with lead.

Tilghman and the others ran out from the house as the gunfire died away in the hills and examined the two bandits. Both were dead.

Little Bill Raidler and Dynamite Dick had intended to accompany Bitter Creek and Pierce. Only a drinking bout had kept them from doing so. When they learned what had happened at Bee Dunn's, they separated. As luck would have it, Dynamite Dick managed to ride right into the hands of Deputy Marshals Steve Burke, E. D. Nix, and Will Jones at a country store on Black Bear Creek, west of Pawnee. They recognized him before he could get out of the saddle. When he went for his gun, they riddled him with lead. He was still alive, however, when they picked him up. They took him by wagon to Perry and on to Guthrie by train, where he died of pneumonia a few days later.

Of the original eleven members of the Doolin Gang, if Ol Yountis is included, the marshals had killed seven. Arkansas Tom was in prison. Only Doolin, Little Dick West, and Little Bill Raidler were left.

XXV

The Horseback Outlaw
Fades Into History

A GREAT deal of nonsense has been written about Little Dick West, the "wild man who, no matter what the weather, refused to sleep under cover." That he was a range waif who could not read or write is undoubtedly true. Drifting around from one outfit to another as he matured, he became a cowhand, and a good one. He knew cow, as the old saying had it, and in the saddle he had few equals. Having worked together on the H X Bar, Doolin had won the full measure of the little man's loyalty.

The death of Dynamite Dick, following the shoot-out at the store on Black Bear Creek, left the two other men—West and Raidler—unaccounted for. For weeks, neither had been reported as having been seen. And then one day in Pawhuska, an Osage Indian told Heck Thomas that Raidler was hiding out on the Sam Moore ranch, forty miles north of town, near the Kansas border. Thomas waited in Pawhuska for Tilghman to join him. The two of them then set out to capture the always scowling, poetry-quoting outlaw.

Moore and his wife acknowledged that Raidler was hiding out in the hills to the east. Just where, they didn't know. However, Mrs. Moore told the marshals that Little Bill rode in three or four times a week, turned his horse into the corral, and ate supper with them. That was enough for Tilghman and Thomas, and they settled down to wait for him to show up. He put in an appearance on the following evening. He turned his horse into the corral and started for the kitchen door. The two marshals had flattened themselves against the rear corners of the cabin, and when Tilghman ordered Little Bill to throw up his hands, the startled outlaw leaped into the air and came down with a gun in each hand, and they were spitting fire.

Tilghman and Thomas had no choice but to start blasting away at him. Little Bill went down, but he was not dead. By wagon they took him to Elgin, Kansas, and from there, on a cot in a baggage car, to Guthrie over the Missouri Pacific and the Santa Fe. He proved how tough he was by surviving his wounds, stood trial, and was sentenced to twenty-one years in the Ohio State Penitentiary (which by arrangement received federal prisoners).

Raidler had served less than half of his sentence when he was pardoned. He married shortly thereafter and lived his remaining ten years as a model citizen. Of all the Doolin Gang he was the only brand saved from the burning.

The capture of Little Bill Raidler left Doolin and Little Dick West very much on the loose. Marshal Nix never disclosed from whom he got the tip that Bill Doolin was living on his farm near Burden, Kansas. However that may have been, he at once assigned to Bill Tilghman, his best man, the not inconsiderable task of bringing him in.

In Burden, Tilghman learned that Doolin had not been seen in several weeks. But from the postmaster he learned that Mrs. Doolin, alias Barry, was receiving several letters a week postmarked "Eureka Springs, Arkansas," possibly from her husband. Tilghman thought it so likely that he lost no time heading for Eureka Springs, a small health resort whose waters, it was claimed, were beneficial in relieving nervous afflictions. Doolin, who was still suffering from the injury he had sustained at Ingalls, had been advised by a neighbor to try the baths at Eureka Springs, and he had gone there.

Tilghman, wearing a hard hat and ministerial garb as a disguise, encountered his man a few minutes after reaching the Springs. Doolin did not recognize him instantly in such clothes. It gave the marshal the advantage, and after a tremendous physical struggle he disarmed the outlaw leader without a shot being fired. "Bill," said Tilghman, "I'll spare you the humiliation of taking you to Guthrie in irons if you'll promise not to try to bust away from me. All I want is your word."

Doolin thought it over for a moment and nodded his head. "Marshal, you've got it." [1]

A crowd of several hundred men and women had gathered at the Guthrie jail to see Doolin being brought in. In the weeks that passed as he awaited being brought to trial, he was never without visitors. Although there was a mountain of evidence against him and he seemed certain to be convicted, he laughed a great deal and did not appear depressed. He made friends with his jailers, and if a guard or turnkey wanted a laugh, he could always find it at the door of Doolin's cell. He also told them fantastic tales of the money the gang had buried and where—or almost where—they could dig it up. He enjoyed their attempts to pump him for more information.

On Sunday evening, January 3, 1896, as a blue norther was starting to blow, a turnkey making his rounds, stopped to exchange a few words with him. Doolin soon had the man laughing hilariously, and as he threw back his head in merriment, Doolin reached through the bars and plucked the turnkey's revolver out of the holster. The merriment was over; he ordered the turnkey to open the cell door, and when that was done, he traded places with him and proceeded to release the other prisoners.

Without a hand being raised to stop him, Doolin walked out of the jail. A block away, he ordered a young man and his girl to get out of the rig in which they were riding and drove off at a fast trot. At the edge of town he unharnessed the horse and, mounting bareback, dashed to freedom. Seven months were to pass before the law caught up with him again.

Bill Doolin's whereabouts in the months that followed are

unknown. Whenever a country bank was robbed, the immediate suspicion was that it was his work, although later evidence often proved otherwise. It was rumored that he had made contact with Little Dick West and that the two of them were riding once more, which was equally untrue; following the Woodward robbery, they never saw each other again.

Little Dick had thrown in with that inept, bungling bunch of amateurs known as the Jennings Gang. But not for long. Disgusted with the way things were going, he tossed his saddle on his bronc one morning and pulled out by himself. Not long thereafter, Deputy Marshal Bud Ledbetter and his posse cracked down on the Jennings Gang, and Al and Frank Jennings and the two O'Malley brothers, Morris and Pat, were packed off to prison. But in the meantime Little Dick West had disappeared and the law could not flush him out of hiding.

Edith Doolin had disposed of the Kansas farm and had returned to Lawson, where she and young John, her son, who was almost two, were living with her father, the Reverend Ellsworth. The marshals knew she was there, and Tilghman visited her on one occasion. Being convinced that she was in touch with Bill, he urged her to try to persuade him to give himself up and take his chances with the law. Nothing came of it, but Nix had the house watched, believing that sooner or later Doolin would risk capture in order to spend a few hours with his wife and son. He did so on several occasions but without the marshals' catching sight of him.

Lawson was the tiniest of hamlets—a post office, a general store, a smithy, a church and half a dozen widely scattered houses. The Ellsworth home was to the northwest on a bend of a small creek, known locally as Camp Creek. The nearest doctor was at Ingalls, twenty miles to the south.

Obviously Doolin was among friends at Lawson, who informed him when it was safe to come in and when it was not. With Bill Tilghman being needed elsewhere, Heck Thomas had been put in command of the stakeout. He established his headquarters at Ingalls. In making this move he was deliberately baiting the trap for Doolin to visit his family, figuring that, becoming overconfident, the outlaw would trip himself.

After pursuing that idea for a month without tangible results, Thomas turned to bribery, inducing the Noble brothers, who were known to be favorable to Doolin, to turn informer.[2] The Noble brothers, blacksmiths and well diggers, were in a position to hear what was happening in the community. Late in August they flashed word to the marshal that Doolin was visiting his wife and son and getting ready to leave the country with them.

Their treachery paid off, for when Thomas and his posse closed in on the Ellsworth house on the moonlit night of August 25, they saw a team and loaded wagon drawn up at the front door, a saddle horse tethered to the end-gate. They realized that they were just in time; in another few minutes the quarry would have slipped through their fingers. Two men were sent around to cover the back door; Thomas and a posseman took up a position in the black shadows cast by the willows that fringed tiny Camp Creek. They were barely in position when Doolin stepped out the front door, his rifle cradled in his left arm. He had allowed his beard to grow, but Thomas recognized him at once.

Doolin glanced about suspiciously as he waited for his wife to join him. She stepped out a few moments later, her son sound asleep in her arms. He kissed the boy and placed him in an improvised bed in back of the seat and helped his wife to get into the wagon. He patted her hand as she took the reins.

"Drive down to the creek," Thomas heard him tell her. "I'll walk on ahead; there may be someone in the willows."

Heck Thomas, no stranger to such moments, knew it was now or never. He was armed with an eight-gauge shotgun loaded with buck, the deadliest of all weapons at thirty yards. The gun half raised, he stepped out of the shadows and ordered the famous outlaw to throw up his hands. Doolin's rifle leaped to his shoulder. The hurried snap shot missed its target. Both barrels of the shotgun thundered and Doolin went down, riddled with buckshot. He was dead when Thomas reached him. Mrs. Doolin had leaped out of the wagon and flung herself, sobbing, on the prostrate body of her husband.

The killing of Bill Doolin can be justified on half a dozen counts. But it was accomplished by treachery, and there was no glory in it. Undoubtedly that was in the minds of many in the throng of several thousand who attended the funeral services in Guthrie, for along with the morbidly curious there were hundreds of Oklahoma's leading citizens, including Tilghman, Thomas, Hixon, Madsen, and the other marshals who had hunted Doolin for years.

Outlawry did not end with the passing of Bill Doolin. Henry Starr was to go on his rampages until he was shot down in the act of robbing the bank at Harrison, Arkansas, on February 18, 1921. He was among the first and certainly the last of Oklahoma's horseback outlaws.

Nix and his field marshals had completely lost track of Little Dick West. He had not been seen or heard of in so long that it was widely believed that he had gone to Mexico. Actually, he had not been more than fifty miles from Guthrie in all the months that the search for him was being pressed.

In the days when Bill Doolin was cowboying on the H X Bar, Herman Arnett, a young man of German ancestry, was regarded by Oscar Halsell as one of his top hands. He was thrifty, took himself seriously, and was determined to have a spread of his own one day. Perhaps the fact that Halsell himself was of German stock tipped the scales in Arnett's favor, for he arranged with Colonel Zack Mulhall to sell Arnett a piece of range on Beaver Creek and then stocked it for him on credit. Arnett prospered, built a house, barn, and corral, doing most of the labor himself, and, in 1897, he took a wife. It changed his life considerably, for he now had someone looking over his shoulder, telling him what to do and what not to do.

It had been Arnett's practice to take in any drifting cowboy or range waif who came along, feed him, and get a day's labor in return. Mrs. Arnett said she would have no more of it; that it had to stop, objecting strenuously to the frequent coming of a dirty, hairy-faced little man who reeked of dried sweat and whose cold gray eyes frightened her. He always arrived in the evening, turned his horse into the corral and left the following morning with a bag of food.

"I can't turn him off," Arnett protested. "I've known him ever since the time when the two of us were working for Mr. Halsell."

Gossiping with a neighbor woman, Mrs. Arnett mentioned the little man and her fear of him. The talk was passed on and eventually reached the wife of the clerk of the District Court. When she informed her husband, he lost no time getting in touch with Marshal Nix. Instead of dismissing the tale as so much tittle-tattle, Nix summoned Field Marshals Tilghman and Heck Thomas to his office. They agreed that the meagre description of Arnett's visitor fitted Little Dick West.

But was it possible that after the long, fruitless search for the little outlaw that he should turn up within a dozen miles of where they sat conferring that morning? Nix thought so and ordered an immediate investigation. Deputies Frank Rinehart and Bill Fossett were called in and ordered to accompany Tilghman and Thomas.

"Until we know to a certainty that Arnett's visitor is not Little Dick, we will proceed on the firm conviction that he is," Nix told them. "You know that Little Dick is deadly and will not easily be taken alive. You will proceed accordingly." [3]

The four marshals left Guthrie at midnight, and at daybreak, April 7, 1898, began moving up Beaver Creek. After proceeding several hundred yards, they tethered their horses in the willow brake and on foot reached the small peach orchard that Arnett had set out in back of the barn. There was a horse in the corral. A man came out of the barn, a currycomb in one hand and a brush in the other, and began grooming the animal. As the light strengthened, Tilghman and Thomas recognized him. It was Little Dick.

"Hands up!" Tilghman commanded.

Comb and brush went flying, and with the incredible swiftness of a wild cat, Little Dick's hands came up clutching his .45's.

Before he could locate a target, the marshals blasted him into eternity. As Tilghman said later, "The currycomb and brush decided it; the split second it took him to get his hands out of the straps made the difference."

With the elimination of Dick West, the only member of the Doolin Gang left alive was Arkansas Tom, and he was behind the gray walls of the Lansing, Kansas, penitentiary and would be for another seven years. The law had erased the others. It didn't mean the end of outlawry, for in the wings, waiting to take over, was a new and utterly ruthless brand of desperadoes. They were to supplant the horse with automobiles for a fast getaway from the scene of a robbery and/or murder. The .45 and the Winchester were discarded for the automatic and the submachine gun.

The exploits of Frank and Jesse James, the Youngers, the Daltons, and the Doolins were to become a fading memory as the doings of Verne Miller, Al Spencer, Al Karpis, Pretty Boy Floyd, Machine-Gun Kelly, and others of their caliber monopolized the headlines. They spread terror over half a dozen states until the government made kidnapping and certain other major crimes federal offenses, which allowed the FBI and its dreaded G-men to cross state lines and force a showdown on Karpis and the mad dogs with whom he associated.

Some were killed by lawmen's bullets; others were sent to prison for long stretches. At least one died in the gas chamber of the Missouri State Penitentiary. Marshal Tilghman, nearing seventy and still in harness, expressed his opinion of them. "They're just young punks, mad dogs who shouldn't be mentioned in the same breath with such men as Bill Doolin. Bill never shot a man in the back and never killed a man who wasn't trying to kill him." [4]

Although the horseback outlaws have passed into history, some of the myths surrounding them have survived. The hardest one to down is that there was a blood strain of lawlessness in them that was passed on from father to son. This is sheer nonsense and springs from the fact that the Daltons were second cousins by marriage to the Younger brothers. It is completely refuted by the fact that no son of any prairie bandit ever followed his father into outlawry.

Jesse James' son, Jesse, Jr., became a leading member of the Kansas City bar. Jesse's daughter Mary had three sons. All became leading members of the church in Excelsior Springs. One of them became an ordained Methodist minister. Frank James' son, Robert F., became a prosperous farmer and lived a long life, untainted by criminality. Four of the Dalton boys—Ben, Henry, Charles, and Littleton—lived and died respected citizens. Bill Doolin's widow married a second time and her son John Doolin was adopted by her new husband, the Reverend Jonathan Meeks, and grew to manhood as John Doolin Meeks, becoming a popular minister in Ponca City. And there was Roosevelt Starr, Henry Starr's son, who rose to a position of prominence in the state government.

Other names could be added to the list of boys who didn't go wrong. Plainly it was the forces of circumstance rather than any hereditary urge that drove men into outlawry.

Notes

CHAPTER I

1. In the Treaty of Guadalupe Hidalgo, signed at the conclusion of the Mexican War, the United States agreed to recognize all land titles granted by Mexico. But for twenty years the United States Land Commission rejected the petitions of seven out of every eight claimants to come before it, constituting, says Julian Dana in *The Sacramento—River of Gold,* in the Rivers of America Series, "the most flagrant government confiscation of property in modern times."

CHAPTER II

1. John Rollin Ridge, a mixed-blood Cherokee Indian, was the son of John Ridge, the grandson of Major Ridge, and the cousin of the celebrated Cherokee leader Stand Watie and of Elias Boudinot. The family was identified with the Treaty Party, as opposed to the No Treaty faction headed by Chief John Ross, in the feud that split the Cherokee Nation after its removal to present Oklahoma.

2. Joseph Henry Jackson in *Bad Company.*

CHAPTER III

1. Tom Bell's farewell letter to his mother:

Dear Mother:
   As I am about to make my exit to another country, I take this opportunity to write you a few lines. Probably you may never hear from me again. If not, I hope we may meet where parting is no more.
   In my prodigal career in this country, I have always recollected your fond admonitions, and if I had lived up to them probably I would not have been in my present condition; but dear Mother, though my fate

255

has been a cruel one, yet I have no one to blame but myself. Give my respects to all my old and youthful friends. Tell them to beware of bad associations, and never to enter any gambling saloons, for that has been my ruin.

If my old Grandmother is living, remember me to her. With these remarks, I bid you farewell forever.

Your only boy,
Tom

Chapter IV

1. For the story of the so-called Sydney Ducks in California, see this writer's *Notorious Ladies of the Frontier* and Herbert Asbury's *The Barbary Coast*. Their crimes were largely confined to San Francisco and its environs. They gave it the reputation of being "the wickedest city in the world."

2. Being young and handsome, it was inevitable that many early writers, combining fiction with fact, should provide Dick Barter with romantic adventures. After he broke up his gang, it was said that on a number of robberies his lone companion was a beautiful young woman. There is nothing in the record to suggest that she ever existed, other than in the imagination of her creators.

Chapter V

1. The fascination that the shaggy-haired little man held for women, some of them respectable enough, is not easily explained. Perhaps it was his untamed, animal-like ferocity that captivated the opposite sex. Sooner or later, such men are often betrayed by a woman. That was not the case with Tiburcio Vasquez.

2. This was a singular circumstance. If the loan of a gallows by one county to another ever occurred elsewhere, it has escaped the writer's years of research.

Chapter VI

1. This is the Wells, Fargo confidential list of the twenty-eight stage robberies of its property by Black Bart, in all but one of which he also robbed the United States mail. It should be noted that it does not include the losses suffered by the independent lines and attributed to him:

1. Stage from Sonora to Milton, July 26, 1875, 4 miles from Copperopolis. John Shine, driver.

2. Stage from San Juan to Marysville, December 28, 1875, 10 miles from San Juan. Mike Hogan, driver.

3. Stage from Roseburg to Yreka, June 2, 1876, 5 miles from Cottonwood. A. C. Adams, driver.

4. Stage from Point Arena to Duncan's Mills, August 3, 1877, between Fort Ross and Russian River.

5. Stage from Quincy to Oroville, July 25, 1878, 1 mile from Berry Creek.

6. Stage from Laporte to Oroville, July 30, 1878, 5 miles from Laporte. D. E. Barry, driver.

7. Stage from Cahto to Ukiah, October 2, 1878, 12 miles from Ukiah.

8. Stage from Covelo to Ukiah, October 3, 1878, 10 miles from Potter Valley.

9. Stage from Laporte to Oroville, June 21, 1879, 3 miles from Forbestown. Dave Quadlin, driver.

10. Stage from Roseburg to Redding, October 25, 1879, 2 miles from Bass Station.

11. Stage from Alturas to Redding, October 27, 1879, 12 miles above Millville.

12. Stage from Point Arena to Duncan's Mills, July 22, 1880, 2½ miles from Henry's Station. M. K. McLennan, driver. Mr. W. J. Turner and wife, of San Francisco, passengers.

13. Stage from Weaverville to Redding, September 1, 1880, 1 mile from Last Chance. Charles Cramer, driver. Took breakfast next morning at Mr. Adkinson's on Eagle Creek.

14. Stage from Roseburg to Yreka, September 16, 1880, 1 mile from Oregon state line. Nort Eddings, driver.

15. Stage from Redding to Roseburg, November 20, 1880, 1 mile from Oregon state line. Joe Mason, driver.

16. Stage from Roseburg to Yreka, August 31, 1881, 9½ miles from Yreka. John Lulloway, driver.

17. Stage from Yreka to Redding, October 8, 1881, 3 miles from Bass Station. Horace Williams, driver.

18. Stage from Lakeview to Redding, October 11, 1881, 2 miles from Round Mountain post office. Louis Brewster, driver.

19. Stage from Downieville to Marysville, December 15, 1881, 4 miles from Dobbin's Ranch. George Sharpe, driver.

20. Stage from North San Juan to Smartesville, December 27, 1881.

21. Stage from Ukiah to Cloverdale, January 26, 1882, 6 miles from Cloverdale. Harry Forse, driver.

22. Stage from Little Lake to Ukiah, June 14, 1882, 3 miles from Little Lake. Thomas B. Forse, driver.

23. Attempt to rob stage from Laporte to Oroville, July 13, 1882, 9 miles from Strawberry. George Helms, driver. George W. Hackett, Wells, Fargo & Company's messenger, fired at robber and put him to flight.

24. Stage from Yreka to Redding, September 17, 1882, 14 miles from Redding. Horace Williams, driver.

25. Stage from Lakeport to Cloverdale, November 24, 1882, 6 miles from Cloverdale. Ed Crawford, driver.

26. Stage from Lakeport to Cloverdale, April 12, 1883, 5 miles from Cloverdale. Connibeck, driver.

27. Stage from Jackson to Ione City, June 23, 1883, 4 miles from Jackson. Clint Radcliffe, driver.

28. Stage from Sonora to Milton, November 3, 1883, 3 miles from Copperopolis. R. E. McConnell, driver.

2. In a novel entitled *The Case of Summerfield,* the leading character was named Bartholomew Graham, called *Black Bart* for short. The famous road agent had read the book and adopted the name.

3. Contrary to widespread belief, Bart left samples of his poetry behind him on only two of his many robberies.

4. Many accounts have it that Jimmy Rolleri's shot carried away Black Bart's hat, which was later found by the posse headed by Harry Morse and Sheriff Thorn. Old Martin, the hunter at whose cabin Bart stopped on his flight from the Sonora–Milton stage robbery, does not mention his visitor being hatless.

5. See *U.S. West, the Saga of Wells, Fargo,* by Lucius Beebe and Charles Clegg.

CHAPTER VII

1. Beebe and Clegg, *U.S. West, the Saga of Wells, Fargo.*

2. Named for General Jesse Lee Reno, the Civil War hero who was killed at the Battle of South Mountain in 1862.

3. The major part of the loot taken in the Verdi robbery was recovered. The Express Company, with its policy of secrecy in such matters, never disclosed the amount. The leniency shown Davis by the court suggests that it was in return for his help regarding the money turned back to Wells, Fargo.

CHAPTER VIII

1. The frequency with which Carson, as a place name, is encountered in Nevada is readily explained by the fact that Kit Carson, the famous frontier scout, passed that way when he guided Lieutenant John Charles Frémont through the Sierra Nevada to California.

2. In Nevada's freshman years, when new strikes were being reported, here or there, every few weeks, the thousands of men and women who joined the stampede to get to the scene of discovery often found they were chasing a dream. Not so Hamilton and Treasure Hill, which produced in excess of $60,000,000 in silver before its mines were exhausted.

CHAPTER IX

1. Virginia City's most popular strumpet was Julia Bulette. She was not a "madam," as some accounts have it. Her neat white cottage at the head of D Street, with potted geraniums from San Francisco blooming in the windows, was her only "castle." She loved diamonds, and her wealthy admirers drenched her with them. The same source had supplied her with a carriage and pair. When she drove up and down C Street of an afternoon, teamsters greeted her with a cheer and pulled aside so that she might pass. The members of Fire Engine Company No. 1 elected her an honorary member, which was akin to knighthood in Virginia City.

Eventually she was murdered for her diamonds. After her death, the Virginia and Truckee Railroad named its newest and plushiest club car "Julia Bulette" in her honor.

2. Mike Tovey, the redoubtable Wells, Fargo Express messenger, was killed in California on June 15, 1893, in an attack on the Ione-Jackson stage. For twenty-eight years he had guarded the company's treasure chests.

3. The chest contained $100,000 in negotiable securities, which explains why it had been dispatched from Bodie under heavy guard. The securities apparently did not interest Milton Sharp, for they were recovered intact.

Chapter X

1. Dave Neagle achieved nationwide notoriety long after his Panamint days when, as a deputy United States marshal assigned as bodyguard to Associate Supreme Court Justice Stephen J. Field, he shot and killed Judge David Terry when the latter attacked Judge Field in the railroad eating room at Lathrop, California. Field had tried the sensational lawsuit brought by Sarah Althea Hill against Senator William Sharon to decide whether she was his wife or his mistress. Field had ruled in favor of Sharon. Terry had subsequently married Sarah and had sworn that he would kill Justice Field on sight.

2. Angelenos whose memory goes back half a century can recall the days when the Nadeau Hotel was the town's leading hostelry. It retained their patronage even after the Angelus and Alexandria were built. Remi Nadeau also gave Los Angeles its first five-story office building.

Chapter XI

1. Lewis and Clark reached the forks of the Clearwater and the Snake on October 10, 1805. Great modern bridges span the rivers today, connecting Lewiston with much smaller Clarkston, Washington, both links in the Lewis and Clark Highway.

2. White Idahoans were onlookers rather than participants in the conflict which erupted in 1877, when the Nez Percé refused to give up their homelands and be rounded up on a reservation designated by the federal government. The resulting clash gained nationwide attention when Chief Joseph led his starving people on a masterful one-thousand-mile retreat across Idaho, only to meet crushing defeat at Big Hole, Montana.

3. Big Ben Holladay, the "Stagecoach King" and his Overland Stage Company, dominated early stagecoaching in Idaho. He early established service across the Territory from Eagle Rock (today's Idaho Falls) to Boise and the Boise Basin. An informative account will be found in John K. Rollinson's *Wyoming Cattle Trails*.

4. McConnell was appointed United States marshal of Idaho in 1865. Being a minority Republican, he was thwarted by the Democratic opposition in his attempts to bring law and order to Idaho and was forced to resign in 1867. But he was to have his day eventually. In 1893 he was elected governor of Idaho.

Chapter XII

1. Granville Stuart was a steadfast friend of the Indian and a critic of his debasement by the white man. In 1862 Stuart married Aubony, a Snake

Indian girl, and by her had nine children, among them Mary, the future wife of Teddy Blue Abbott, the well-known cowboy and ranchman.

2. These districts lay so close to one another that it was difficult for them to maintain their identity. Nevada City was less than a mile below Virginia City.

3. The townsite got the underground as well as the surface runoff of water after every storm. Some wag later put a "card" in the *Montana Post* announcing that he was applying for a permit to conduct a ferry service at the flooded corner of Wallace and Jackson Street.

4. Cleveland fired the first shot, but he was rolling drunk and the bullet went wide of the mark. Plummer's marksmanship was not much better, his first shot plowing into the ceiling.

Chapter XIII

1. Original on file in Montana State Historical archives.

2. All but five of the twenty-six were eventually apprehended and lynched.

3. Although the Territorial government was organized in Bannack, that camp was never the official capital of Montana.

Chapter XIV

1. The cattle that Bass and his companions had driven north had been turned over to them on credit by Texas ranchers. On being paid in cash for the herd at Ogallala, Nebraska, they decided at once that instead of returning to Texas to collect their share of the money, they would divide it among themselves and head north.

2. For the best life of Hickok, see Joseph G. Rosa's *They Called Him Wild Bill*.

3. Charles L. Martin's *A Sketch of Sam Bass*, with an Introduction by Ramon F. Adams, is both colorful and authentic.

4. See *Notorious Ladies of the Frontier* by Harry Sinclair Drago.

5. *U.S. West, the Saga of Wells, Fargo* by Lucius Beebe and Charles Clegg.

6. See Agnes Wright Spring's *Cheyenne and Black Hills Stage and Express Routes*.

Chapter XV

1. Dr. George Cooper, a member of the Swan River posse, severed Singleterry's head from the body and carted it to Alma, where it was put on display, as had been done with Joaquin Murrieta's head.

2. At sunrise, late on November 25, 1864, Colonel John Chivington, at the head of 950 troops and supported by four cannon, attacked the sleeping winter camp of the Cheyennes on Sand Creek without warning, slaughtering an estimated 300 Indians, mostly old men, women and children. Chivington was censured and removed from his command.

3. Among his other accomplishments, Gilly had his master's papers as a deep-water sailor. The last word his American friends had of him was

that he was running ammunition to the Popular Front in the Spanish Civil War in 1936.

CHAPTER XVI

1. For the best (if biased) account of the sacking of Lawrence on August 3, 1863, see William E. Connelley's *Quantrill and the Border Wars*.

2. A carefully detailed account of Pearl Starr will be found in Edwin P. Hicks' *Belle Starr and her Pearl*.

3. A comment by Paul Wellman directed at the Pinkertons, of whose accomplishments in Missouri he is extremely skeptical.

CHAPTER XVII

1. The reader will recall that a John Rollin Ridge, the grandson of Major Ridge, was the author of *The Life and Adventures of Joaquin Murrieta, Celebrated California Bandit*.

2. Quoted from *The Rise and Fall of Jesse James* by Robertus Love, the most reliable of many similar accounts.

3. Homer Croy in *The Last of the Great Outlaws*, a documented and realistic biography of Coleman Younger.

CHAPTER XVIII

1. In his *The Last of the Great Outlaws*, Homer Croy says that the bandits missed the jackpot by twenty-four hours; that on the following night the eastbound Chicago and Rock Island express was carrying $45,000. He doesn't cite the source of his information.

2. Stewart Holbrook, in his fascinating *The Story of American Railroads*, devotes a chapter to the "Ballads of Rails."

3. Frank and Annie James were the parents of a son, Robert, who served in the army in the Spanish-American War and was highly regarded by his neighbors. For a time he conducted the Jesse James Museum at the Samuel homestead. Jesse's wife bore him two children, a boy and a girl. The son, Jesse, Jr., became a respected member of the Kansas City bar.

CHAPTER XIX

1. Bridge Square has not changed greatly with the passing years. Many of the old buildings are still there, bearing the scars and bullet holes they received that September day in 1876.

2. Cole Younger in his little paperback *The Story of Cole Younger by Himself*, demolishes the story as fiction.

CHAPTER XX

1. Clarence Hite soon contracted what used to be known as galloping consumption. He was released from prison and sent home to die.

2. "General Jo Shelby, the Confederate cavalry leader, noticeably under the influence of the Bourbon with which his admirers had toasted him that

morning, took the stand as a witness for the defense. Glaring about the courtroom with the look of a shaggy old unvanquished lion, he demanded: 'Where is my old friend and comrade in arms? Ah, there I see him! I should like to shake hands with my fellow soldier who fought by my side for Southern rights!' He started to rise from his chair but the bailiff restrained him. . . . The case against Frank James was decided then and there."

3. You may read that Jim Younger committed suicide because a woman with whom he had fallen in love had rejected him. The story is not supported by any trace of evidence.

CHAPTER XXI

1. Daisy Bryant was held as a material witness in connection with the Wharton robbery, but was released for lack of evidence. Writers interested only in the sensational, after the killing of Bob Dalton, had her wearing male clothes and riding at the head of her own gang of bandits, which can be dismissed as nonsense.

CHAPTER XXII

1. "I've heard that story a thousand times," Emmett Dalton told me in Hollywood, in 1928. "I've never believed it. If Bill had known we were in trouble, he wouldn't have turned back; that was not his style."

2. Ayers survived, the bullet that felled him only creasing his scalp. He is said to have exchanged shots with Bob Dalton, which is not true; his hastily borrowed rifle had not been fired.

3. Because Emmett's attempted rescue of his brother rather closely follows Cole Younger's rescue of Bob Younger at Northville, Burton Rascoe ridicules it as never having happened. And yet he has high praise for Eye-Witness, who first published it. He ignores the fact that John Kloehr and Carey Seaman confirmed it.

CHAPTER XXIII

1. Croy gives the recorded details of this marriage in *He Hanged Them High*. See also Drago's *Outlaws on Horseback*.

2. Watson was not the quiet, inoffensive man he appeared to be. Croy picked up his trail in the Belle Starr country and followed it to Florida, where Watson was killed in a blaze of gunfire.

3. So stated by the Reverend Leslie McRill, twice minister of the Methodist Episcopal Church, North, at Ingalls, in the early 1900's, and well acquainted with many of the old-timers who had witnessed the battle.

CHAPTER XXIV

1. Evett D. Nix was the antithesis of the ex-gunfighter turned lawman. He was head of the firm of Nix and Company, wholesale grocers of Guthrie, and his silent partner was Oscar Halsell, owner of the famous H X Bar ranch. He had demonstrated his executive ability. As United

States marshal for Oklahoma Territory, he made law enforcement a business by putting together the greatest organization of frontier field marshals this country has ever known.

2. Arkansas Tom was indicted for the killing of Houston, Speed, and Shadley. He was convicted of manslaughter in the Houston case and sentenced to thirty years in prison, of which he served less than seventeen, when he was pardoned. After operating a restaurant in Drumright for two years, he slipped back into outlawry and was subsequently killed by a Joplin, Missouri, policeman as he was fleeing from a robbery.

3. J. C. Seaborn was a prominent figure in Missouri politics and had been state auditor. McDonald County, Missouri, and the American Bankers Association offered rewards totaling fifteen thousand dollars for the arrest and conviction of his killers. It was never collected.

CHAPTER XXV

1. The story of the capture of Bill Doolin by Marshal Tilghman first appeared in print in Mrs. Tilghman's little paperback *Outlaw Days*, and was repeated by her in her later books.

2. Rose Dunn, the celebrated Rose of the Cimarron, married Charles Noble, the younger of the Noble brothers, in 1898, two years after the betrayal of Doolin. It was a long marriage, lasting thirty-four years. Her marrying Charlie Noble casts further doubt on the tale that she had been Bitter Creek Newcomb's sweetheart.

3. Excerpted from *Oklahombres* by Gordon Hines and E. D. Nix.

4. On the evening of November 1, 1924, in the oil-mad town of Cromwell, Oklahoma, Bill Tilghman, while serving as town marshal at the governor's request, was murdered by Wylie Lynn, a drunken young punk and so-called gangster-controlled "prohibition agent."

A Selected Bibliography

Abbot, N. C. (Teddy Blue), and Smith, Helena Huntington. *We Pointed Them North*. New York: Farrar & Rinehart, 1939.

Aikman, Duncan. *Calamity Jane and the Lady Wildcats*. New York: Holt, 1933.

——. *The Taming of the Frontier*. New York: Prospect Press, 1931.

Angel, Myron. *History of Nevada*. San Francisco: published by author, 1881.

Appler, Augustus C. *The Younger Brothers*. Chicago: Regan Publishing Co., 1930.

Asbury, Herbert. *The Barbary Coast*. New York: Alfred A. Knopf, 1931.

Atherton, Gertrude. *The Splendid Idle Forties*. New York: Harper, 1936.

Bancroft, Caroline, and Nafziger, Agnes. *Colorado's Lost Gold Mines and Buried Treasure*. Boulder: Johnson Pub. Co., 1961.

Barnard, Even G. *A Rider of the Cherokee Strip*. Cambridge: Harvard University Press, 1936.

Barsness, Larry. *Gold Camp*. New York: Hastings House, 1962.

Beebe, Lucius, and Clegg, Charles. *U.S. West, the Saga of Wells, Fargo*. New York: E. P. Dutton & Co., 1949.

Bennett, Esteline. *Old Deadwood Days*. New York: Sears, 1928.

Block, Eugene B. *Great Train Robberies*. New York: Coward-McCann, 1959.

——. *Great Stagecoach Robbers of the West*. New York: Doubleday & Company, 1962.

Botkin, B. A. *Treasury of Western Folklore*. New York: Crown Publishers, 1951.

Brown, Dee, and Schmitt, Martin F. *The Settlers' West*. New York: Crown Publishers, 1958.

——. *Trail Driving Days*. New York: Crown Publishers, 1952.

Buell, James. *The Border Outlaws*. Chicago: Regan Pub. Co., 1892.

Burns, Walter Noble. *Robin Hood of El Dorado: the Saga of Joaquin Murrieta*. New York: Garden City Press, 1932.

265

Chapman, Arthur. *The Pony Express*. New York: G. P. Putnam's Sons, 1932.

Clemens, Samuel (Mark Twain). *Roughing It*. New York: Harper, 1913.

Connelley, William Elsey. *Quantrill and the Border Wars*. Cedar Rapids: Samuels' Book Store, 1910.

Croy, Homer. *He Hanged Them High*. New York: Duell, Sloan, and Pearce, 1952.

———. *The Last of the Great Outlaws*. New York: Duell, Sloan, and Pearce, 1963.

Dalton, Emmett, and Jungmeyer, Jack. *When the Daltons Rode*. New York: Doubleday & Company, 1930.

De Quille, Dan. *The Big Bonanza*. New York: Alfred A. Knopf, 1913.

Dillon, Richard. *A Biography of James B. Hume*. New York: Doubleday & Company, 1968.

Dimsdale, Thomas. *Vigilantes of Montana*. Missoula: a reprint, 1946.

Drago, Harry Sinclair. *Wild, Woolly and Wicked*. New York, Potter, 1961.

———. *Outlaws on Horseback*. New York: Dodd, Mead & Company, 1963.

———. *Notorious Ladies of the Frontier*. New York: Dodd, Mead & Company, 1969.

Drury, Wells. *An Editor on the Comstock Lode*. New York: Farrar and Rinehart, 1936.

Eberhart, Perry. *Treasure Trails of the Rockies*. Denver: Sage Books, 1961.

Ellis, Amanda M. *Legends and Tales of the Rockies*. Colorado Springs: Denton Printing Co., 1954.

Eye-Witness, anonymous author of *The Dalton Brothers*. Chicago: Laird and Lee, 1892.

Fredrick, J. V. *Ben Holladay, the Stagecoach King*. Glendale: Clark, 1940.

Glasscock, C. H. *Big Bonanza*. Indianapolis: The Bobbs-Merrill Company, 1931.

Hafen, LeRoy. *The Colorado Gold Rush*. Glendale: Clark, 1940.

Harlow, Alvin F. *Old Waybills*. New York: Appleton-Century, 1940.

Harmon, Samuel W. *Hell on the Border*. Fort Smith: Fort Smith Pub. Co., 1899.

Harrington, Fred Harvey. *The Hanging Judge*. Caldwell: Caxton Press, 1951.

Hicks, Edwin P. *Belle Starr and her Pearl*. Little Rock: Pioneer Press, 1963.

Holbrook, Stewart N. *The Story of American Railroads*. New York: Crown Publishers, 1947.

Holdredge, Helen. *The Woman in Black*. New York: G. P. Putnam's Sons, 1960.

Horan, James D. *Desperate Men*. New York: G. P. Putnam's Sons, 1949.

———. *Desperate Women*. New York: Crown Publishers, 1952.

Howard, Joseph Kinsey. *Montana, High, Wide and Handsome*. New Haven: Yale University Press, 1945.

Hungerford, Edward. *Wells Fargo: Advancing the American Frontier*. New York: The Macmillan Company, 1945.

Hunton, John. *John Hunton's Diary*. Lingle, Wyoming: Flanery, 1956.

Jackson, Joseph Henry. *Anybody's Gold*. New York: The Macmillan Company, 1941.
———. *Bad Company*. New York: The Macmillan Company, 1949.
———. *Tintypes in Gold*. New York: The Macmillan Company, 1939.
Jennewein, J. Leonard, and Boorman, Jane. *Dakota Panorama*. Mitchell, South Dakota: South Dakota Centennial Commission, 1954.
Karsner, David. *Silver Dollar: the Story of the Tabors*. New York: Crown Publishers, 1932.
Kneise, Louis J. *Mother Lode*. Palo Alto: Stanford University Press, 1941.
Lake, Stuart. *Wyatt Earp, Frontier Marshal*. Boston: Little, Brown and Company, 1931.
Langford, N. P. *Vigilante Days and Ways*. Missoula: a reprint, 1957.
Lavender, David. *The Big Divide*. New York: Doubleday & Company, 1948.
Lee, Mabel Barbee. *Cripple Creek Days*. New York: Doubleday & Company, 1958.
Lewis, Oscar. *The Big Four*. New York: Alfred A. Knopf, 1938.
———. *Silver King*. New York: Alfred A. Knopf, 1947.
———. *Lola Montez, Victorian Bad Girl in California*. San Francisco: Pioneer Press, 1938.
Lyman, George D. *The Saga of the Comstock Lode*. New York: Charles Scribner's Sons, 1947.
MacDonald, A. B., with Sutton, Fred. *Hands Up*. Indianapolis: The Bobbs-Merrill Company, 1927.
Masterson, V. V. *The Katy Railroad and the Last Frontier*. Norman: University of Oklahoma Press, 1952.
Monaghan, James. *The Overland Trail*. Indianapolis: The Bobbs-Merrill Company, 1947.
O'Connor, Richard. *Wild Bill Hickok*. New York: Doubleday & Company, 1958.
Paine, Swift. *Eilley Orrum, Queen of the Comstock*. New York: The Bobbs-Merrill Company, 1929.
Parkhill, Forbes. *The Wildest of the West*. New York: Holt, 1937.
Quinn, John. *Fools of Fortune*. Chicago: Donahue, 1892.
Rascoe, Burton. *Belle Starr, the Bandit Queen*. New York: Random House, 1941.
Rosa, Joseph G. *They Called Him Wild Bill*. Norman: University of Oklahoma Press, 1964.
Schaeffer, John G. *Early History of Wells Fargo Express*. New York: G. P. Putnam's Sons, 1928.
Shirley, Glenn. *Law West of Fort Smith*. New York: Holt, 1957.
Sprague, Marshall. *Money Mountain*. Boston: Little, Brown and Company, 1953.
Spring, Agnes Wright. *Cheyenne and Black Hills Stage and Express Routes*. Glendale: Clark, 1949.
Stegner, Wallace. *Gathering of Zion*. New York: McGraw-Hill, 1961.
Streeter, Floyd Ben. *Prairie Trails and Cowtowns*. Boston: Chapman, 1926.
Stuart, Granville. *Forty Years on the Frontier*. Cleveland: Clark, 1925.
Tilghman, Zoe. *Marshal of the Last Frontier*. Glendale: Clark, 1936.

Wellman, Paul I. *A Dynasty of Western Outlaws*. New York: Doubleday & Company, 1961.

Wells, Evelyn. *Champagne Days in San Francisco*. New York: Press of the Pioneers, 1939.

Wilson, C. C. *Chinatown Quest: the Life of Donaldina Cameron*. New York: Appleton-Century, 1940.

Winther, Oscar O. *Express and Stagecoach Days in California*. Palo Alto: Stanford University Press, 1936.

Younger, Cole. *The Story of Cole Younger, by Himself*. Kansas City: Published by author, 1903.

Index

269